MESSAGE AND
EXISTENCE

MESSAGE AND EXISTENCE

An Introduction
to Christian Theology

LANGDON GILKEY

THE SEABURY PRESS · New York

1981
The Seabury Press
815 Second Avenue
New York, N.Y. 10017

Printed in the United States of America

Library of Congress Cataloging in Publication Data
Gilkey, Langdon Brown, 1919–   Message and existence.

1. Theology, Doctrinal—Popular works. I. Title.
BT77.G478   230   79-17612
ISBN 0-8164-0450-X
ISBN 0-8164-2023-8 pbk

Second printing

In gratitude to three friends
      DAVID BURT
      JERALD BRAUER
      DAVID TRACY

CONTENTS

PREFACE

MY intent to write a relatively short and easily understandable contemporary statement of the Christian faith had its immediate cause in the discovery, through teaching an introductory course for "beginners in theology," that few such statements had appeared in the recent past. A second, and deeper, ground of this intent was the desire, increasing in intensity in the past half decade, to think out and express a general overview of Christian faith, a hopefully consistent and integrated interpretation of all the major symbols of that tradition. My own previous works had dealt either with particular issues or symbols in theology (creation, Church, providence) or with the relations of theology to aspects of cultural life (for example, to modern secularity or to science). The effort to express on the grand scale the whole faith results, of course, in a "systematic theology," the massive summation of the theologian's lifework. As the major recent examples of this genre (for instance, the works of Barth, Brunner, Tillich, and Rahner) show, however, such works presuppose on the part of their authors an immense range of scholarship and a rare originality of thought with regard to every major area or issue within Christian doctrine. An unavoidable realism about the level of my own present learning and capacities, and the length of time remaining to

I

improve either one, have together cautioned against such an ambitious and demanding project.

In the place of the vast systematic theology has appeared, therefore, its diminutive stand-in, represented by an introduction for beginners to Christian belief as a whole. Still, a "baby systematic" of this sort in its way can provide the opportunity for a total and coherent interpretation, covering as it must, every central Christian symbol. Since, however, it seeks to remain on the beginning level by giving to each symbol only a simple, uncomplicated, and so incomplete and undefended interpretation, it eschews (or, more accurately, "dodges") the stupendous and intimidating scholarly and intellectual requirements of a full systematic theology. Such an introductory statement, largely unfootnoted and providing minimal reference to academic discussions of each issue, at best can offer a suggestive or fruitful perspective on the faith as a whole; at worst, it can appear ungrounded in its claims and superficial in its understanding. Where the latter seems to be the case in this volume, the author can only apologize and hope that the disgruntled reader may have the patience to refer to some of my other, more extensive works where scholarly documentation and detailed arguments give more adequate grounds for most of the perspective offered here.

This volume is professedly an introduction to Christian theology or, more accurately, a simple, reflective statement about the content of the Christian faith. If one looks at books for beginners in theology, a goodly number spend most of their time telling the reader what theology is, what its sources and its methods of inquiry and of verification are, and thus where it fits in among the other scholarly disciplines. They concentrate—as all of us in academia are wont to do—on method, on procedures, on all the various arguments about both, and ultimately on "how theology should be done." One might call this the Driving School

approach; at its best such writing results in that very useful volume, "The Complete Driver's Manual to Religious
Philosophy." Such volumes on techniques and procedures
have their obvious uses and their equally evident limitations.

I am going to try to avoid this temptation and to keep a
quite different aim in mind. This is to introduce interested
beginners, not into the pursuit of theology as an academic
discipline, but into the various views or beliefs about life
and destiny held by the community of Christians, that is,
into the contents of the Christian faith as it can be understood today. This will, if it succeeds, be more a reflective
description of what is seen on the theological journey than
a manual for driving, though as we shall see, in theology,
as in most other explorations of the mind, procedures and
terrain covered can hardly be separated; but my goal is a
travelog and not a driver's manual. In any case, my volume
is strictly for beginners and not for professionals in theology. The temptation to write for one's colleagues and so to
raise, discuss, and try to resolve all the intricate problems
of a professional discipline will be strictly avoided—as far
as possible. The result will be that while, if successful, this
book may (we hope) seem to the beginner readable and
intelligible, that very success will make it appear to the
professionals embarrassingly naive, deceptively simple,
and in fact inexcusably fuzzy, if not elusive, on every fundamental issue of the trade.

I am not, let it be said, too sanguine about the chances of
success at this point. The first book I wrote (*Maker of
Heaven and Earth*) was explicitly intended for that model
gentleperson, the intelligent layperson, well-educated but
unadorned with competence or training in theology. As a
consequence, I wrote every sentence with my college
roommate in mind. When I sent my friend a copy on its
publication, I received somewhat later a grateful but

apologetic note: "Thanks for the book, and congratulations on its publication. I regret I could not finish it, try as I might; I could barely understand a single sentence. Yours, Dave."

This volume is dedicated to three friends. Books of this sort are usually dedicated to persons with whom we have a "primal," that is a familial, relationship: to mother and father; to wife, husband, or beloved; to daughters and to sons; to sisters or to brothers. This practice (which I have in the past also followed) is utterly sound. These relations not only create, shape, and uphold us as persons; they also constitute the deepest bases of joy and fulfillment in life—as I have come more and more fully to realize in relation to my own immediate family. A year ago at New Year's, however, David Burt, the college roommate mentioned above,—after several years of mutually indifferent noncommunication—phoned from Connecticut, visited shortly thereafter in Chicago, and reestablished by that act what had been lost to both of us.

With that experience I realized that this other sort of relation, also of the deepest significance to our personal being, to our intellectual or artistic achievements, and to our emotional joys, is almost never celebrated in dedications, namely, the rare but precious relation one sustains to a friend. Books by professors are frequently dedicated to "colleagues and students," but that is a bit different from what I here intend. Dedications of that sort are of course inclusive of intellectual respect, of affection, and of appreciation for companionship. Usually they are not, and do not seek to be, inclusive of the deepest levels of personal dependence on the one hand and of creative giving on the other and thus of the corresponding emotional tone of love. These three, dependence, giving, and love, as well as admiration, respect, and companionship, are present with those persons whom we name friends; and they appear in our existence almost as rarely as do the relations that bind a family together. In many other cultures this special relation of friend to friend has been formally celebrated and honored. In ours, while it is probably equally significant for us all, often—for a hundred dubious reasons beginning with the blurring of acquaintance with friend and ending with the fear of seeming unmasculine—the forms of love that cement this relation are unadmitted, the depth and significance of the relation is all too frequently ignored, and so this crucial type of human communion remains uncelebrated and overlooked. In the end, forgotten, it is allowed to slip away so that our whole existence is left impoverished. To recognize and celebrate this relation— and even more the three friends here honored—this dedication is made.

These three friends are themselves diverse, as most friends are. And they represent varying sorts of relations in a variety of contexts and epochs in my now disturbingly extensive life span. The first, David Burt, sculptor and musician, is now my oldest close friend; tennis singles opponent and doubles partner in summer tournaments and roommate in Eliot House, best man, confidante, he is now a mature and seasoned element in the most essential structure of my existence. Jerald Brauer shared with me an office and early vocational discussions, enthusiasms, and "causes" in my first job at Union Seminary; fifteen years later, as Dean of the Divinity School, he helped to rescue my own then faltering career by calling me to Chicago; and since then my wine-expert friend has been a loved companion and wise helper in most aspects of our common, but actually bizarre, human existence. David Tracy, present theological colleague, is a full two decades younger, and yet bonds of mutual affection, respect and

confidence, and always-shared intention grow apace each
time we discuss important issues, chatter about silly ones,
or merely drink and laugh together.

I wish to commend my immediate family, Sonja, Amos,
and Frouwkje, for their understanding as well as their love
while this book was being written last summer and rewrit-
ten last fall—and what good sails we had after a difficult
paragraph had been completed! And I am exceedingly
grateful to Carol Jean Brown for being willing to type a
difficult manuscript and to Martha Morrow for her help in
completing it.

THE DIVINITY SCHOOL
THE UNIVERSITY OF CHICAGO

1
INTRODUCTION

NOT surprisingly, the question of how it is possible to make a brief overview of theology moderately intelligible is directly related to what theology is. Christian theology (and theology is always a definite *kind* of theology: Christian, Jewish, Islamic, Buddhist) may be described as an inquiry with two poles, an "elipse with two foci," as Albrecht Ritschl said. It can be defined as *reflection on our human existence*, on its character and its destiny, and on the "world" (in the widest sense of the term) in which we live from the perspective of the Christian faith ("in the light of the Christian fact," as David Tracy puts it). Or it can be called a *coherent reflective explication of the contents of the Christian faith*, a delineation in contemporary terms of the "revelation" on which the Christian community and thus the faith of those who are in it are founded. Theology is, then, an explication of common experience from the perspective of a religious tradition. Theology in this sense is characteristic of most religious traditions that have moved to a reflective level of culture—though in other contexts the labels "Buddhist philosophy," "Hindu philosophy," and so on may be preferred. Thus although I shall henceforth be speaking specifically of Christian theology, many of the same procedures and principles that I discuss will be applicable to the reflective thinking that takes place in other religious traditions.

To make clear the ultimate interrelatedness and unity of the two definitions of Christian theology outlined above—an examination of general experience and an explication of Christian symbols—will be one of the purposes of this book. Briefly put (as almost every theologian would agree), this unity stems from the fact that the contents of the Christian faith on the one hand, its set of major symbols, are such that they interpret, illumine, and clarify the basic nature of our human existence and history—their goals, possibilities, obligations, problems, and destiny. Correspondingly, the character of our human existence and history, their problems, possibilities, and hopes, is such that they can only be understood fully in the light of that content, as interpreted through these Christian symbols—as human life in history, so I believe, can be most authentically and creatively lived in the light of that faith. This "correlation" between our human existence and history and Christian revelation, between our ordinary experience of self and community and the symbols characteristic of the Christian tradition, is fundamental for all theology. All the arguments among theologians about how to proceed in theology boil down to questions of how these two poles are related, with which one it is necessary to begin, and what means one should use for talking about each and for putting the two together.

A good introduction, consequently, has two seemingly mutually exclusive and yet deeply interdependent aims in view. The first—in order to be intelligible—is to "start where we all are," to begin with the reader's and the author's own situations, with her or his experience of themselves and of their history and so to make whatever is subsequently explained about the Christian faith meaningful and relevant. Little that is said to us is meaningful if it lacks touch with our self-understanding, and theological statements that fail to enter the world of our experience—

of nature, of ourselves, of our relations with others, of our communities, of history—and that fail creatively to shape and to realign that world, will be empty of meaning to our minds and void of relevance to our actions.

Thus most introductions have an "apologetic" form. They begin with ordinary experience, and they seek to develop the understanding of Christian symbols or doctrines on the basis of that "common ground" of shared experience. If such a book should argue *solely* from that shared experience to the validity of certain Christian doctrines and define those doctrines in the light of that argument, its argument would be termed an example of "natural theology," a theology developed solely by rational interpretation of common experience. If, however, the volume does not derive Christian doctrines from ordinary experience but merely insists that these symbols cannot be understood or appropriated except in correlation with ordinary experience (as, for example, Reinhold Niebuhr and Paul Tillich did), then it is not a "natural theology," although it is an "apologetical theology" in form. It seems to me difficult to write an introduction (or any theology) that makes sense to the reader (or to its author!) without a strong apologetical element; this volume will reflect that aim and thus this mode of procedure. The Holy Spirit, we are told, always meets us and speaks to us "where we are"; it may therefore not be unwarranted for the theologian to assay a modest earthly parallel to this exemplary procedure and in his or her reflection also to begin "where we are."

A second aim, and in fact, as noted, the major aim, of an introduction, however, is to delineate as fully as possible the contents of the Christian faith, what it is that is believed and has been believed by Christians. In many religions, and certainly in Christianity, what is believed is not identical with, though it is related to, our ordinary experience of life. First, both religious experience and faith point to a realm, a dimension, or a depth beyond the ordinary world and the ordinary history we inhabit, to a higher level of consciousness (as in Buddhism), or a deeper and more enduring reality or energy. In the case of Christianity this referent of religious experience and of faith is named God, and what is believed in Christian faith consequently has mainly, if not exclusively, to do with God and his/her actions among us.[1] As a consequence, much of the discourse of Christian theology concerns matters not immediately evident in ordinary experience, in the home, or bedroom, the shopping center, the business office, though, as I shall seek to show, it has a very significant relation to all of these aspects of ordinary experience. Second, when Christian faith reflects on things that are a part of ordinary experience, on, for example, the character and problems of being human in home, school, or office, or the problems of our wider communities, of history, it understandably views them in a significantly different light than when they are looked at simply on their own terms. They are seen in the light of their relation to God, as reflected in and through that relation. Consequently, the character, the problems, the questions, and the possibilities of human life in history take a significantly different form than they do when we start with ordinary experience. If ordinary human experience and ordinary historical action were the "sources" and thus provided the substance of Christian theology, nothing new or ultimately significant could be said to the world through the Christian message. This is, however, new wine; and it is not just *my* new wine, or even my epoch's!

Both because it speaks, and must, of God as known in the experience of faith and because it sees the world in a new light because of that experience, Christian theology is in important discontinuity with what is usually considered—on both a simple or a very sophisticated level—as our ordinary experience of the world and as the wisdom of the world. Yet because it seeks to be intelligible and meaningful in what it says both about God and about our human existence in history, Christian theology must also be in important continuity with our ordinary experience. And surely, however it ends up, it must (like the Holy Spirit) start there. To combine in one both of these perspectives or directions, as obviously we must—the one, so to speak, proceeding "from below," the other proceeding "from above"—is quite a trapeze act and demands, if one is to succeed, a great deal of precision and speed on the part of the performer. This double requirement is one reason that the motions of most theologians seem to the amused observer who follows them closely to be fantastically complex, perilously confused, hopelessly awkward, and always escaping by some unexpected leap (Was it good luck or genius?) a fatal plunge into vacuity or contradiction.

It is this dilemma, of wanting both to begin where we are and yet to declare the contents of the faith given to us, to explore reflectively human existence, its problems, and possibilities, and yet to speak of God and of what God has done for us, that explains the form of each of the subsequent parts of this volume. The basic form, expressed in the title of each part, is declaratory or confessional, an attempt to expound clearly, coherently, and persuasively—and adequately to the traditional sources—an interpretation of the Christian faith that is intelligible to a contemporary person and so to the contemporary Church. Thus I have built the successive parts around four of the central motifs of the oldest Christian confession, the so-called Apostles' Creed. These motifs are: I believe . . . in God the Father Almighty . . . and in Jesus Christ His only Son Our Lord . . . and in the Holy

Spirit. The second half of each part, then, is devoted to giving a contemporary interpretation of that motif and thereby an elucidation of central elements of Christian belief.

Since, however, I also want to begin my exposition of the historic faith—or of a revised, reinterpreted, or reconceived edition of that faith[2]—with our experience of ourselves and our history, another element is necessary and will be considered in the first half of each part. This is an examination of our experience of ourselves, our ordinary life, and our history—that is, of our "being," as that being relates to the creedal theme or motif under discussion. Thus in relation to "I believe," I shall explore the character of ordinary human beliefs and thought; in relation to "God the Father," I shall explore the character of our human creatureliness or finitude; in relation to "Jesus Christ His Son," I shall inquire into the problem and tragedy of our existence, our sin or estrangement, that calls for redemption; and in relation to the Holy Spirit, the character and possibilities of human relations in community and so in history.

In these beginning sections of each part an effort will be made to make contact with our ordinary experience of ourselves and our history and thus to establish the meaningfulness and relevance of the central doctrinal symbols correlated with that aspect of our experience. However, it should be clearly noted that these introductory sections, while in continuity with ordinary experience because of their subject matter (for example believing and belief, human nature, the human predicament, etc.), are by no means "outside" or "prior to" theology and therefore nontheological or neutral, if there is such a position. Rather they each represent a *Christian* interpretation of that aspect of human experience. In the first half of each part, then, I shall in fact be explicating or proposing a

Christian "doctrine" about human experience: about believing and culture, about creatureliness, about sin and estrangement, about community.

God and man, said Calvin, are only to be understood in the light of one another, when the two are, so to speak, set in juxtaposition and in union. Each chapter of this volume will seek to do just that; only each one will begin with the human-ward and the historical side first, as that hither side in continuity with our ordinary experience is Christianly understood, that is, as our understanding of ourselves, our world, and our history reflects the affirmations about God—Father, Son, and Holy Spirit—that are fundamental to the faith.

Theology concerns, as has been said, an essential interrelation between human experience and divine revelation, human and creaturely being, and God's presence and action. It is reflective discourse about that interrelation as it is understood and affirmed in a given religious tradition, in this case, Christian faith. As there are two different emphases here, so there are also what may be called two "levels" to which I will continually refer. The first is what is usually termed the "existential" level; it points to the way we actually exist or *are* in our lives as individuals and in community. If we speak on this level of "questions" or "problems," we do not refer to queries in our heads, intellectual puzzles, or blocks in intellectual understanding. Rather we refer to problems in our life, to our actual existence or our being, as a question, as a problem, as a contradiction: to anxiety, loss of courage and confidence, estrangement, injustice, conflict, alienation.

Correspondingly, when on this existential level we refer to "answers," we do not necessarily mean intellectual answers to mental queries, formulae, or articles of wisdom, doctrines, or even explicit beliefs. We refer to the advent of confidence, purpose, courage, self-affirmation, humility, and the power to love; to justice and peace in a community rather than a new social theory: to trust rather than belief in the mind; to a new mode of being rather than a new set of views or an increased stock of information. On this existential level, as Søren Kierkegaard said, all persons are equal; here intellectual endowments and training can be as much of a hindrance as a blessing. Or, as psychoanalysts like to point out, intellectually understanding a theory of neurosis is very different from deeply and existentially understanding or appropriating *oneself* as neurotic, comprehending one's own particular problems and thus being open to healing. This is the "religious" level, the level of true religion, of personal faith, of love—of Christian authenticity. Correspondingly it points also to the level of genuine or actual lostness, of sin, injustice, and despair. Theology continually refers to this existential level as an essential part of the substance or object of its words and concepts. As reflection and discourse, however, theology itself exists on another level related to and yet differentiated from the first.

Persons are thinking and reflective as well as merely existing beings. They have unanswered puzzles in their minds as well as unrelieved estrangement in their souls. They have skeptical doubts about the truth they possess as well as despair about the meaning of the life that is theirs. They are curious about intellectual answers as well as hungry for a new mode of being or existing. And clearly these two levels, the existential and the intellectual-reflective, are interacting and interrelated all the time. All this is obvious: the life of the mind, the pursuit of knowledge and of understanding, the development and refinement of new theory or new symbolism concerning what is experienced are all fundamental to being human. Such reflective efforts represent, of course, the main center of concern for the intellectual classes of any society. Here questions and answers refer to intellectual questions and intellectual answers, to puzzles and queries, on the one hand, and to new evidence or new theories, on the other. Natural, social, and psychological science, philosophical, ethical and political reflection—all of these areas of intellectual discourse exist on this second level as forms of reflection on life rather than life itself, as theory about and understanding of our existence in the world, though as Kierkegaard, Marx, and Dewey reminded us, the point of reflection and of theory is to transform existence rather than merely to contemplate and understand it.

As reflection upon religion or upon faith, theology of course subsists on this second level. Though like all important thought its continual purpose is the transformation of life, still it is the reflective clarification of the contents of the religious faith in and through which persons exist on the first level. It is thus theoretical in character in the sense that it seeks to provide theoretical answers to intellectual questions. By intellectual questions in the arena of theology, I mean: What is human being in the Christian view? How is God to be defined and described, if at all? What is the meaning, if any, of my life and of the human story as a whole? What sort of actions for my neighbor or for society are implied in Christian obedience?

Clearly, as Schleiermacher said, to know an amount of Christian "doctrine," however thoroughly, is a theoretical accomplishment only; it indicates little about the depth of that intellectual's religion, of her or his relation to God, trust, courage, serenity, humility, and power to love. But since cognitive problems, theoretical contradictions, intellectual errors, and wrong views—not to mention intellectual despair about the possibility of the truth—can create genuine crises in personal life and especially in social life, the light of the understanding—truer theory, more universal understanding, deeper insight—is crucially important for creative life as well as for clear thought. In personal and social life alike a more accurate understanding of the self and of community, and of the relation of both to nature, in effect a new consciousness, is requisite to new personal and social health. Correspondingly, in the Christian tradition God's revelation brings truth as well as grace, wisdom as well as power, enlightenment as well as health, life, or a new mode of being. Thus, because we must as humans understand as well as exist, and understand *truly* if we are to *be* "truly," so reflection on religion is an aspect of all religious being, and theology is a genuine aspect of being Christian.

As reflection, as a mode of inquiry into the truth, theology establishes relations, and must do so, with all other modes of inquiry concerning all our other sorts of questions: What is real in the world about us and how does it work? What is the life in which we participate and what are its significant levels? What is a human? What is a society, a community? What is history? These reflective questions about the world, ourselves, society, and history characteristic of the sciences are parallel in various ways to the kinds of reflective questions theology must also ask about the same subjects in their relation to God. And, thus, theological answers to these same questions naturally are deeply related to our secular (scientific, historical, philosophical, and ethical) answers on these matters. Hence arises the essential interrelation of theology to its intellectual and cultural matrix where these questions, and many others, are asked and answered—however dependent on "revelation" the ultimate perspective of a theological tradition may be.

Much as an existing human may live as a Christian in her or his culture, and however "authentically Christian" she or he may seek to be, will reflect in various ways and in different degrees that cultural context in most of their habits, norms, aims, and views of what is or is not true, so Christian theology, however authentically it may explain the faith, reflects the cultural and intellectual context within which it arises. Any study of the history of orthodox Christian theology—or of Jewish or Buddhist thought as well—will reveal this strange mingling in each epoch of the authentic message of the gospel with the cultural situation in which this Christian reflection arose. Though it seeks to speak truly of God and of human being and history, theology is a form of cultural reflection, and so it speaks always in the accents of its historical time and place.

This little volume, therefore, even if it succeeds in being simple, clear, intelligible, and even obvious, and despite its intention to state the faith in truth, will not, and could not, succeed in unambiguously stating the *universal faith.* Inevitably, as a product of human and thus of cultural reflection, it will itself exhibit the perspectives and the biases of its cultural time and place, of the class, race, nationality, and sex of its author, and heaven knows what other quirks and idiosyncracies of any "particular" in history. And as a constructive effort seeking to give relevant and intelligible, and thus *new,* form to the symbols of the faith, it involves the risk of misinterpretation and thus of error.

Merely to repeat past formulations is to abjure the theological task and to guarantee a theology that is anachronistic and thereby void of living meaning; for the task of theology is to express the message in contemporary form, in terms relevant and meaningful to its own time and place. To take up that task, however, is to embrace *new* forms of relativity and to court *new* possibilities of distortion. The theologian reflecting on the faith of the community, like the believer existing within that community, has the intention of authentic re-presentation, the one of the faith that is believed, the other of the existence that is graced. However much on each level there is growth in grace, both are in the end insufficient and even wayward. As relative, in part wayward, and in fact biased, both are justified by faith, that is, by the divine mercy and by the grace of the Holy Spirit that can make perfect whatever is fragmentary in our existence and our thought.

Each theological effort, then, arises out of the community of Christians, on the one hand, and out of the culture of that time and place, on the other. Each theological effort represents not so much a culmination as only a proposal to the Church and the world, a proposal that this tradition be interpreted for our time in this way and an argument that such an interpretation satisfies our available criteria as an approximation to the truth about our existence, the world, and God. As a Christian, each theologian (I believe) is confident that an adequate contemporary statement of the Christian perspective, witnessing and pointing as it does to God's revelation in Christ, is as close to the truth as it is possible for human beings to get. But she and he know that any particular formulation of that perspective, and even the tradition as a whole, reflects only part of the truth to which it seeks to witness. Thus she and he also share a confidence in the continuing work of the Holy Spirit in the Christian community and in the world to complete what is fragmentary and to refashion what is biased in any given theological proposal, as those communities ignore or reject, accept or refashion each proposal of the truth that is offered to them.

NOTES

1. Several theological colleagues (for example, Gordon Kaufman, *An Essay on Theological Method* [Missoula, Mont.: Scholars Press, 1975] prefer to *define* theology as "talk about God." While this makes good sense in relation to Christian theology, I prefer, as indicated here in the text,

to define the word in relation also to other religious traditions, namely as reflection on the meaning and validity of the symbols of a religious tradition and/or reflection on the meaning of human existence from the perspective of a religious community. In that sense almost every religious tradition has a "theological" aspect or component. To me that reflective component—as for example in Buddhism—is more accurately and helpfully described as "Buddhist theology" than as "Buddhist philosophy," mainly because the fixed starting-point in the case of every "Buddhist philosophy" is the situation or perspective of a member of that particular religious tradition, a trait not characteristic of philosophy. If theology is reflection looking at its world from the point of view of a religious tradition, then Buddhist, Jewish, and Christian reflection are in the fundamental shape of their modes of thinking "theology."

2. Since my friend and colleague, David Tracy, has published his excellent book, *Blessed Rage for Order* (New York: Seabury Press, 1975), as an example of "revisionist theology," I have frequently been asked if I consider myself to be a "revisionist theologian." On thinking carefully about this, I have realized that unquestionably I am. Every time I read something I have written before, I think to myself, "That *really* needs revision!"

SUGGESTED READINGS

Recent Classics

Barth, K. *Anselm.* Meridian Books, 1960.

Brunner, H. E. *The Divine-Human Encounter.* Westminster, 1943.

———. *Our Faith.* Scribners, 1936.

Horton, W. *Christian Theology: An Ecumenical Approach.* Harper & Bros., 1955.

Micklem, N. *Ultimate Questions.* Abingdon, 1955.

Niebuhr, Reinhold. *Beyond Tragedy.* Scribners, 1937.

Temple, W. *Basic Convictions.* Harper & Bros., 1936.

Whale, J. S. *Christian Doctrine.* Macmillan, 1946.

Current Discussion

Capon, R. F. *Hunting the Divine Fox.* Seabury, 1977.

Cobb, J. B., Jr. *Living Options in Protestant Theology.* Westminster, 1962.

Gilkey, L. *Catholicism Confronts Modernity.* Seabury, 1977.

———. *Religion and the Scientific Future.* Harper & Row, 1970.

————. *Naming the Whirlwind*. Bobbs-Merrill, 1969.

Jennings, T. W. *Introduction to Theology*. Fortress, 1976.

Kaufman, G. *An Essay on Theological Method*. Scholars Press, 1975.

————. *Systematic Theology: A Historicist Perspective*. Scribners, 1968.

Kelsey, D. *Uses of Scripture in Recent Theology*. Fortress, 1975.

Lonergan, B. J. F. *Insight*. Longmans, Green & Co., 1964.

————. *Method in Theology*. Herder & Herder, 1972.

Ogden, S. *The Reality of God*. Harper & Row, 1964.

Pannenberg, W. *Theology and the Philosophy of Science*. Westminster, 1976.

————. *The Apostles' Creed*. Westminster, 1972.

Rahner, K. *Foundations of Christian Faith*. Seabury, 1978.

Schillebeeckx, E. *The Understanding of Faith*. Seabury, 1974.

Sykes, S. *An Introduction to Theology Today*. John Knox, 1974.

Tracy, D. *Blessed Rage for Order*. Seabury, 1975.

Wiles, M. *What Is Theology?* Oxford Univ. Press, 1976.

PART ONE

"I Believe . . ."

2

FAITH, COMMUNITY AND TRADITION

I SHALL begin with a discussion of the first two words of the Apostles' Creed: "I believe, ..." This topic is appropriate not only for its historic role in creedal statements and in fact in the interpretation of theology itself; theology has, since Augustine, been defined by most if not all of its practitioners as the enterprise of understanding what it is we believe. It is also appropriate because it introduces us to many of the crucial categories and polarities essential to the understanding of theology: to the interplay of tradition and autonomy, to the nature of faith and assent, to revelation and event, to symbols and the media of revelation, and to several additional issues in the relation of theology and culture.

The phrase "I believe," with its dominating first-person pronoun and its clear reference to an individual's deepest commitment and thus to the center of his or her unique and personal existence, seems to point inescapably to the inward, the individual, the idiosyncratic. Thus, when we hear someone say "I believe," we think at once of the inescapable variety of tastes and of beliefs in a world filled with diverse individuals each looking at things in a different way. Correspondingly, the category of belief, and especially the personal affirmation of religious belief, seems to represent a subjectivist principle utterly opposed to all that is connoted by such words as universal, rational, sharable, communal. The world of belief, and thus the world of religion, seems in this perspective to lie *inside* each of us in our private imaginations and dreams. On the other hand, the common objective world where all live, the world known by science, lies *outside* of us in objective reality and is therefore universal, sharable by all who choose to look objectively at it. This sharp contrast or dichotomy between a private, imagined, almost unreal world in the subject and the real, universal world of objects has been characteristic of our modern culture and has caused a great deal of misinterpretation of the category of belief and of religious belief. Such a private and individualistic interpretation of what we do when we believe something is, however, both untrue to the historic meaning of the creedal phrase "I believe" and an inaccurate account of the actual role of believing in our objective cultural and social life.

The man or woman in the early centuries of the Christian tradition who with great seriousness and excitement said "I believe" and then repeated the Christian community's confession of faith was not attempting to state the personal beliefs of a private individual. On the contrary, the primary intention and meaning of that affirmation was to identify herself or himself as a participating member of a community and a tradition, both of which were quite objective to the individual and, in fact, formative of that individual's new life. Fundamental, important beliefs thus point not so much to a private subjective world as they point to some historical tradition and to the community that bears that tradition and lives from or within it. The symbolic contents of the creed, what was believed, were thus actually more creative of the individual's inner or subjective life than the reverse; and that public content had that crucial shaping role because it was, in turn, the significant factor creative of the tradition in question, of the community in which every individual lived and acted, of the "world"—nature, history, the divine—surrounding the persons in that tradition and community. "Belief" on the deepest level has reference to the symbolic forms that structure the perspectives, the norms, and thus the life of objective historical communities. These forms are creative of the social worlds in which humans live. This is evident enough in religious communities where there is an explicit correlation or coherent unity among beliefs about reality (expressed in a creed or its equivalent), rules or law covering ordinary behavior, rituals and practices, and thus a total and all-encompassing style of life shared by the whole community. To say "I believe" in that context is first of all to associate oneself as participant on the deepest level in such an objective religious and yet also social world borne by a given historical religious tradition and embodied in both the inner and the outer life of each member of that community.

As modern anthropology and sociology have taught us, this character of religious communities or religious traditions is shared in a less evident way by every "secular" community, that is, one that is not formed around an explicit religious center. For here, too, there is a particular "cultural world" that, in turn, shapes the community and its social existence and as a consequence shapes the lives of each of its participating members. That cultural world, cultural vision, or "ethos" has—as does its religious equivalent—several aspects: it includes a view of reality, of nature, of history, and of what is and is not real within them; an understanding of what is or what is not true and of how that truth is to be uncovered; and of what is of value (the good) and thus of what are the fundamental aims of an authentic life and an authentic society. This ethos finds explicit expression in basic symbolic forms that appear regularly when the community describes itself, its life, and its destiny in history, at crucial moments of crisis and decision, at its important ritual functions, and when it seeks to justify its acts, its institutions, and practices. Because this cultural vision is also expressed in and through all the important, shared facets of the community's life, it is imperceptibly and steadily communicated to each of its members. This communication takes place primarily through its language, which primordially shapes and structures each member, institution, and custom; through the explicit views of the community about life, reality, and human being ("common sense"); through its most detailed habits of life and its lesser institutions. Finally, it is explicitly communicated through its objective cultural creations: its art, social and ethical theory, literature, science, and thought.

Granting the depth, significance, and all-encompassing character of these symbolic structures, they are not at all easy to formulate precisely—though they are crucial to the life of the community, and thus "everyone" knows perfectly well what they point to or mean. It would be impossible to formulate precisely what America means to Americans or Russia to Russians. But that in both cases there is included in a fundamental vision, however vague, a view of reality—of history, of truth, and of value—and of the role of that community in each area; that these shape in large part the institutions, habits, and customs of its people and structure its education and political action; and that the great literature and thought in each case seek to express them, there can be no doubt at all. Some levels of such a vision of history, of authentic community, and of authentic human being are quite distinctly formulable in terms of certain definite social theories, for example, capitalistic economic theory, liberal democratic political theory, and similarly their Marxist equivalents. Alternatively, this ethos is objectively and clearly enshrined in certain communally accepted procedures for making social decisions and for enacting policies and customs. Other levels, however, expressing the *ultimate* views of history, of community, and of authentic communal relations within this ethos are expressible only in vaguely defined but powerful symbols such as "democracy," "equality," "liberty," "progress," and similarly in their Russian or Marxist equivalents. Although, therefore, there are scientific, theorizible, and philosophical elements within such a symbolic structure, the structure as a whole is *symbolic* rather than *theoretical* in linguistic form, and, however significant and full of meaning it may be, it cannot be formulated with complete coherence and precision.

To be a participating member of such a community means, therefore, to share inwardly in some important measure in this objective cultural world, to assent to this vision or ethos, and thus to be shaped inwardly as a thinking, feeling, acting individual human in terms of this outward objective communal ethos—as any "standard" American would do with regard to free enterprise, democracy, and our way of life and as would most Russians—though neither "believer" would necessarily be able to formulate what they so believed. To be "alienated" from a cultural community or a tradition is to refuse to share inwardly in its ethos, to repudiate basic practices or procedures legitimated by that ethos, and thus to participate in some other (well-or ill-defined) tradition, as would any new leftist in the United States, Marxist radical in Western Europe, or "liberal dissident" in Eastern Europe and in Russia. Again, belief on the deepest level means a personal participation in the life and ethos of a community and its tradition and an assent to the fundamental symbolic forms of that tradition as true and as normative, that is, as directing or guiding one's own thought, goals, and patterns of behavior.

Belief in ordinary life is thus not an act of subjective fancy; it represents *the* important spiritual link between ourselves and the objective social world in which we all live and act.

We should note, moreover, that while political communities (such as America or Russia) make particularly good examples of this relation of belief to communities, traditions, and symbolic forms, the same structure appears in nonpolitical societies (besides religious communities), such as, for example, the scientific community. To be a scientist means also to participate in the quite definite ethos (the "scientific spirit") of a tradition borne by a particular community—the community of scientists. In this case the positive and very important view of reality and its relation to experience shared by this community remains implicit and not defined. (For example, the community holds that common experience is not in the end "maya" or illusion.) Only the *procedure* ("method") of inquiry into what is taken to be real in experience is regarded as determinative of this community's shared life and must be accepted and affirmed if one is to participate. For this reason, devoted as it is to its *method* of truth rather than to particular truths, the scientific community would prefer to avoid using the word "belief" to describe itself. Nevertheless, the same kind of self-commitment to the procedures, norms, and goals of that community; the same assent to its fundamental views of reality and truth; of submission to its criteria and its judgment; and of dependence on its continuing creative role in universal history, all represent the essential interrelation of believing to community, tradition, and ethos I have outlined. To be human, even in an advanced secular political society or in the sophisticated scientific community, means to participate inwardly (to assent to or to believe in) some shared and objective ethos structuring and shaping a historical community and its world; thus it means, in turn, to be shaped in one's own thinking, valuing, and acting by the symbolic forms of that tradition.

A most curious character of each example of the ethos of communities is that, however secular they may be (that is, having no essential relation to a "religion" in the ordinary sense of that word, for example as in the case of Russia or America), these cultural visions quickly take to themselves a "religious" character. By that is meant that they each claim (or are claimed by their participants) to be *ultimate* in character, to possess the *truth* about history, society, and human existence, and thus to represent *the* essential message, center, and goal of history. Certainly the modern European and American West believe this to be true of itself and of its role in a progressing history of civilization (begun in Egypt, passed on to Greece and Rome, taken up again in modern culture, and now located "for the duration" in the hands of an advancing America)—and that sense of its own relation to the meaning of history (the theory of progress) was central to its ethos. Certainly Russia as the center of "Marxist Science" believes this about itself. And certainly the scientific community has, until recently, taken this for granted.

These ultimate claims, or claims to ultimacy and absoluteness, are not surprising. As has been noted, such cultural visions communicate to their participants a view of reality, a set of norms for their self-direction, and a context for the meaning of their life. It is, therefore, by *them* that life is lived and through *them* that life is given meaning. They are, thus, matters of "ultimate concern," as Tillich put it. Consequently, if they are shattered or questioned, the coherence, unity, and meaning of experience—the reality of what is in experience and the truth of what we believe about experience—are all rendered precarious. There is in each cultural vision an unconditional dimension, a dimension of the ultimate and the sacred, that gives power, form, and meaning to the life lived in that society. The loss of that dimension consequently spells the disintegration of both the cultural ethos and the community that bears it—as the scientific community would disappear if there occurred among its members a widespread loss of confidence in its method or a loss of concern for the kind of truth it promises. Thus, these cultural visions, however secular, not only, as has been noted, function like a religion in shaping, preserving, and guiding the community; they also share certain characteristics of religions in claiming ultimacy and sacrality, in claiming to embody an ultimately valid view of reality and history, ultimately authentic norms and goals, and thus to represent what is of ultimate concern for human beings.

In this description of these social objects of belief, the ethos or vision of a community, a see-saw (or dialectic) familiar to social history has appeared between ideology and relativism. Since Marx's profound understanding of society, we have all been aware of the pervasiveness of ideologies. Ideologies are views of the whole of reality, especially of historical and social reality, which are believed by a community, which claim to be the truth about the whole, but which actually represent a particular point of view or bias, and (here was the main point for Marx) which in that bias represent and further the interests of a certain class or group. Thus did Marx describe the entire "cultural vision" of the bourgeois nations—their Christian religion, their idealistic philosophy, their Victorian morals, their romantic art, their common law and democratic political theory, and even their science—as a rationalization justifying bourgeois society and thus serving the interests of the bourgeois class. And, as we all can now see, there was—and is—a great deal of truth in this critique of both Victorian and contemporary capitalistic societies. Thus have many of us described the "cultural vision" or ethos of fascist or segregationist societies as representing views of reality, truth, and goodness which were merely rationalizations serving the interests of given national groups or races. Clearly, societies or traditions in conflict or potential conflict see each other's cultural visions as mere ideologies and decry the "blind faith" their opponents give to such false visions of reality. And, clearly, it is precisely the religious dimensions of their own cultural vision that fuel the fire of their zeal to overcome and destroy the enemy, for now the "enemy" (for example communism) is seen not only as a threat to our own security but also as a threat to *all* truth, meaning, and value in history. Yet, equally obviously, to regard all of these systems of "belief" as merely "ideologies," as false, biased, and thus only rationalizations of special interests, is, if this analysis is correct, to be unable oneself to think, to judge, and to act. For each of these latter activities presupposes a vision of reality, truth, and value or meaning shared in some communal tradition (be it as esoteric as can be).

Even the skeptical, questioning, critical "tradition" (the intellectual or philosophical side of a capitalistic society) requires a certain vision of reality, history, truth, society, human being, and of the procedures for inquiry into these realities which must be presupposed, participated in, and believed if creative criticism is to be possible. And to regard all beliefs but one's own as ideologies is to be back in the traditional role of the fanatic. The claim to ultimacy in cultural life seems, therefore, both inescapable and infinitely dangerous, while its opposite, the loss of all confidence in the value of any tradition and thus of any pattern of constructive thought, appears to represent a situation in which both creative community and creative individual life are impossible. Social and personal existence seems to be essentially dependent on religiouslike dogmas and religiouslike beliefs and yet infinitely threatened by them.

And to see this dilemma is to face on the other flank an equally debilitating relativism.

Every recent social philosophy—naturalistic, Marxist, Freudian—has attempted an explanation or interpretation of these strange and paradoxical characteristics of social history: its uses and misuses of myths and symbols, its recurrent fanaticism, its ideological bias, and the perils of relativism. All have seen these perils as peculiarly characteristic of religion and expressed confidence that this "religious disease" of absolutism might be cured by intelligible, "hard-headed" thinking and by social reconstruction. Some, for example, Emile Durkheim and the sociological tradition that has been influenced by him, have admitted the seeming permanence of this "religious dimension" of social life, though they gave a naturalistic, nonreligious explanation of their data. To understand these data fully and coherently, however, requires, I believe, a *theological* interpretation (as well as a psychological, political, and social one), namely a view of society and of the individual, of social ethos and belief, that centers its interpretation on the essential and active presence of the divine in human existence, and that interprets human being, both individual and social, in terms of its relations and responses to that presence.

If, as I shall argue in the next part, the divine creative power is present in all of life, giving reality, order, and new possibilities to each moment, then any vision of what is real, of what is true, and of what is of value will reflect that unconditioned and sacral presence. Each cultural vision or cultural ethos, then, appears in history as a vision, not only of the finite creaturely world around us—of nature, society, and ourselves—but as a vision saturated with these religious elements of ultimacy and sacrality. The continuity between cultural life and religious community—that is, the religious dimensions of cultural life—that has here been elaborated reflects the continual presence of the divine in all human experience, its creative role in the reality, order, and possibilities of that experience, and the dim consciousness in us all of this presence, an awareness objectified in the religious characteristics of social existence. Social history hardly reveals the intentions or the character of "God"; however, it does manifest that creative presence—and as shall be seen later—the divine judgments. In every cultural vision, however perverted that ethos may be, there is a vision of reality, truth, and value set in the framework or horizon of an ultimate sacrality. That vision reflects an awareness of the divine presence giving power, order, and possibility to life. It is an aspect, therefore, of what I shall call in a moment the universal revelation or self-manifestation of God.

My emphasis has been on the social and traditional aspects of belief, the way believing relates a person to a community, a tradition, an objective view of the world. This is, however, not to deny the more obvious point that the phrase "I believe" also points in the opposite direction: to the principle of individual and personal participation, to the principle of autonomy. We all begin to be as members of community, shaped by language, family, and group; and only slowly do we become self-aware and then self-directive in belief, thought, and action. The history of the race apparently repeats this process of individual development on a grand scale; only slowly has the overwhelming power of community and of tradition in both primitive and archaic cultures been successfully challenged by the appearance and development of personal autonomy. The Liberal West has seen this emergence of the self-directing individual as the clue to the meaning of history. However, the devastating results of a rampant individualism, of the loss of community and of "the common good" in the modern West—not to mention the collectivist reactions to that loss—have reminded us that community and individuality are in polar relationship, each depending on the other for its own reality and fulfillment. As Tillich has perceptively insisted, there are no genuinely self-directing individuals without participation in community; and there can be no real community without such individuals. "I believe" does rightly point in both a communal and an individualistic direction.

This principle—manifest in the emphasis *I* believe—contains several facets each illustrative of personal autonomy or individual self-direction. There is first of all the intellectual facet established by the seventeenth- and eighteenth-century Enlightenment: the autonomous *mind* affirms nothing to be true but that which reason—that is, my own reason or independent thinking—has shown to be true. Kant defined Enlightenment as "the maturity of the race" which "dared to think for itself" instead of merely receiving truth ready-made from the established authorities of community, state, or church. Thus the principle of intellectual autonomy carries with it the important requirement of criticism, of a questioning, even "suspicious," attitude towards what is given by tradition in order that its conclusions, if accepted, may be reestablished on new and contemporary grounds. As a consequence, the principle of autonomy also carries with it the requirement of continual revision, reinterpretation, or re-presentation of what is received or believed—and thus in the long run it entails an acceptance of the relativity, the historicity, and fallibility of every particular expression of truth.

First formulated by the scientific community about its own truth, this principle of the historical relativity of all particular expressions of truth and the need for their continual criticism and revision into new, more relevant forms has gradually moved into other disciplines as well—even (and now especially) theology. This was the essence of the liberal and modernist movements in nineteenth-century theology. Whatever the power of tradition and community as providing the "substance" of what is believed—in the social, the political, and the religious realms—no longer is that role of tradition one of an absolute or unquestionable authority. Correspondingly, no longer is the "I believe" merely a matter of passive or blind reception of what has been delivered to us by the past. We must reformulate and reestablish for *ourselves* what is believed if genuine assent is to be offered. It is, therefore, through the dialectical principle of *autonomy* that its polar principle of *tradition* has become itself enriched or fulfilled, namely become living or historical, subject to creative change as culture itself changes, and alive and relevant in each new epoch.

There is not sufficient space to discuss in detail the other aspects of the principle of autonomy that modern culture has uncovered, explored, and brought to prominence. Following on the Enlightenment's concern for autonomous intellectual assent, the romantic movement emphasized personal experience in every relevant realm. Whatever the subject matter—scientific inquiry, the appropriation of art, of religion or even of wisdom about life—for the "I believe" to be asserted, it is, said the Romantics, necessary for me to enjoy my own experiencing of what I affirm; otherwise I make my confession only "second-hand," on the authority of another's experience. Later under the powerful influence of Kierkegaard, this principle of personal experiencing was deepened and widened to the principle of personal decision or commitment, of self-constitution, so to speak, as mandatory for authentic human existence: to be a person (and thus a lover, friend, citizen, believer), I must "choose myself"; I must decide through an inner act of will what I am to affirm and cleave *dialectical character of belief*

, community
, autonomy

to, what norms or goals I am to recognize, what relations and commitments I am to embrace, in short, who I am to be. Human existence simply is not *there* until it is established by this act of self-constitution; without it, we merely *seem* to be persons, but we are in fact empty inside, mere standard "objects" in human form. (As romanticism was a reaction in the name of individual experience to Enlightenment universal reason, so contemporary existentialism has been an individual reaction to a standardizing consumer culture.) With this emphasis upon self-creation and its correlate, self-direction, the principle of autonomy has in this tradition come almost to define human existence. The familiar existentialist formula: "Man has no essence (no given, already defined substance from tradition or community); he is only his existence" (he is only what he creates himself to be) thus expressed the culmination of this principle—and signaled the reaction in the twentieth century to find and secure community again!

Belief, then, has itself a complex, essentially dialectical character. *On the one hand,* it entails participation in an objectively given tradition and thus in the community that bears that tradition. It involves at this point assent to and affirmation of the symbolic structure of that tradition and community, providing through those symbolic forms a perspective on or vision of reality, truth, and value. It thus entails submission to certain procedures of inquiry and of settling issues common to that community and entailed in that symbolic understanding. To say "I believe" means to enter as a self into and participate in a communal world under a particular symbolic horizon and involved in particular ways of thinking and knowing, of feeling and experiencing, and of doing, acting, and relating. *On the other hand*, to say "I believe" entails personal intellectual assent to that symbolic horizon and thus the requirement of criticism and reformulation, of personal experiencing and appropriating of the world thus embraced, and personal self-constitution and self-direction on the deepest level of our own being and acting. What we are and are to be is at once given to us by our destiny and yet is also self-chosen and refashioned by our freedom. Both a communal destiny and a personal act of commitment and assent are involved in genuine believing.

Both of these poles of this fundamental characteristic of our existence are expressed in the "I believe" and are to be uncovered, as has been shown, in every important realm of cultural life. These polarities and paradoxes of our existence have been particularly apparent in the history of religious community: tradition and authority as opposed to autonomy; and their correlate, the requirement of orthodoxy as opposed to the possibility of heresy; the changelessness and universality of dogma as opposed to the variety of individual experiences and points of view; the necessity of selfless identification with the community and the necessity of personal decision and commitment for that identification. However, in its use of both tradition and authority, in the crucial importance of symbols and procedures, and in the historical relativity of its formulations combined with the relevance of present experience, religion and religious believing are in the deepest continuity with other aspects of cultural life.

SUGGESTED READINGS

Berger, P., and Luckmann, T. *The Social Construction of Reality.* Doubleday/Anchor, 1967.

Durkheim, E. *The Elementary Forms of the Religious Life.* Free Press, 1947.

Eliade, M. *The Sacred and the Profane.* Harper & Row, 1961.

———. *Myth and Reality.* Harper & Row, 1963.

———. *Myths, Dreams and Mysteries.* Harper & Row, 1967.

———. *Patterns of Comparative Religion.* Meridian Books, 1958.

Geertz, C. *The Interpretation of Cultures.* Harper/Colophon, 1973.

Gilkey, L. *Catholicism Confronts Modernity.* Seabury, 1976.

———. *Religion and the Scientific Future.* Harper & Row, 1970.

Nisbet, R. *The Sociological Tradition.* Basic Books, 1966.

Parsons, T. *Essays in Sociological Theory.* Free Press, 1949.

———. *The Social System.* Free Press, 1951.

———. *Sociological Theory and Modern Society.* Free Press, 1976.

Schneider, L., and Bonjean, C., eds. *The Idea of Culture in the Social Sciences.* Cambridge Univ. Press, 1973.

Tillich, P. *Theology of Culture.* Oxford Univ. Press, 1959.

———. *My Search for Absolutes.* Simon & Schuster, 1967.

3

REVELATION AND THEOLOGY

IN the theological interpretation of belief and culture just completed, five essential elements have been uncovered: tradition, community, personal autonomy, symbols, and procedures. Together these form the context within which the particular perspectives on reality and truth, the values and norms for action, the meanings and goals in any culture's life are both objectively borne along in history and inwardly and personally appropriated and refashioned by participating members of the community. And because of the religious dimension intrinsic to all of this—its objective character as ultimate and sacred and its subjective character as an ultimate concern to each participant— I spoke of that cultural vision of reality, truth, and value as a "revelation" or self-manifestation of ultimate reality, truth, and value ("God"), as a way in which the divine creative presence manifests itself in the historical and cultural life of men and women everywhere. As the prologue to John and the early Church theologians insisted, the divine Logos (the divine order and goodness) is universally present to all cultural life, and every truth known and every value affirmed reflects through its own cultural form that universal presence.

When we turn to a theological interpretation of our own explicitly religious community and tradition, the Christian community and tradition, and enter the realm of theological symbols or doctrines directly, we find important aspects of both continuity and of discontinuity with the life and tradition of any culture so interpreted. The same central five elements are there in an understanding of Christian belief: tradition, community, personal autonomy or acceptance, symbols, and procedures. Only because they are now set within a quite new context, these elements take significantly· different form. For now we are interpreting a *religious* community, that is, one explicitly formed around its religious center and understanding itself explicitly by the religious tradition that constitutes it. What in a secular community is implicit, indirect, often hidden, and thus "in the background"—the religious dimension of cultural life—moves out into the open and to the center of the stage as the defining, empowering, and directing principle of the community's life. Thus the religious community, in interpreting its own life, understands itself as called, created, preserved, shaped, and guided by the divine presence.[1] That is, on the one hand, it understands itself as established by a divinely initiated "event" or "revelation," and, on the other, it regards its most fundamental principle of spiritual unity, illumination, and direction to be the continuing divine presence itself—in the Christian tradition named the Holy Spirit. The religious beliefs, practices, and moral norms of the community become central to defining its own self-understanding; the social, institutional, and practical aspects of the community's life recede to the status of necessary but secondary aspects. Thus, while historical inquiry, sociology, political and economic theory, and anthropology naturally serve to uncover the center of a secular culture's existence, and a theological or religious interpretation only reveals in an ancillary way the religious dimension of that culture's life, in the case of religious communities, theological interpretation is necessary to make visible the animating center of the community; and social, political or even historical understanding, while important and valid, fail to reach and reveal that center. In the self-interpretation of the Christian community, therefore, the categories of revelation and of the presence of the Holy Spirit are central: as a religious community, it is to be *theologically* understood if it is to be understood at all.

The first task, therefore, is to say something about the meaning of "revelation" as the Christian community understands it as its central originating, shaping, empowering, and thus defining principle. The Christian community has historically understood itself as established on a unique and unsurpassable—"final"—divine self-manifestation in Jesus of Nazareth, in the Hebrew tradition that preceded and formed him, and in the continuing presence of the Holy Spirit through which Jesus as the Christ remains as the empowering, illuminating, and directing center of the community's life. By "final" here, as I have already insisted, is not necessarily meant that God does not reveal himself/herself elsewhere. On the Christian understanding here proposed, the divine power, order, and meaning are indirectly manifest universally as the principle of each culture's ethos. And it seems evident to most, if not all, contemporary Christians that the God known in the Christian tradition is also, in obviously greater or lesser clarity, manifest in other religious traditions. What the word "final" means, therefore, is not that Christian revelation is the sole or the exclusive revelation. Rather, it indicates that for those committed to it and participating in it, it provides the all-determining criterion and measure for the reality and nature of God, for what is in the end taken to be real, to be true and to be of value; that, therefore, on this basis the character of authentic human existence, individual and social, is to be determined; and that here the hopes—and fears—concerning our historical and transhistorical destiny are to be grounded.

As has been noted, every cultural vision, and certainly every religious tradition, if taken to be ultimate for one's existence and one's thought, functions in this same way, providing the perspective and the norms by which the real, the true, and the good are appropriated and through which other traditions, while respected, are interpreted and assessed. If such an ultimate norm for one's existence, one's thinking, and one's judgments is not "religious," this problem of an ultimate center or stance in life is not thereby escaped. Rather, the all-determining perspective and norm will merely be the secular ethos of one's own particular cultural heritage—perhaps the liberal, democratic, capitalist or the Marxist heritage. For this reason this Christian position, so interpreted, is no more exclusivist than is any other position, secular or religious. In its recognition of truth, if not of *the* truth, in other religious positions, it is parallel, to my knowledge, to the way in which any tolerant Hindu or Buddhist would regard other positions.

From a Christian perspective each cultural vision—whether Hellenic, Chinese, modern Western, or Marxist—is at once a creative if dim foreshadowing of what is ultimately true and of value, an understanding of all things which through its positive creativity leads up to and points to a completion and fulfillment beyond itself in some deeper and truer understanding. On the other hand, each cultural vision represents a "fallen" understanding, an ideological bias, and therefore a serious deviation from what is true and good. Thus each, even, or especially, our own "American" vision, stands under the higher criticism or judgment of the divine understanding of authentic human existence and the fulfillment of history. And thus, as shall be seen later, the Church itself—its doctrines, its morals, and its immediate aims—also stands under the same transcendent judgment. Augustine remarked that each community sought security, justice, order, and lasting peace; but because of its predominating self-love, the security it sought and gained was always insecure, its justice always in part injustice, its order disorder, and its peace precarious and ephemeral. Each community, therefore, he said, foreshadows and yet also denies the eternal life, the complete justice, the love, and the final peace of the Kingdom of God.

Our own understanding of the relation of universal revelation in history and culture to final revelation in the Christian gospel will try to re-present a similar continuity and discontinuity to that expressed in Augustine's formulation. Christian revelation, in short, neither merely accepts nor transcends an ambiguous cultural life; nor does it merely judge and reject it—and certainly it should not simply represent or bless it. Rather, Christian revelation both deepens and critically redefines in the light of its own vision of human existence in history the understanding of life characteristic of each culture. This principle of the negation of ordinary secular life, of worldly wisdom and of routine justice, balanced by the deeper affirmation of each, represents the central—and paradoxical—thrust of Christian understanding. It is a dialectic I shall explore throughout this volume.

Revelation, then, means the self-manifestation of the divine power and meaning on which all depends and in and through which all is fulfilled, that is to say, in our tradition, "God." At its most fundamental level, therefore, revelation means the communication of the divine *power* (being, life, health, and eternal life), of the divine *truth* (order, illumination, insight, and meaning), and of the divine *love* (mercy, forgiveness, and renewing, reuniting love). The content of Christian revelation and thus of each of these three aspects (the divine being, truth, and love) will be more fully explored in the following three parts.

As is evident, revelation as the communication of the divine power, truth, and love represents a polarity between the gift, on the one hand, of a new level of being or life—the "impersonal" base of our existence—and that, on the other, of a new *consciousness*, a new understanding, trust, and love—the "personal" center of our existence. Protestantism saw correctly that a sacramental interpretation of Christianity which emphasized only what lies below the level of consciousness and of personal apprehension was external, inadequate, and, in extreme cases, magical. But Protestantism's exclusive concentration on *conscious* intellectual belief, on *moral* action, or on *conscious* religious experience has resulted in the long run in weakness in liturgical and sacramental life, in loss of the categories of the holy and the transcendent, and in an inability to deal with the religious dimensions of health, of contemplative techniques, and an incapacity to aid the achievement of spiritual unity and serenity. As contemporary medical and psychological studies have also shown, human existence is a unity of body and spirit, of unconscious and conscious, of the impersonal and personal dimensions of our life; in short, both "ontological" and "personal" categories are necessary to describe it. This unity of the ontological and the personal has always been affirmed of *God* as at once the source of our ontological being and yet as personal, as the giver of life and of eternal life and yet also as one whose judgments, intentions, and "will" were the final object of our personal trust or faith. Revelation thus fulfills our human being, individual and historical, as well as evokes our personal trust; it is a communication both of a new way of existing and a new way of understanding or of believing.

On the reasonable premise that there is a manifestation

or visibility, however dim, of the divine power and wisdom everywhere that God is active, most of the Christian tradition has affirmed that the ultimacy and the sacrality inherent in the divine presence are "there" to be seen—in some fashion or another—throughout both the course of nature and the sequence of historical events. As Tillich notes, and most of us have experienced, the constant order of nature has frequently been a medium or vehicle for an awareness of the divine wisdom and faithfulness (for example, in the Logos conception of Hellenic culture and the Tao of China), while strange, unruly, or extraordinary powers and events of nature (the sea, sacred mountains, volcanoes and other awe-inspiring and overwhelming realities) have been media for an awareness of the divine power and transcendence. Correspondingly, an (apparently) benevolent sequence of historical events has frequently seemed to indicate the presence of a providential goodness ruling those events (for example, the glory and success of a tribe or a state or the sense of historical progress that the modern West enjoyed), while a chaotic sequence seemed to reveal either only the divine anger or judgment or only a history quite void of purposive rule. As with the revelation through culture, the enigmatic forces of nature and of history certainly "lure" us to worship and glorify their necessity, power, and beauty; but they also tempt us to idolize in them what is merely finite, creaturely, and partial. Thus while both the natural order and the sequences of history can be vehicles of revelation, if criticized and corrected by a perspective anchored elsewhere, both also are in themselves opaque and ambiguous. The divine is as hidden as it is manifest through nature and history, though neither can be fully understood without theological interpretation; and as a result no definitive clue to the power and meaning of existence as a whole comes to us through them.

It is, therefore, through some special event or special

sequence of historical events that a clue to the power and meaning latent in existence is possible, that any definitive or "final" revelation in the sense that has been spoken of occurs. As noted, this special sequence can be centered around the history of our nation, our race, or our culture—as, for example, in China it was centered around all three; in the West around single nations, the Caucasian race, or the developing Western culture; or in Marxist countries around the special history of the proletariat and the Party. The luring power in each is obvious; the temptation to idolatry—without very much of an inherent or built-in antidote—is equally obvious.

In the Christian tradition, accordingly, the locus of the clue to the ultimate power and meaning of process lies neither in nature nor in general history, nor again in any particular cultural tradition. Rather, it lies in the special history or sequence of events culminating in a person, in and through which special sequence God is believed to have given a definitive manifestation of his/her power, purposes, and will. The special history in question is constituted by the events through which Yahveh established, preserved, judged, and reestablished Israel as a people. The person was, of course, Jesus of Nazareth who was formed by that Hebrew communal tradition, who, in Christian eyes, both completed and refashioned that tradition, and who provided in his person, his words, his destiny or fate, and his response to that destiny, definitive manifestation of that same God's being and will.

Thus a sequence of objective, historical events and a person are, for Christian belief, the culminating media or vehicles for revelation. Through them the being, power, and intentions or will of God are manifest, and shorn of the ambiguity and hiddenness characteristic of nature and history generally and of any particular culture. Clearly it was the *factuality* of this revelation—that God was in fact encountered there by these communities as actually and gratuitously manifesting himself/herself—that established or constituted for them these media as revelatory. No "choice" was made either by the Hebrew or by the Christian community of these media as revelatory because they were "superior" to others. In most forms of religion, humans experience revelation, if that category is used, as in this sense "given" to them, not as found, discovered, or chosen by them. Nevertheless, after the fact it may be noted that events and persons, as vehicles or media of the divine, unite the central realms or dimensions of experience, namely the natural, the historical, and the personal; and, as noted, that they "fit in" with the nature of God as experienced in this tradition as at once the source or ground of finite being and thus of nature, the ruler of the processes of social history, and the personal creator, lord and "co-respondent" of human and thus of personal existence. There thus is latent in this tradition, as in no other I believe, the possibility of a union of nature, history, and personal existence that is genuinely inclusive of the best (and often greater) wisdom in many other traditions and also that is essential to our present dilemmas. In any case, here revelation is centrally given and received through a particular sequence of historical events and in a person, his words, and the events of his life.

"Nature," as we ordinarily use that word, however, is not just "there," "already out there real" (as Lonergan says) before we experience and know it. As a symbol, nature is also what is known about nature; it is nature interpreted and understood by a tradition of experience, of inquiry, of reflection, and of judgment. Correspondingly, "history" as a given sequence of events is never merely "there" to be observed; it also is already interpreted if it is to be known or referred to at all. It is remembered, organized by a theme into an intelligible sequence of ordered relations (of causes and effects, we say), of successive epochs or periods, and thus given some sort of intelligibility and meaning, beginnings, endings, and some principle of the union of the two. Likewise when we speak of revelation through nature, through history, or through a sequence of historical events and a person, immediately implied is an interpretation and a mode, form, or tradition of interpretation. The power, meaning, and character of Yahveh's acts in history are in the Old Testament revealed to the prophet. The "Word" of Yahveh given to them provides, say the prophets, the insight into this sequence of events that makes it possible for Yahveh's purposes and promises to be revealed there. Correspondingly, in the Christian community, it is the witness of the community of disciples—the "apostolic witness"—that opens up or uncovers the deeper or transcendent meaning of the events of Jesus' life, words, and death, and that witnesses to his resurrection. Thus, just as nature and history are uncovered or unveiled and known by the *interpretation* of human experience and inquiry, so the nature and purposes of God as manifest within historical events and persons are uncovered, interpreted, and proclaimed by the responding *witness* of the community. Objective event and creative word, historical sequences and linguistic interpretation, unite in the manifestation of the divine. Even before the appearance of written Scripture, therefore, these polar media of event and Word of interpretation, event and witnessing community, are present.

As a consequence, revelation refers to a relationship, a relation that has both an objective and a subjective side—as do "world," "nature," and "history." All refer to a correlation between some aspect or aspects of objective reality and responding human participation, inquiry, judgment, and acceptance. In the case of revelation, the response begins, first, with conscious and self-conscious *acknowl-*

edgment, acknowledgment that a revelatory event has occurred, creating a new openness to receive, understand,
and appropriate that event. This acknowledgment, insofar
as it is conscious and autonomous or free, the self-directed
act of an integral person, involves, second, *understanding* as
the condition of inward, personal, uncoerced assent.
Third, since revelation is the communication not only of
insight and illumination but of a new mode of existing, this
response leads also to new forms of *action* and to new *ways
of relating* to other people. It directs and guides as well as
illumines and heals. Finally, the response results in *witness*
or *speech* to others about the event, to new modes of responsibility to others, of care for others, and thus to new experiences and new forms of communal life. In short, the
objective event of revelation creates a new community
with a new center of loyalty, new modes of understanding, new styles of action, new forms of relationship to
one another and to the world, and a new message—a
community whose ultimate goal and norm is the Kingdom. A tradition thus begins, a new community is
formed, and new ways of being human in history become
possible.

As is evident, a distinction should be made—as Tillich
helpfully does—between "originating revelation," the
event or events that begin a religious community and its
tradition, and what he calls "dependent revelation," the
continuing process over extended time of the reception of
that revelation by subsequent generations. The earliest
community, the disciples and apostles, were the original
respondents to the event of Jesus as the Christ. In their
response they acknowledged, understood, interpreted, and
witnessed to that event. The results of that response were
the nascent and then explicit community: the ecclesia or
Church; the early proclamation, or kerygma, of the leaders
and of many others who spread news of the event and its

meaning; the new forms of community, of its practices and worship—the early liturgies and sacraments; and finally the oral and then the written traditions of Gospels, histories, and letters (the New Testament canon) that recount the event, and that set it in relation both to its preceding tradition (the Hebrew Scriptures) and to the processes of history generally. This sequence of responses—altogether called "tradition" by the early community—becomes subsequently the "media" for those events of dependent revelation through which our acceptance or acknowledgment, our understanding, our new mode of existence, and our witness—*our* belief or faith—become possible. Each one of these media—Scripture, preaching, worship, sacrament, the witness and life of members of the community (and even theology, maybe)—can be called "revelatory" or an instrument of revelation in the Christian tradition *only* insofar as they *re*-present the originating event, that is, as they bring persons over time into relation with Jesus of Nazareth. Word (Scripture and preaching), sacrament, and—possibly most effective of all—the love exhibited by Christians have historically thus been regarded as the "means of grace" of the Christian community, continuing the community by relating each subsequent generation of Christians to the originating event of revelation on which the community and its new life were founded.

It has always been assumed by the community—and by theologians seeking to understand the mystery of this continuous reenactment of the event of revelation—that the possibility of this reenactment (of, say, a man or a woman in the twentieth century "encountering God in Jesus Christ," "being born again," "being grasped by the power of the New Being," or "coming to faith"—there are many possible ways of expressing it—depends on the continuing and active presence of God within both the life of the community and the life of the individual. For both the establishment and the presence of a deep relation to God and of "faith" require the presence of God and not just the words (however persuasive), the actions (however loving), or even the life (however noble) of another person. Thus, it has from the very beginning been affirmed that the power of Word, of sacrament, and of a loving life either to establish or preserve the faith of persons in the community lay, not primarily in the abilities of members of the community, but lay in the working of the Holy Spirit in the community and through these media. It is the Holy Spirit resident in the community that continues the original revelation over time, that empowers the believing community to be the preaching, worshiping, and loving "Church" (whenever it *is* that), and that relates and re-relates each person and each generation of Christians to God. That the Holy Spirit has been at work in the Christian community, and that it is promised that the Spirit will continue to be there, no believing Christian can doubt. That the spirit of God works elsewhere as well, bringing the gifts of grace to other persons outside the Church, where the Church is either not known (as in other religions) or not heeded (as among, say, humanists) is also something no one can doubt who knows the universal presence, the justice, the all-encompassing love, and the mercy of the God preached by Jesus and witnessed to in the Christian community.

The basic form of originating revelation, then, is that of revelatory event and human response, and the basic form of continuing or dependent revelation is that of tradition (or media) and autonomous acceptance and understanding. It is this fundamental structure of event and response and of tradition and autonomy that in turn shapes our understanding of the role and authority of the Scriptures and of the Church, the role, authority, and procedures of theology, and finally the status of Christianity among other religions. On each of these issues important changes have occurred in the self-understanding of the Christian community.

Perhaps the most important development in modern culture with regard to theology has been the growth of "historical consciousness," namely, the awareness that every cultural product of history, be it a set of laws, a philosophy, a social theory, a theology, a religious document or scripture, is "relative" in the sense that it reflects the perspectives, aims, and norms of its time. More through the influence of this development of modern culture than its own insight about itself, modern theology (since ca. 1800) has first discovered to its surprise and then admitted into its essential understanding that the human responses to revelation, and thus the creations or products of that response (preaching, Scripture, doctrine or dogmas, and moral precepts), are *human* and not divine, part of our response to revelation and not themselves directly revealed. Thus, the Scriptures have come to be viewed as *human* documents reflecting the ideas, biases, hopes, and fears of their age and so filled with the errors about nature, historical events, psychology, etc. of that age—not to mention the less than perfect moral and social standards of that age. They *witness* to a divine revelatory event or events, but the witness is human and thus historical and fallible. They have been and can again be "media" of dependent revelation, that is, a continuing experience of the divine by the community. But they are not *themselves* directly revealed as if they represented complete and perfect truth. As Archbishop William Temple said, "There are no revealed truths; there are only truths about revelation, witnessing to revelation." Correspondingly, the Church's statements, even its dogmas and sacred laws, have come to be viewed not only as "developing" over time but, more important, as influenced at each stage by the views, the philosophies, the goals, and the standards of that time in which they were produced, and, thus being relative to their own age, in continuing need of reinterpretation and revision. In short, for contemporary theology (and what a revolution this was!), the media of revelation—Scripture, church authority, dogmas, doctrines, laws, in fact the whole corpus of the Christian "religion"—have become, while still *media*, relative, historical, fallible, and thus subject to continual criticism and transformation.

While, therefore, Protestantism has lost its infallible Scripture and Catholicism (for many) its infallible ecclesia, nevertheless both remain "means of grace," witnesses to the original revelation and thus vehicles of dependent revelation through which God continues to manifest himself/herself to us. As the primary witness to the originating event, Scripture remains the ultimate source and the final norm for the life, the thought, and the practice of the continuing community. However, as our principle indicates, what is given in revelation and thence in tradition must be acknowledged, understood, and interpreted anew to be received at all. Hence, the community and its tradition always interpret Scripture, refashioning its message in the light of the cultural situation and, through the work of the Holy Spirit, transforming in turn their cultural "situation" in the light of the revelation communicated to them through the witness of Scripture. It is only the Holy Spirit, not their own absolute or infallible status, that can make Scripture, community, and the Christian religion generally a genuine witness to revelation and so can give to each whatever healing, illuminating, and saving power each of them possesses.

Theology, I said in the introduction, is the enterprise of understanding reflectively and thus, in our own cultural terms, the contents of the Christian faith or, correlatively, of interpreting the human situation in its widest extent in the light of that faith. It is now possible to understand much more precisely how theology, involved in that dual task, proceeds, what are its sources, and what procedures and instruments it uses. For we have established that the contents of the Christian faith in their entirety refer to what I have called originating revelation, that series of events that established and preserved the Hebrew community, that culminated for Christians in the life of Jesus of Nazareth, and in response to which the community of the Church was founded. Further, the primary present source for our knowledge of those events is the witness of each of these two interrelated communities, the Old Testament and the New Testament Scriptures. Finally, it is evident that that witness, set in the terms of its own time, must be interpreted by each successive age, including our own, and that our present interpretation, being itself historical, is itself the child of generations of interpretation.

Again it is apparent that theology represents an interrelation, a correlation, of a number, in this case four, different resources. First, its primary and normative source is Scripture as the central witness to the originating events of revelation. This means that for the responsible theologian whatever in his or her work does not seem to accord with the witness of Scripture is not authentic and must be reworked. Correspondingly, the essential responsibility of the theologian is to be faithful to the witness of Scripture, and his or her main theological arguments are directed to give warrants for the authenticity of his or her interpretation of Scripture. Second, since Scripture is always interpreted, the second if not the primary and normative resource is the tradition of the interpretation of Scripture, the tradition of theology. A responsible theologian should not only criticize, as is necessary, that tradition to make room for his or her new interpretation. He or she should also seek to show continuity with the spirit if not the letter of

major elements of the theological tradition, with the historic
as well as the original contents of the Christian faith—if a
given theology is to claim to be an authentic expression of
that faith.

For the moment, before I move on to the third and the
fourth resources of theology, I will make more precise how
the theologian is "faithful" to the scriptural source and
how he or she shows a continuity with the spirit of major
elements of tradition. Does this mean the theologian copies
or repeats the words, the categories, the propositions of
Scripture or tradition; that he or she makes a précis of
Scripture or writes a commentary on accepted dogma? If
copying or repeating is futile because anachronistic, what
is it that the theologian "draws" from this source and this
resource? In our discussion of cultural and religious traditions an important element in the "ethos," the cultural
vision of any community has been uncovered, namely, the
symbolic structure through which that community viewed
reality, truth, and value and thus through which it expressed its perspective on the world and on itself. Correspondingly, each religious tradition, reflectively viewed,
represents a definite, unique symbolic structure through
which, or by means of which, it views reality, truth, and
value. In the area of belief, of intellectual conviction, the
differences between religions are represented by the crucial
differences in the symbols each finds expressive of what is
real, in the procedures each adopts to find what is true,
and in the values and goals for life it correspondingly
cleaves to. Just as, therefore, to express reflectively what
"democracy" or "Marxism" means is to bring into a coherent, intelligible unity the central symbols that make up
each of these social theories, so to express reflectively the
contents of the Christian (or the Jewish or Buddhist) faiths
is to bring to coherent, intelligible unity the central symbols of the Christian (or Jewish or Buddhist) tradition.

These symbols and the ways they are related to one another—for these symbols tend to define and qualify each other—differ in each religion, as in each social tradition. The uniqueness of each tradition is, therefore, located intellectually in the uniqueness of that particular gestalt of symbols.

In the Christian tradition these symbols find their normative expression, and for theology their source, in the Scriptures since their primary reference is to the events of revelation to which the Scriptures witness. It is these symbols that are reinterpreted in various ways in tradition; and it is they that the theologian must reinterpret, re-present in a manner intelligible to us and yet "appropriate" or faithful to their sense in their original locus. Because of the theocentric character of Christianity as a religion, in our tradition these symbols have to do primarily with God: God as creator (*ex nihilo*), God as sovereign lord of events, God as judge, God as electing, choosing, or covenanting, God as giver of the law, God as redeemer, as faithful, etc. Correspondingly, since here God reveals himself/herself too and creates a community, there are also important symbols about Israel and its life: the covenant, the elected people, the law, betrayal and sin, the new covenant, the Messiah, the new age to come, etc.

In the New Testament this battery of symbols reappears but in a quite new synthesis, recentered around the historical event and person of Jesus. Thus, "Christological" symbols appear: incarnation, atonement, resurrection, ascension, trinity, the second coming, etc. These theological and Christological symbols refer to and express the prime referent of Christian faith, namely God, his revelation in Jesus of Nazareth, and the community (ecclesia) established and continually reestablished by the latter. Associated with them, therefore, are corresponding symbols expressing a Christian view of human being, history, and its destiny. And, finally, entailed in both are normative or ethical symbols (e.g., "love") expressing the obligations and aims implied in such an understanding of God and of human being. "Biblical theology" is the attempt to give a unified account of these symbols as they appear in the Old and the New Testaments; historical theology is the story of these symbols as they have been reinterpreted in the tradition.

Theology as a whole, then, concerns itself with these symbols and with their power to illumine our existence. The awesome and risky task of "constructive" or "systematic" theology is to provide or propose a unified *contemporary* understanding of that same complex of symbols, an understanding that is (a) faithful to their original sense in Scripture and tradition, (b) adequate to our own general experience, and (c) intelligible to our time.

It is now time to consider the third and fourth resources of theology. It is they that provide, so to speak, the materials for the *re*interpretation or *re*-presentation of the traditional symbols, that is, the task of constructive or systematic theology. They stand in theology for the principle of *dis*continuity with tradition as fidelity to the complex of symbols represented the principle of continuity with tradition. The third resource is what Tillich called the "situation" of the contemporary world, the entire understanding of reality, of human being, and of history that animates and dominates present-day life and thus the minds of both theologian and reader, preacher and listener, priest and worshiper. This is the "cultural vision" or "ethos" of which I spoke in an earlier chapter. Very sketchily put, this general understanding and self-understanding has, in our own epoch, been formed largely by two intellectual currents, by two social realities, and by two communal aims. The intellectual currents are the rise to domination of science and the appearance, as noted, of historical consciousness;

the correlated social realities are the dominance of indus-trialism and urbanization on the one hand and the domi-nance of technology on the other; the communal aims are for freedom or self-direction on the one hand and for jus-tice and community on the other—both being aims for *this* existence in *this* world and in *this* history.

The development of this modern self-understanding has resulted, as everyone knows, in a view of almost every-thing vastly different from the traditional view. Our con-temporary understanding of nature, of social and human life and their interrelations, of time, of causality, of human history, and of the factors that make it work, of where history is going and where it ought to go, of what is au-thentic in life and what is not, and so on endlessly, differs dramatically from the understanding of these things in the cultural epochs when our theological tradition was formed. If Christian faith is to be relevant to us who live in this new world, it must re-present itself in the categories and forms of that new world. How can we speak of the religious dimension of health, of the wholeness that comes through faith, without relation to—as well as transcen-dence of—the procedures, the knowledge, and the modes of curing represented by modern medicine not to mention modern therapy? The modern "situation" in the light of which the gestalt of traditional symbols must be reinter-preted includes, therefore, the natural and human sci-ences, literature and the arts, contemporary legal and social theory, and especially philosophy's union of this self-understanding into contemporary epistomology, ontology, and ethics. How this interrelation of traditional symbol and of cultural situation is to take place is the crux of the question of theological method and is too complex to em-bark upon here. Theology, however, can neither avoid the issue nor, if it is to be intelligible and relevant, avoid making union in some way with the situation of contemporary men and women.

To be intelligible and true to us, a contemporary explication of Christian symbols must be deeply related to this whole "modern" mode of understanding: to our consciousness of nature and of historical passage, to our understanding of causality and of space, to our interpretation of human existence and its goals. In the case of each of the symbols I shall discuss, I shall propose a sharp *re*interpretation of that symbol so as to give it expression in the context of this modern self-understanding, as I have already done with the symbol of "belief." The primary task of the theologian, therefore, is to reinterpret the classical symbols of the tradition, for example, creation or providence, incarnation and redemption, in terms that are at once intelligible in our world and yet faithful to the original and continuing sense of that symbol in the tradition.

Lest, however, this principle of method whereby traditional symbols are reinterpreted in a modern light seem to connote a simple "capitulation" to modern culture, it should be noted that this same principle cuts both ways. That is, it entails as well that modern experience is in turn interpreted in a *Christian* way; that is, that this experience is *shaped* by those traditional categories. Thus, as will be increasingly clear as I develop this interpretation, the resulting theology, which is hopefully *intelligible* to a modern person, is *by no means* itself merely representative of "modern thought." On the contrary, at basic points it represents a significant opposition and challenge to modern thought. The view of reality is *not* naturalistic but theistic, dominated by the transcendent figure of God. The view of human nature is not humanistic but classically Christian, characterized by created goodness and present estrangement. The view of redemption is Christological and not immanentist; that is, it is dependent upon a transcendent grace and not on our own powers. The view of history is theonomous and eschatological, not autonomous and progressivist. Anyone who thinks this represents a view in which "modernity" remains the main or determining criterion simply knows nothing of what kinds of views "modern thought" represents. The result should be a *Christian* interpretation of *modern* experience. If it be not Christian, that is, "appropriate" and faithful to Scripture and tradition, it will bring no new message and thus no healing to modern existence; if it be not an interpretation of *modern* experience, it will not touch that experience enough to have effect. Thus do its *sources* lie in tradition and its *resources* in various aspects of present experience. There are few orthodox or evangelical interpreters of the gospel who do not, implicitly if not explicitly, follow this same procedure.

Since, moreover, no symbol means anything to us, however sacred it may be, unless it touches and thematizes, that is, gives creative, healing, and directing shape to our ordinary experience of life, any relevant theology must continually relate its interpretation of Christian symbols to the more significant experiences and obligations of our common existence in the world.[2] It is this necessary and essential touch with the modern situation and its obligations that gives theology both its interest and its risk. It is risky because what is required is a *new* interpretation not a repetition, and a new interpretation, the creative effort of the theologian, is always in danger of failure, that is, of a one-sided and incoherent or even a profane presentation of the symbol. It is exciting because only as a result of this reinterpretation is theology relevant to life and to action and so genuinely transformative in its affect. Thus is it enabled to become what it should be, namely, a reflective Christian interpretation of our com-

mon human situation and itself possibly a small but important means of grace to our existence and our action in the
world.

Although the fourth resource is the most enigmatic in its
results on Christian theology, it is as unavoidable in our
modern situation as are the others. This is the resource for
Christian theology latent within other religious traditions.
Because this is for me as for others an almost unexplored
terrain, only very preliminary remarks are possible based
on principles already established in the above. The first
principle is that since it is evident to most, if not all, contemporary reflective Christians that God's revelation extends far beyond the bounds of the biblical tradition,
clearly there is "truth" to be found in other traditions,
truths about reality as a whole, about nature, about human
existence, about the possibilities of consciousness, and thus
contemplative techniques, which the Christian tradition
has either ignored or never attained at all. The second
principle is that since the Christian tradition as a *religion*,
and therefore as a body of reflective theory (doctrines) and
as a set of practices and rules, is thoroughly human, a
human response to God's activity, Christianity as a religion is both partial and fallible, inclusive of some perspectives and exclusive of others. Much that might potentially
have been included within its scope but was not—for cultural and historical reasons—is therefore to be learned
from other traditions, as they have learned much from the
biblical perspective. Both because of the width of the divine revelation and the narrowness of our human reception, even of the revelation in Jesus as the Christ, the
traditions of other religions can be a creative and authentic
resource for Christian theology. How this resource might
be used is suggested in the following.

As I have noted, Christian faith—and any other tradition for that matter—always interprets itself in the light of

a particular cultural gestalt or vision. In the earliest period it was the Hellenic culture of Greece and the Hellenistic culture of the Roman Empire that provided the situation and the perspective through which Christian symbols were interpreted and transformed from their original biblical setting. Patristic theology represents a reinterpretation of biblical symbols in the terms of Hellenic and Hellenistic cultures. In contemporary life it is, as I said, in the terms of modern culture that the classical symbols are now again reinterpreted. In each case of reinterpretation, as any study of historical and of contemporary theology shows, new and creative elements in the gospel have been uncovered—as when the new social consciousness of the nineteenth century uncovered the ethical implications for political action of Christian symbols in the social gospel and the liberationist movements. Now, as the presupposition of their theological work, requiring as it did an interpretation or reinterpretation of biblical symbols in Hellenic and Hellenistic terms, the theologians of the early Church spoke of "God's covenant with the Greeks" paralleling the "covenant with the Jews" and thereby legitimatizing the union of Greek philosophy and of biblical symbols that constituted all Patristic theology. God, so they reasoned, has revealed himself/herself in some measure through Greek culture, and thus on the basis of that "covenant" they could use Greek philosophy and its categories as means through which to express their own Christian faith. If this process of using Greek philosophy to reinterpret the Christian faith is "orthodox"—and what else is?—then we can equally speak, as a defense of modern theology, of a "covenant with modernity." In this very traditional way, a modern re-presentation of traditional symbols within the terms of modern culture may be legitimatized. Modern culture may, to be sure, be "pagan," but it can hardly be more pagan than the Greek philosophy that preceded the event of the Christ.

Finally, if God's presence and self-manifestation are really universal, essential for each cultural and religious tradition, it is also possible to speak of a covenant with Buddhism, with Islam, or with Hinduism. For theology such an understanding means that, just as viewing biblical symbols through the eyes of Hellenic, Hellenistic culture and then of modern culture has been "enlightening," so it can be illuminative of both the weaknesses and the strengths of the Christian tradition—and there are vast heaps of both—to view its symbolic understanding through the eyes of, say, Buddhist questions and categories. This does not represent a synthesis of two different religions, nor does it represent an abandonment of the final sources of Christian theology in Christian revelation and tradition. What it does do is to seek to criticize, and so to deepen, our understanding of our own tradition and perspective by examining it in the light of another tradition. In this limited but potentially very radical way, other religions can be a creative resource for Christian theology.

To sum up: to say "I believe" is, as can be seen, a most complex affair. On the cultural and historical levels, it means to associate oneself by personal participation, by assent, by understanding, and by transformative action within the tradition of the Christian community. In turn, that means to view one's own existence, one's world, one's history, and one's obligations in the light of the symbolic structure and the norms of that community. If one really means that affirmation, it entails that this commitment to this tradition—its symbolic understanding and its norms—transcends one's similar commitment to the social group, the nation, class, race, or culture to which ultimate loyalty would otherwise be given. This becomes, then, the *real* community within which one lives out one's history.

On a deeper level, to say "I believe" means to relate oneself—or, better, to witness to a relation that has occurred—through that community and its tradition to (1) an event of originating revelation in Jesus as the Christ, (2) to the long and significant preparation for that event in the Hebrew community, and (3) to the presence of the Holy Spirit in the tradition and in one's own experience of that tradition. Thus in this case the originating event, the tradition itself and one's own autonomous acceptance of both, are qualified, supported, and even initiated by the divine presence, the divine activity, and the divine intention. To say "I believe" is, in other words, to witness to the presence of God in the event of Jesus, in the continuing life, Scriptures, and understanding of the community, and in the autonomous acknowledgment, understanding, and commitment discovered in oneself. There are two levels here: a visible, cultural, historical level and a deeper, religious, or theological level. Both are essential to Christian experience, to theological understanding—and both will continually reappear as the contents of faith and its relation to human existence are explored further.

NOTES

1. The words in the text ("called," "created," etc.) are, of course, directly relevant only to the Jewish and the Christian religious communities, and possibly the Islamic. Since the relation of the "divine presence" to the community—and the conception itself of the divine presence—is understood in different religious traditions in *very* different ways, needless to say, a quite different set of words would be appropriate to other traditions. In all cases, however, it would be *those* words, specifying the relation of the community to its religious center, that would define the community—and that is our point.

2. For a fuller discussion of this requirement that meaningful theological concepts be related to ordinary, daily, "secular" experience, see the author's *Naming the Whirlwind: The Renewal of God-Language* (Indianapolis: Bobbs-Merrill, 1969), especially pp. 91–106, 190–203, 260–84, 454–70.

SUGGESTED READINGS

Recent Classics

Baillie, J. *Our Knowledge of God*. Oxford Univ. Press, 1946.
———. *The Idea of Revelation in Recent Thought*. Columbia Univ. Press, 1956.
Barth, K. *The Epistle to the Romans*. Translated from the 6th edition. Oxford Univ. Press, 1950.
———. *The Word of God and the Word of Man*. Harper Torchbook, 1957.
———. *Dogmatics in Outline*. Philosophical Library, n.d.
Brunner, H. E. *Revelation and Reason*. Westminster, 1946.
Gadamer, H. G. *Truth and Method*. The Seabury Press, 1975.
Kierkegaard, S. *Philosophical Fragments*. Princeton Univ. Press, 1946.
———. *Concluding Unscientific Postscript*. Princeton Univ. Press, 1944.
Niebuhr, H. R. *The Meaning of Revelation*. Macmillan, 1946.
Tillich, P. *Systematic Theology*. Vol. 1. Univ. of Chicago Press, 1955.
———. *Dynamics of Faith*. Harper & Row, 1956.

Current Discussion

Ebeling, G. *Word and Faith*. Fortress, 1963.
Kaufman, G. *Relativism, Knowledge and Faith*. Univ. of Chicago Press, 1960.
Pannenberg, W. *Revelation as History*. Harper & Row, 1968.
Schillebeeckx, E. *The Understanding of Faith*. Seabury, 1974.

PART TWO

"... In God the Father Almighty ..."

4
THE SYMBOL OF HUMAN CREATURELINESS

THE central theme in this second part is the nature of God as "Father [or Mother, or, best of all, Parent] Almighty," the source, ground, and sovereign of all that we are and experience. I shall, therefore, be concerned with those symbols, words, or notions about God that express or define this "almightiness," namely, God as the creator (as the creed adds, "Maker of Heaven and Earth") and providential ruler of all that is.

In thus discussing God as source or ground of the reality and fulfillment of everything finite, as creator and providential ruler, we are dealing with God's universal and necessary relations to all things, activities God must, so to speak, be doing if anything else is to be done at all by anyone. Obviously, if God, as creator, were in any given instance not so related or not at work in these ways, that instance would never *be* at all and would itself thus be unable to *do* anything. Thus (to subside for the moment into technical jargon) I am outlining God's "ontological" or "metaphysical" characteristics, those aspects of his/her essential nature that are necessary and thus universal factors in the reality or being of things. However they may be known, by revelation or reason—and that is a complex matter—the symbols of creation and of providence deal with God's *being* in his/her relation to all finite beings and with his/her *universal activity* in relation to all creatures. To know in this sense that God is "Parent-almighty" is, therefore, to know much that is significant about both the being, nature, and work of God and about the being and nature of finite creatures. As the succeeding chapters will indicate, however, it is not yet to know all that Christian faith wishes to say about either God or about creatures.

The method of this volume is to begin each chapter with our own experience of ourselves as that experience reflects the aspect of God—or more precisely of the creed—under discussion. The ground for this was, first, that I wish to begin "where we are" and in that way to make my discussion as intelligible as possible. And second, I start with our experience of ourselves because it is a well-recognized rule in meaningful theology that God can only be understood in relation to ourselves and our experience—just as the latter can only be made intelligible, bearable, and creative in relation to God. If it is, then, my method to begin with our human being as it is reflected in the Christian witness to God, clearly that aspect of our human being which is relevant to God as creator and preserver—namely what it is about us that God "creates" and "preserves"—is represented by our finitude, that is our *reality* or *being* as finite entities in a universe of finite entities. This finitude characteristic of our being is termed in Christian parlance our creatureliness; it can be described as our self-transcending finitude and, on the deepest level, as the image or "symbol" of God.

What, then, is the Christian view of human finitude or creatureliness? The wise theologian or Christian—at least in this day—does not pretend to know through the witness of his or her faith, or even through theological training, all that is useful or true to understand about men and women. For most of this, as we recognize, we must go to the life sciences, psychology, social science, and history, to our analyst, to personal and social experience, to literature and the arts, to the daily press and X-rated movies; to our hospital terminal wards and our city morgues; to our kitchens, bathrooms, and bedrooms—if we are to know what is to be known about ourselves and others. The essential point of a *Christian* or a *theological* interpretation of men and women is that all of this common experience, commonsense knowledge, and even scientific knowledge of ourselves makes little sense alone. Or, more precisely put, it only makes patches or pockets of sense that together make no sense, and, separated from one another, these perspectives on ourselves are unintelligible. Unless this whole conglomeration of "old saws," or knowledge, of formulae, of insights, perspectives, and myths is seen in the light of God, unless the men and women we know and experience are understood in their relation to God, we find appearing a fundamental confusion and misunderstanding about ourselves and a fundamental incoherence in our understanding of our own life and its meaning.

This example provides a good working rule for what theology on its own theological grounds can legitimately talk about. It does not and cannot know *everything*: how the earth was made and when, how we are related to and different from animals, how big the universe is, ad infinitum. These are matters for science and historical inquiry, for exploration and common sense to tell us about if they can. Theology as theology can discuss "creatures"—all of us in the universe—*only* in their relation to God and ourselves only as we are related to God—or, as Tillich put this, only insofar as an issue is an "ultimate concern" for us, an issue of our being and non-being, can theology deal with it. The theologian can, of course, also talk about a lot of other matters—and I shall. But in that case he or she does so as an interested student of other disciplines or as an observer of human affairs and of his or her own motives and problems, not as a "theologian."

I shall start with a description—which I hope is recognizably accurate—of our common experience of our own creatureliness. That we are "creatures" is at present drummed into our minds repeatedly by the "sciences" of human being—though the fact of science itself with its extraordinary powers to know and to control our world shows we are at the least unusual creatures—and by most contemporary naturalistic philosophy: "We are merely animals who laugh, speak, play, dream, etc." In our day we are intellectually exceedingly conscious of our relation to the animal world and through them to nature's processes—though ironically it is precisely in forgetting that relation in its own *technological* and *industrial* existence that modern life is most in danger of self-destruction. I will try, then, to explore our awareness of this creatureliness as it appears in our experience of ourselves.

For most humans—particularly, it seems, modern people—the predominant sign or evidence in experience of that finitude or creatureliness has been our temporality. Temporality is a word standing for the fact that we are, whether we will or not, immersed in an ongoing temporal passage, "thrown into it," appearing in *medias res*, coming to be, so to speak, on an already-going conveyer belt or, better, on a rushing river that hurtles us on careening from moment to moment—and will hurtle us off or immerse us at the end. We come and then we go, everything—and our life—zooms by, and the duration of our appearance in existence is very brief indeed. We did not choose to be here, to have this self in this world, these parents in this community, these quirks, meager talents, and paltry opportunities—to be in this canoe on this creek with this paddle. Our thinking, our understanding, and our deciding start here, within this given rushing world and our immersion in it. Nor does any of this "given" from our past stay, so we can sum it up or really learn to cope with it. It, too, rushes and changes and gives little indication where it, and we, are going. Above all, it requires us to use and manage it. For we are also given practical charge of our passage; we are, so to speak, handed the paddle, and we are called inexorably to steer while the river takes us careening into the next moment—a next moment whose peculiar threats as well as unique chances are now unseeable, mostly unknown, and certain to appear largely unannounced. We have neither a map nor time to look at it, and yet we have to find our way—and our own way. Clearly in such a difficult, if not desperate, situation, our most direct temptation is merely to watch others to see how they handle their passages and thus, in case they have a poor technique, to go under with them.

This is, I suggest, our primordial experience of our own temporality. It is a strange experience of double directionality. The future comes at us and becomes, far too fast, the present. The present (especially a summer vacation, one's youth, or when one's children are young) slips by and out and, like a train rushing through a station, soon vanishes, out of sight and out of touch, into the past. The excitement and often panic of this ferocious speed come from the experience of the movement of time itself out of the future, into the present, and then into the vanishing past. Meanwhile, we experience ourselves and our world—whatever "being" there appears to be anywhere—as moving at an equal pace in the opposite direction, out of their past, out of what is given, into a present where we are necessarily in charge and must make decisions, and on into a future that is undecided and thus open. Time seems to move one way, being or process another—which is why both the new eschatological theologians and the process philosophers are right.

Now what I shall call "destiny"—the given in our existence—comes out of our past complete with our present selves and our present world; it is the entire given world and our selves in that world which at the moment are together actual and which represent whatever *is*. "Destiny" thus presents us with a present, an actuality in space and in the now, the whole set of conditions, including ourselves, in which we are and in which we now must act. In this same present we dimly discern possibilities ahead of us in the future, and we feel our own inescapable role in the enactment of those possibilities and so in the shaping of what will be the destiny for the next present— that is, for our next present and for the present of others. Our careening passage through time is characterized, then, by two sets of polar categories: (1) *destiny*—what we and our world have been given and so what they are—and *freedom*—the capacity to shape both ourselves and our world into the future; and (2) *actuality*—what is now arising out of what has been—and *possibility*—what might be or become in the still undecided future.

Who, then, are we who experience in this way our temporality? What is the essential structure of our creatureliness uncovered by this analysis of our experience of passage? It is, says Christian symbolism, viewing this experienced reality of temporal human being as reflected in our relation to God, a *creatureliness* which is made in the *divine image*. Certainly, such experience of being in passage as we have described it is first of all an experience of radical finitude, of contingency, and of dependence. It is an experience of creatureliness, of ourselves as finite. Clearly, we are the causes neither of ourselves nor of our world. Rather, we are given ourselves from beyond ourselves by causes that long preceded us; and we are given our world without a single "yes" from us. Thus are we in every regard dependent on other beings, and thus is the fact that we are here at all radically contingent, contingent on an infinity of other events and entities over which we have little or no control. As a consequence, who we are and what world we are in, is so far as we can directly see, a monstrous, but for us at the moment, a happy accident, a concatenation of a million "good lucks" that result in us, that is, results in all these particular "thises" that together make it possible for ourselves (*this* "this") and our particular world to be at all. The radical contingency of our being—and that of all around us—has been noted by theologians and philosophers since the beginning. Only in modern culture has it, because of our new controls over life, seemed questionable. It is also experienced by us "from the inside," as Tillich puts it, first, in the sense of *wonder* at being at all and perhaps of a strange and unexplained gratitude and, second, in the continual experience of an equally unexplained *anxiety* that we might not be at all!

Yet we are not just *in* passage and not just radically dependent on everything else in the universe. We "face" this passage as it comes towards us, and only thus are we so starkly aware that we are in passage and so anxious and easily upset about it. Moreover, while we have not chosen ourselves or our world, we cannot avoid deciding in part who we are going to be and what we are going to do in the light of those unavoidable possibilities thrown at us. (As we discover to our chagrin, sometime in our teens, even to stay in bed and so to avoid decisions, is itself a decision—and we are responsible for it if for nothing else.) In fact, moreover, we can recognize and understand such possibilities as are now given to us by remembering (in part) the past now vanishing, and we find ourselves enacting those possibilities in the light of a probable future that can, therefore, be partly envisioned. Thus do we "transcend" temporal passage with our minds and our wills in the very condition of being immersed within it. As temporal we represent a self-transcending finitude that continually synthesizes past and future into a new present, that relates our given destiny to our present freedom, and that unites in thought and deed our present actuality and our future possibilities. This is the basic structure of our temporality as we experience it and reflect on that experience. Being temporal as we are contains the possibility of self-creation and of the new and thus, if its destiny is benevolent, can it be filled with excitement and meaning. It also contains, however, possibilities of infinite risk, of deep loss, and of not being at all, and so is it frequently experienced as threatened and even overwhelmed by a "fate" which its freedom and its powers cannot control.

Much modern, secular analysis might recognize our description of the human, though it might well wish to use other categories. "To be human is to be in, yet above, time; to remember what has been, to hypothesize about what will be, and to act on the basis of both past and future effecting thereby a new actuality, the present, out of both"—a self-transcending finitude. Secular analysis might also admit into this discussion such categories as reason, will, even spirit, as well as the categories appropriate to biological and physiological inquiry, to describe all of this. But why have I called this (as the Bible does) a creatureliness "made in the divine image"; why are this religious dimension and this religious language involved in speaking about the human? If one already believes in God as our creator and preserver, this may (or may not) make sense. But could it make sense to anyone wondering about God, skeptical about God, or quite ignorant of God?

Or, to put this question another way, in describing the human, there can be little question that humans share with the animals not only life, but dependent, fragmentary, contingent, and mortal life, life supported, driven, and threatened by powerful forces from outside and determined in large part by strange, exciting, and frequently useful impulses from within. Like theirs, ours is an existence governed by the external order of nature and the precarious inner order of instinct and habit. But in us also appears that illusive, rare, and precious order of reason. Because of our participation in both the order of nature and the order of reason, we experience the necessity and the opportunity to plan and to play, to work and to laugh, to feel consciously and to think and know. We are *in* the flux of nature and subject to its determining order and disorder, but we are also in strange ways *out* of it, transcendent to it, able to remember our past and envision possibilities for the future, and thus able to create our own new order and disorder—and to be anxious about what kinds of disorder (or order) the future may bring. The human is thus "naked" ape, *homo faber*, "rational" animal, the organism who (note, not "that") *plays*, who *laughs*, who *dreams*—or as the theological tradition has put the same point: we share in both ontological necessity and the freedom of spirit, in the organic, the psychological, and the spiritual dimensions of being.

Are we also, then, *religious* animal, *homo religiosus* or *mythicus*, a creature made in the divine image? Empirically and historically this is certainly so. Humans everywhere have been religious in one way or another. But the question persists: Is this an *essential* characteristic? Or is it not the case that, as most of modern, intellectual culture has thought, to be religious has been a human possibility, to be sure, but nonetheless a mistaken one, a "deviation," be it harmful or harmless, from full humanity, an early infantile illusion that it is advisable for us to outgrow with maturity's grasp of cold reality? Many of my remarks in these chapters are directed at this question. I shall begin now by pointing to certain aspects or traits of our creatureliness that clearly indicate our human being to be a creatureliness in relation to God, as well as a self-transcending finitude. In fact, as I shall argue, these two, self-transcending finitude and creatureliness in relation to God, are the same thing said in slightly different modes of speech, for neither one can make much sense without the other.

First, the temporal passage in which we participate—which produces and sustains us and lures us into the future—is, I believe, unintelligible unless it too reflects or manifests a ground, power, and order beyond itself. The flux itself, what we often now call Nature, or, in more sophisticated language, Process, is not God. As far as we can see from our careful inquiries, it is made up of all the interlaced causes and effects that produce, threaten, and interest us. All of them arise and then pass—even the great stars and vast galaxies that people our universe. Evidently on reflection none of these can be God. But—and this is my point—none of this can become intelligible unless it is in turn the manifestation, the creature, of some divine ground, something that in a deeper but analogous way is itself in but not of this flux, a kind of self-transcending infinitude. Although, as I shall note in a moment, this deeper level of reality, the divine power and energy, has recently been widely reexperienced in the new religious movements, there are also *reasons* for inferring its presence. For the flux is, I said, unintelligible without it. The reasons for this in terms of argument—as opposed to an experience of its presence—are philosophical. It may, therefore, be said that the following sketchy line of argument is an example of "natural theology."

If finite reality is really or thoroughly a *temporal* process, as it seems to be, then there occurs inexorably the vanishing of present immediacy into a quickly receding, speedily nonexistent and consequently noneffective past. But if the immediate past now vanishes into "not being there," how can that past affect the present? How can it remain so as to provide both the reality and the structure of the present—as this room persists from the past into my present space? How is it that destiny—the power and reality of the past *in* the present—is "given" to us as the basis of all that is and can be, as the ground of the actuality of the present? The weight and influence of the immediate past is experienced alike in our sense of our own reality, of our self, of our world, in our effectiveness, in our sense perceptions and our knowing; and it is expressed by the traditional categories both of substance and of causality. This cumulative "effect of the past" requires that the past, while vanishing, still also endures and is effective in the present. This requirement of experience and of reflective thought alike is inexplicable without some deeper ground of the passing flux and the vanishing present. The effectiveness of the past—and thus the continuity of the flux itself—depends upon a continuing reality or power of being that does *not* vanish or recede—as does each entity in process—but on the contrary brings the receding past into each present as that present is given a starting point. This transcendent and yet immanent power of being is one of the aspects of God; it is one of the "necessary" and "universal" things God is or does as creative providence.

We experience our present as the locus or "place" of self-actualization. It is in the present that plans are hatched, decisions made, and creative action takes place. Or, in the terms of the previous description, it is in the present that past actuality ("destiny") and future possibilities are brought together by our freedom to form what is: ourselves and our social world. Because of our obvious continuity with nature, it is presumed that nature undergoes an analogous process of given destiny and of present self-forming "freedom" expressed in categories appropriate to that level of being. Thus is there self-actualization, or freedom, in the present.

We do not, however, cause our freedom, our capacity to decide and to shape. It, too, is given to us as a basic power that is ourselves, that is itself the basis for all we do or create. Nor is our freedom caused by the heavy pressure of the past, for then it would not be the freedom to reshape and even to transform the past. Further, we can no more escape this gift or burden of freedom than we can escape time and passage, or the past. As not caused either by itself or its world, freedom too, therefore, must have a ground beyond both. As Schleiermacher said, we experience our freedom as *itself* caused and thus as "caused" by some deeper power. This immanent and yet transcendent ground of the present, and of our freedom in the present to reshape and redirect the given, is one of the aspects of God, one of the things God does universally as creative providence, creative of our freedom and thus of the totality of our human being.

Our present is saturated with possibilities. Some of these represent the possibility of the reappearance of the old, but often they are the possibility of something quite new—forms of action, of matter, of life, of institutions never before seen on land or sea. Passage thus has a history; it enters into change and into novel change because of these possibilities and especially because of possibilities that never have been actual. Possibility, what is not yet actual, is nevertheless clearly an effective factor in actuality, and yet (like the past) it is not. And so, like the vanishing past, "not-yet-possibilities" must be related to what is in order to be at all and to be effective—as they clearly are. This ground of possibility, the supreme and all-embracing actuality that envisions the entire range of possibility and thus relates all of possibility to concrete actualities in passage, is one of the aspects of God, one of the things he does as creative providence. Creative providence establishes us in and on our past, constitutes us as self-creative beings despite our dependence, and lures us through new possibilities into the open future.[1]

The reality we experience in our own temporal being is constituted by past, present, and future, and thus is it a union or synthesis of a vanishing past, a self-actualizing present, and an impinging future of not-yet-possibilities. This experienced reality, if it is to be made intelligible, points beyond itself to its own transcendent ground that on a deeper level, and as the possibility of our finite synthesis, unites past, present, and future in its own thereby "eternal" and unconditioned life. This transcendent, creating, preserving, and directing reality represents in Christian faith the beginning of the understanding of God. A part of what we mean when we witness to God the Parent Almighty, creator, preserver, and providential ruler is, therefore, represented here: the power of being whereby past actuality is given as the base of our present, the ground of freedom through which we and our present are constituted, and the "place" of future possibilities as the lure of our present as it moves into the new. The presence of this transcendent ground, as power, as freedom, as possibility or lure, is immanent in each moment and in our experience of our own being in each moment. It is this "ontological" or "metaphysical" presence, necessary and decisive for each instant and consequently for each facet of our being, that gives to our existence its continued experiencing of ultimacy and of sacrality, in short its strange, creative, and disturbing religious dimension.

Second, as was demonstrated in the first chapter, our social existence is itself saturated with a religious dimension and thus presupposes a dim awareness of this ultimate and sacral presence I have here begun philosophically to describe. Traditional cultures always joined the political and the religious, the king and the priest, in varying and strange but always essential interrelations, the only legitimate ruler being he or she who is in touch with the divine. Correspondingly, this religious dimension, now implicit rather than explicit, characterizes even secular politics with its claims to ultimacy, its mythical speech, its requirement of total commitment, and its concern for orthodoxy.

Another example in ordinary experience of the religious character of the human is very much before us today in the rise all around us of new and old religious movements. What is of interest to our present theme is that, contrary to all modern expectations and quite outside traditional Christian or Jewish religious communities—where the power of habit and custom could be invoked—obviously a religious reality has been widely sought and even more widely experienced in the midst of a modern scientific and technological culture. Whatever their varied forms—Hindu, Buddhist, Sufi—these religious phenomena in our midst point to a reality transcendent to the material and social horizons of modern culture. These phenomena are all-encompassing, all-engrossing, and healing in their effects; and when once experienced, they each become the most real and the most sacred of all realities for their devotees. Many men and women have found again that they can become human only in transcending (through contemplation, meditation, Yogic exercises, the dance) the flux in which they are immersed, in unity with the ultimate energy, reality or nothingness—whatever its name—that grounds and lures that flux but is infinitely more than appears within it. In becoming "symbols" themselves, that is, media, vehicles of the divine ground because transparent to it, or empowered, made real, and grounded by it, these men and women have found their frequently broken or empty humanity filled, unified, and centered again.

To return in conclusion to my initial theme: for us to be is to be in temporal passage, and this temporality bears negative and positive implications crucially significant to our lives. On the one hand, it means continually and inescapably to lose our present into a receding and vanishing past and thus to experience frequently a devastating sense of unreality and loss of being.[2] It means, furthermore, to face a future that is not-yet and that can—and frequently does—threaten what being we have as well as promise a renewal of that being. And, finally, to be in time is to face an end, not only of the term paper's or the vacation's allotted time, but of our life's time. Temporality is apparently the sole place of our being and yet also the sign of our lack of it, of the non-being that surrounds and permeates our creaturely life. Time reminds us of our dependence, of our contingency, of our mortality. As Tillich noted, the deep, ever-present echo of this dependent, rushing, and bounded character of creaturely life is *anxiety*. This anxiety is felt when we realize how each present has vanished into a past; when our freedom finds itself helpless, locked in a possibility-less room; when we contemplate a menacing future; when in panic we realize the time for the term paper has run out and we have no more time. In these anxieties we experience directly in new form our finitude, and we yearn for a ground, a power which can overcome and conquer that void. In anxiety the absence of God is felt even if who it is that is absent is not yet known.

There is, on the other hand, also the possibility of another experience of our temporality that overcomes or conquers this deep anxiety, this overwhelming and frequently stifling sense of unreality and of crushing mortality. When the uniting ground of past, present, and future is experienced and its purposes over the course of time apprehended, the separateness and negativity of time are overcome. The past no longer vanishes into non-being, the present is no longer dominated by fate, nor the future closed to new possibilities. Then what is given to us as an actuality from what has been, our destiny, is full of creative possibilities and capable powers. The present is filled with the tone of exhilarating freedom, of the possibility of self-actualization, and of the exciting capacity for creative work. And the future is open, glowing with unrealized but real opportunities for enlargement. In such experiences time and temporality become "good," full of possibilities, of promise and so meaningful, a fit place for the Kingdom itself to be realized. And human being in time—and so in community and history—is good and feels good, full of wonder and courage, of self-affirmation and so of hope, of the power to create, and thus to love. Such experiences, as I have argued, presuppose and reflect the divine power that unites, structures, and directs time—the past, the present, and the future—and that grounds our creative destiny, our creative freedom, and our creative possibilities. To experience human being in its temporality this way is, therefore, both to experience the goodness of creatureliness and to experience the providence of God. It is to understand human being as made in the image of God and God as the all-determining Parent.

To confess in faith, "I believe in God the Parent Almighty" is to bring to explicit awareness and acknowledgment—and commitment—this dim awareness of unity, support and possibility in our temporal life. It is to begin to name and thus to relate to the deep, transcendent, and yet immanent ground of our passage: the power that gives us our past and preserves it, that creates and recreates our freedom, and that lures and calls us with new possibilities. It is also to receive a new and, I believe, creative—because critical—perspective on the inescapable religious dimensions of our common life: on the religious claims of our politics and our culture and on the religious reality of our churches, synagogues, and mystical cults.

Most important, it is to receive, express, and appropriate a new understanding and vision of the human. In faith this dimly expressed "Power Almighty" that grounds all powers and forms all possibilities, is known further and on other grounds as recreating love and faithfulness, surely as well (or better) expressed by the symbol Mother as that of Father. Thus has the human despite its creatureliness at once the opportunity of knowing security in time, trust for the future—and an obligation to recreate the present so that security, possibility, and creative destiny may be the given for all her creatures.

NOTES

1. These arguments are indebted directly and indirectly to the thought of A. N. Whitehead as well as (as noted) to that of F. Schleiermacher and P. Tillich. Although the third one (the argument vis-à-vis possibility) is directly Whitehead's argument, it should be noted that an essential distinction from Whitehead's view appears in the first two. Whitehead argues (1) that *some* metaphysical factor or principle must be responsible for "transition," for the élan that "effects" the movement of the receding immediate past from vanishing into non-being into becoming an objectified datum for or qualification of the present; and (2) some metaphysical factor must be responsible for "the continual self-creation" of unity out of diversity that is actuality," i.e., the self-creation of each successive entity. As is evident, our argument is *indirectly* indebted to this line of argument (as it is to Schleiermacher and Tillich). However, Whitehead assigns these two metaphysical roles to "creativity"; in fact these two roles exhaustively define creativity, the "ultimate principle," the "universal of universals," for Whitehead. Moreover, he sharply distinguishes creativity so understood from God. Thus by viewing *both* of these roles as aspects of the creative and preserving functions of God, the position presented here distinguishes itself radically from the view of God and her/his role in actuality characteristic of Whitehead and of process philosophy and theology. See Langdon Gilkey, *Reaping the Whirlwind: A Christian Interpretation of History* (New York: Seabury Press), chaps. 5 and 12.

2. I recall meeting a young man who had spent the last four summers of his now well-advanced youth recapturing, as he said, his now vanished boyhood: returning to the latter's scenes, photographing each

house, building, and street with care, and interviewing on tape every person whom he could find that he had known or had known of him. His entire present was thus spent seeking to set into permanent (?) form, i.e., on tape and film, and thus make endlessly "present" (in boxes) his past. So engrossed was he in the importance of this quest for his own past, that he did not seem to realize that he was thereby sacrificing his sole chance for a creative present and for a new future. The non-being of a lost past had lured him into trying to live *there* (and via tape!) and so into losing his creative actuality in the present and his possibilities for the future. A very sophisticated young man, well versed in literary and philosophical matters, he had no notion that he was a "living" (?) embodiment of Beckett's "Krapp's Last Tape" and of Kierkegaard's aesthetic mode of existence.

SUGGESTED READING

Becker, E. *The Denial of Death*. Free Press, 1973.
Browning, D. *Generative Man*. Delta Books, 1973.
Camus, A. *The Plague*. Knopf, 1948.
———. *The Rebel*. Knopf, 1954.
———. *The Myth of Sisyphus and Other Essays*. Knopf, 1955.
Gilkey, L. *Reaping the Whirlwind*. Part 1. Seabury, 1977.
Heidegger, M. *Being and Time*. Harper & Row, 1962.
Kierkegaard, S. *Either/Or*. Princeton Univ. Press, 1971.
Niebuhr, R. R. *Experiential Religion*. Harper & Row, 1972.
Pannenberg, W. *What Is Man?* Fortress Press, 1970.
———. *The Idea of God and Human Freedom*. Westminster, 1973.
Rahner, K. *Hearers of the Word*. Herder & Herder, 1969.
Ricoeur, P. *Freedom and Nature: The Voluntary and the Involuntary*. Northwestern Univ. Press, 1966.
———. *Fallible Man*. Gateway Books, n.d.
Temple, W. *Mens Creatrix*. Macmillan, 1917.
Tillich, P. *Systematic Theology*. Vol. 1. Univ. of Chicago Press, 1955.
———. *The Courage to Be*. Yale Univ. Press, 1952.

5

THE SYMBOL OF GOD

HAVING discussed, however sketchily, human temporality and its relation to its divine ground, it is now possible to talk more meaningfully of those aspects of the "doctrine" of God that relate to our creatureliness. First, in Christian theology those aspects are expressed through the traditional symbols of creation and providence; and, second, these "thematize" (give expression to) the universal and necessary activities of God in relation to all creatures, not to this and not to that creature, but to the creature "as such"—and thus to the nebulae, the amoeba, the dinosaurs, the early Picts and Scots, the Chinese, the Kremlin, you, I, our two dogs, and even the cat. These concern, therefore, the "ontological" or "metaphysical" attributes of God; they are essential and very significant, but, as noted, they are by no means all that the Christian (or Jewish) witness wishes to say about God.

As has already been discovered with regard to other issues, great changes have occurred in the way many contemporary theologians speak of the major symbols of their tradition, changes brought about largely because of the varied influences of modern culture. This is neither new nor surprising. It is not new because vast changes occurred in the meaning of all these symbols when they began to be reinterpreted by the earliest Church in terms of its culture's scientific, philosophical, and social ideas, namely, the Hellenistic culture of the Roman Empire. What resulted from that mingling, as is well known, was precisely the theological orthodoxy that is now fearful of a new mingling with the modern cultural ethos. And it is not surprising, for, as was noted, theology and its doctrines, in order to be meaningful to us and to have reference to what is to us real, must speak in the language of our own time and in the basic categories characteristic of our cultural situation.

Among many important factors in the modern spirit, the central influences that have effected changes in our interpretation of classic theological symbols have come, I believe, from two sources: the rise to predominance of science and of its method[1] and the development of what has been called the historical consciousness.[2] These influences together have resulted in three central presuppositions or premises characteristic, by and large, of our epoch's consciousness; and it is these, I am suggesting, that continually force changes in the interpretation of Christian (and incidentally also in the Jewish and Buddhist) tradition. First, all events and entities in our natural and historical world arise in a complex of finite causes stretching back seemingly infinitely into the past and, being the result of that complex, are relative to it and to be explained in terms of it. Second, despite this complex of causes and the relativity of everything entailed by it, the essential character of the human is its self-direction and self-creation, its autonomy of thought, feeling, willing, and acting. Third, historical life, especially in the future, is open to vast possibilities of enlargement and fulfillment— and thus entails not only new promise but also new obligations for political and social action for the future.[3] Modern thought has not found it easy to put these, its basic presuppositions, coherently together, some emphasizing the "reign of law," others the "free" self-constitution of all existence, and still others concentrating on the immense possibilities of a perfected future, and others uniting all three in various strange and bizarre ways. In any case, few modern theologians fail to reflect deeply these three presuppositions, and my proposal for thinking about God as creator and providential ruler will also reflect each of them. As does every theologian, I shall seek to accomplish the double task of re-presenting Christian symbols in their light and conversely of re-interpreting this queer modern "world" of interlaced causation, of emergent and self-constituting freedom and of immense future possibilities, in the terms of Christian symbolism.

These three notions have had a great effect on the symbols of creation and of providence. In its older, inherited, "orthodox" form creation meant a sudden absolute beginning of time and of the world in its present form and with its present forms of life a short six thousand years ago—and then no more creative activity. Providence meant the all-determining rule of God over every event, as a consequence the divine willing or ordination of every act of his/her creatures, and thus, finally, the divine "causing" of all of history's events and institutions, even those that are clearly tragic and unjust.

Obviously these orthodox interpretations of creation and providence, stemming from another cultural epoch, run directly counter to each of the presuppositions mentioned. It is hard to know whether these older forms of creation and providence offended more the consciousness of law in natural and historical life, the new affirmation of autonomy or self-direction in human existence, or the confidence in development and progress in historical events, of a new and open future. As a consequence, subsequent theology has, sometimes admitting it and sometimes not, sought so to interpret creation and providence that these stark conflicts are overcome. In the previous chapter, in uncovering God as the ground of our temporal being, I have partly unveiled my own proposal; let me now continue that enterprise.

The first change that occurred in these symbols was the disappearance of the sharp temporal distinction between God's creation of the world at an absolute beginning (the fabulous six days six thousand or so years ago) and his/her subsequent providential rule over a fully established and formed world (the time *since* the six days). Creation is seen now to take place throughout the unfolding temporal process, for new forms of life and of institutions were now seen continually to appear during that process. If God creates at all, therefore, he/she creates over time; thus, creation and providential rule seem to melt into one another.

The theological distinction that did remain between creation—bringing into being—and ordering what was already there thus has had to be viewed in a new light. The symbol of God's creation of the world points not to an event at the beginning; rather, it expresses the absolute dependence of the creature and thus of the universe of creatures, on the power and ultimate being of God and on his/her purposes for its own finite being. God—so the symbol of creation out of nothing said—is the sole *source* of our world, the unconditioned being from which that world derives its relative, dependent, and contingent being. "Out of nothing" refers, then, not to a first moment before which there was nothing but God. It means, rather, that God is the sole source or ground of all there is in its entirety. He/she does not, so to speak, find an unfinished universe, dependent for its being on other factors, already there and proceed to work on it; nor is our world the result of the joint activity of several ultimate and everlasting powers. God is its sole source and ground; creation out of nothing is the continuing expression in theological symbolism of monotheism, and thus—however science views the temporal process of becoming—is central for Christian faith. Creation as a symbol, therefore, expresses the unconditioned reality and power of God as the source of all beings, the power grounding all power, the life from which all life springs, and the eternity from which time itself originates.

Because, however, the world—and ourselves—which this unconditioned power has created, have a real if relative autonomy, self-direction and self-constitution—as modernity has particularly emphasized—the symbol of creation *also* points to the mysterious self-limitation of God in producing a creation and creatures with freedom, "over against" himself and thus relatively autonomous.[4] Thus is creation, as traditional symbolism has also emphasized, "good." Their being at all of creatures is absolutely dependent on the unconditioned power of God. But since their being is to be self-creative and self-constitutive, the self-transcending finitude that God produces ipso facto itself limits his/her effective absoluteness. Even in the symbol of creation, then, the paradoxes or polarities of absoluteness and self-limitation, of unconditionedness and reciprocity, of being and even of non-being, in God begin to appear. The discussion in the previous chapter of God's creative providence as the power of the continuing being of "destiny," the ground of our freedom, and the locus of possibilities to come sought to express in modern conceptuality this polarity of absolute source and self-limiting reciprocity.

Providence, on the other hand, was a symbol pointing to the rule—the sovereignty—of God over the creation already established, already in being; how God relates to all creatures, granting they are now there. With the symbol of providence we are more concerned with God's continuing relation to the ongoing temporal process of actual, self-creative entities than we are with the eternal source or ground of that process as a whole in God. As the *sole* source of finite creatures, God is , so to speak, therefore, alone and thus unconditioned, even absolute in his/her creative activity; as sovereign—in whatever sense—of that process, however, God shares with his/her creatures the power to be, to be effective, and to be free. Although there is now no necessary temporal distinction between these symbols, they point to very different aspects of the divine being and activity in relation to the world.

The symbol of providence, therefore, tends, especially in modern theology, to emphasize—as in my proposal— the relatedness, the temporality, the conditionedness, and thus the self-limitation of God "over against" his/her temporal, active, and autonomous creatures. As has been shown, as creative providence, God brings the immediately recent yet completed past into its effective role in the formation of the present; he/she grounds the new freedom which receives, accepts, and reshapes that past in the light of present possibilities; and he/she offers new possibilities to that occasion relevant to its situation. In none of this is God all-determining—neither of the past, which has been formed by past occasions out of their past; nor of the present, which is the locus of self-constitution; nor of the future—for each finite occasion chooses in part, but in important part, its present to come. God is here radically self-limited in order that the created world share in the divine reality, the divine creativity, the divine order, and the divine beauty.

Nevertheless, as the symbol of creation also implies, God is absolute being and eternal necessity as well as divinely self-limiting. Thus, in turn, even the divine providential preservation and ordering entails the unconditionedness, the eternity, and the infinity of God. As a continuing source of the being, freedom, and possibility of *every* creature, God is not essentially conditioned by any preceding "given," nor does he/she pass away; as a reality uniting past, present, and future, God transcends each phase of time; as the unlimited vision of possibilities, God is infinite. These proposals for retrieving the symbols of creation and providence, are, to be sure, by no means identical with traditional accounts. Like many other examples of recent theological re-presentation, however, they seek to express the central and underlying polarities of transcendence and immanence, of absoluteness and relatedness, of unconditionedness and conditionedness, of eternity and yet temporality, characteristically implied in the Scriptural and so the Christian witness to God.

Specifically there are three points where this—and many another contemporary proposal—distinguishes itself from the classical conception of God. Each of them emphasizes the participation of God in and his/her relationship to historical passage, a theme certainly central to the Old and the New Testaments and one which has had an increasing significance in modern culture.

First, God is here affirmed to include potentiality in his/her being. I have said that one of God's central roles is to envision the unlimited possibilities not yet realized in process, that he/she thus "lures" the world into as-yet-unactualized forms. If this be so, then the future God faces is also open, undecided; it is characterized for God, as for us, by possibilities, not by actualities already decided in eternity. This means, on the one hand, that human freedom and self-direction are real, inclusive of the power effectively to decide in part what the future is to be and thus that our freedom shares analogously in the divine creative freedom. On the other hand, it means that history is no longer either a shadow of a timeless eternity nor a temporal unfolding of the already completed "eternal scroll" listing the divine decisions. Here history, and therefore also God's acts in it, accomplish something; a story untold before is here told, new institutions are fashioned, new situations encountered and resolved. The certainty—first established in the Old Testament, repeated in even greater force through the events recorded in the New, and now widely apprehended in modern culture—that the future is open and undecided, that as a consequence in history meaningful, new and creative actions transpire is thus here theologically expressed and underscored.

Second, another direct implication of my proposal about God is that God is also positively related to the world and thus affected by it, by the events that occur there, and by the story that there unfolds. It is surely assumed in the Scriptures that God knows what transpires in his/her world, that he/she suffers with its tragic conflicts and woes and is gladdened by its joys, that he/she judges its sins and out of love responds to its needs. There is here clearly an implicit reciprocity, however "Almighty" God may be said to be. Older forms of piety assumed this relatedness of God to the world, of course—but frequently their official theologies denied it philosophically or made unintelligible its possibility in declaring that God was absolute, unrelated, unaffected, quite unconditioned in every aspect of his/her being. In specifying divine self-limitation in creation and in providence, and even more the difference between what is actual in God's being and what is potential, my proposal makes room for this obvious "passivity" in the divine being, his/her capacity to be affected and so to be in reciprocal relation to a world that initiates new events.

Third, finally, as both the potentiality of God to new forms of experience in being and the relatedness of God to a changing world directly imply, God shares in both the temporality and the changeability of his/her creatures. The future is, for God, open, undecided, known so far as it is known by him/her only a possibility and not as actuality. Thus God's actuality and actual experience move forward with time, as possibilities become realized in each present. God thus "becomes" as the process becomes, and in this becoming the actuallity of God changes.

These attributes of potentiality, relatedness, changeability, and temporality have in past theological epochs been regarded as representing too radical a denial of God's absolute being to be tolerated, as indicating such a lack in God's reality that he/she would simply cease to be "God." To this point there are three things that may be said in defense of such a contemporary "dynamic" conception of God as I have tried to suggest. In the first place, it seems clear that if the God represented in the Scriptures is conceptually described, such dynamic notions as these appear to be required. Certainly the God who acts in historical events, judges, chastizes, repents, renews, promises, and fulfills his/her promise, is a God related to time and to change and thus shares in both.

Further, in the Old Testament accounts, historical sequence and thus change in time are not negatively but positively assessed. As illustrated in history itself, they are real if not ultimately real. Thus, it is with no loss of his/her being but rather through a manifestation of it that Yahveh participates in history's events. The Hellenistic culture into which Christianity spread, and in terms of which Christian theology first formed itself conceptually, had a much more negative view of temporal passage and of historical sequence than did the Old or the New Testaments or than does our modern era. Thus to them participation in time and change signaled a loss of being, and thus only such attributes as unrelatedness, pure actuality, changelessness, timelessness (eternity)—all negations of temporality and historicity—were admitted as characterizing the Godhead. In many respects modern culture represents a stark opposition to essential biblical views; but with regard to its positive assessment of history, change, and temporality, it seems closer to the Scriptural view than were these intervening epochs. For this reason one can argue that a dynamic conception of God appropriate to modern attitudes towards time and change is actually closer to the authentic biblical conception than were the orthodox alternatives.

Also it should be noted that in ascribing potentiality, relatedness, change, and temporality to God, I am not ascribing finitude or contingency to the divine—as surely any Hellenistic philosopher or theologian would have concluded. In being affected and related, in changing over time, God is not dependent on other entities or factors for his/her being, nor is he/she correspondingly threatened in his/her being. As the source of all over time—and thus *in* time—God is not contingent but necessary in being; as the uniting principle of past, present, and future—and thus *in* time—God transcends temporality; as the actuality envisioning the infinite realm of possibility—and thus sharing in potentiality—God is infinite. His/her necessary and self-sufficient being is the source of all, and his/her infinite envisionment of possibilities is inclusive of all that has or will be. In creating the world over time, God brings the immediate past, objectified and now vanishing, into the living present; in this "necessary" act—if there is to be being at all—he/she transcends the passage of time while making it possible. Thus in not arising out of other things nor passing away into them, God is not contingent in his/her being, nor mortal in his/her temporality. God is a continuing source of being as it is actualized in time, the ever-present principle of unity of what is actual and potential, of past actuality, present realization, and future possibilities. In sharing in temporality, relatedness, and change as the continuing ground of each, God transcends all three; as creator and preserver of all that is contingent and temporal, God "is" necessarily and eternally as their source over time. God thus shares without contingency and yet infinitely transcends without negation of them, these attributes of creatureliness. Since, therefore, the concept of God is not that of an ordinary finite, contingent creature, nor one that denies in toto these characteristics of finitude, this seems a paradoxical if not contradictory notion. Certainly it is a unique notion with its own peculiar or idiosyncratic problems and rules. To these, therefore—or to what the tradition has termed the "mystery" of God—I shall now turn.

Throughout both religious and ordinary experience the divine has been shrouded in mystery. Touch with the gods was always a strange, eerie experience, often fraught with danger, carefully circumscribed, surrounded with taboos, fascinating and awe inspiring, as Rudolf Otto and Mircea Eliade have shown. The mystery of God, or the holiness of God, for they are aspects of the same characteristic, is therefore initially an aspect of all religious experience. Since, however, it is also true that the intellectual or rational grounds or reasons for that mystery can be described, mystery is also an aspect of the conception or doctrine of God.

The first reason for the mystery is that, as this discussion has made plain, God, however he/she may be conceived, is not an ordinary entity or object. As the source and ground of all objects, God transcends them all. Where they are circumscribed and bounded, God is not; where they are defined by limiting characteristics, God is not; where they are isolatable (distinguishable from other things), manipulable, analyzable, God is not. All our ordinary ways of perceiving, knowing, and thus describing, whether within ordinary or scientific experience and language, do not work here. God is not an object among other objects to be known by our familiar modes of knowing or talked about the way we talk about other things. In transcending the finite, God transcends ordinary language about the finite. We can understand and even measure, for example, a finite power or force; the "power" which is the source of all finite powers is quite beyond our simple or direct understanding.

On the other hand, we cannot understand God by recognizing this transcendence and then simply negating all finite characteristics. Such a divine "ground," understood as the negation of the world, is, in consequence, not in any creative or transformative relation to the world. As has been shown, however, God is positively related to the world as a creator and as providential ruler. Thus the divine shares, as the source, ground, and guiding principal of all things, many of the characteristics of creatures familiar to us: passage, temporality, actuality and potentiality, relatedness, changeability, and so on. But again those attributes, because of the transcendence of God to the finite, are different in God—are, so to speak, slightly beyond our natural comprehension and yet not completely out of its range. As this proposal has perhaps shown, we can understand in particular God's relation to us and something of the divine role in our being, living, and acting. But the very nature of that role, transcendent in its very relatedness to us and thus related because of its very transcendence, means our understanding is balanced by the mystery of the almighty and holy God.

The second reason for the mystery is that being ultimate and unconditioned, the ground and source of all, God is not a being or entity who appears, so to speak, "on his/her own," that is, directly, immediately before us as "this" and not "that," at least distinguishable by manipulative experiment from other beings. As the source of all entities—as a union of the objectified past, of present freedom, and of future possibility, God appears *through* these direct, isolatable entities: in the order and power of nature, the ultimacy and sacrality of the social community, the strange, unexpected, ambiguous events of history, the serenity and sanctity of certain persons. These creaturely media are, moreover, as has been shown, in part free, self-constituting, and self-directing. Consequently, they reveal in their actions as much of their own powers, natures, wills, and intentions as they do of the power that grounds and preserves them. Filled as the world and time are with ambiguity, evil, and injustice, the meaning of these creaturely events and media is by no means clear. Thus, the divine visage is even less clear in and through them. God's power and order are deeply hidden in both the natural and the historical worlds. Now and again in each—in the beauty and order and wonder of nature, in a fortunate sequence of events—a divine order and purpose seems momentarily clear. But while traces of the divine are never absent from nature and politics, any real unveiling of the divine presence or purpose is quickly shrouded again. The mystery of God is, therefore, as much the result of the *ambiguity* of the finite world he/she creates, preserves, and guides as it was also dependent on the divine *transcendence* and yet relatedness to that world.

The third reason for the mystery is that, besides the transcendence and so the strangeness of God and the free ambiguity and thus the "unclarity" of his/her world, there is also as essential to the divine mystery what is called the "freedom" of God. This category, in relation to God, connotes the power of self-direction, of activities stemming from the deepest personal center of the divine, and thus action subject only to the divine will. And as in humans, the inner will or intention is originally hidden to the observer, manifesting itself only when its subject reveals himself/herself in speech or when that intention is realized in completed action. Thus, the freedom of God connotes an analogue in the divine to the mystery each one of us represents to each other in the inward freedom of our own personal being. We do not "know" each other fully until we open ourselves completely to one another. Even then there are, we say, "depths" in which the totally unexpected lies hidden.

With regard to God, this freedom, or this mystery of the divine personal being, is one of the most vivid characteristics of Yahveh in the Old Testament. Although, as the tradition develops, he/she becomes the sovereign lord of all nations and places, still he/she appears when and only when he/she wills, in definite places and to definite persons; and he/she is, again according to his/her own unfathomable choice, the special lord of one covenant people. God's universal powers and activities do not prevent or circumscribe his/her freedom to manifest a special presence and activity.[5] This is the first aspect of the category of divine freedom. As is obvious, it is essential to the Christian understanding of God as creator and preserver of all, but also as manifesting himself/herself in special events and persons.

Also, as with humans, the divine freedom connotes the capacity in God for the unexpected act or word, for that which is an apparent change or new direction in his/her intentions or will, for the revelation—to put it another way—of a deeper, more authentic purpose. Thus in the midst of the severest anger and judgment, Yahveh frequently "repents" his/her threats of wrath and destruction and thus reveals an unexpected mercy and the unexpected promise of a new beginning for Israel. This same theme is continued in the New Testament where, despite the emphasis on the holy righteousness of God in upholding his/her own divine law and so on the universal judgment of God on human sin, there appears, quite unexpectedly, a new quality of mercy, of forgiving love, and of renewing grace in the teachings, the person, and the destiny of Jesus the Christ. Much of the divine *being* transcends and yet is related to finite creatures; it enshrines, therefore, a depth that represents mystery in a special sense. Correspondingly, in the divine *will* there is also a depth of intention and of purpose that represents both freedom and mystery, the mystery of the divine personal being, of the divine love or mercy in relation to the divine righteousness or justice.

As is evident, it is through these categories under discussion—of freedom and of mystery in their various connotations—that the *personal* character of the divine being is most vividly expressed. In many important ways, God is not "a person" at all. He/she is not a creature among other creatures, a "personal" member of a community; he/she is not located in a body; he/she does not act "ontically" in space and time, and so on. But in the mystery and freedom of his/her being and his/her will, he/she represents in transcendent and yet analogous forms the personal being we find dimly, ambiguously, and waywardly present in ourselves.

It has been evident throughout the preceding discussion that because God is significantly different from ordinary objects, we cannot speak of him/her in precisely the same ways we speak of other, more ordinary persons and things. Thus the words we use—nouns like "thing," "object," or "person"; adjectives like "great," "infinite," "powerful," or "kind"; verbs like "acts," "intends," "loves," or "speaks"—all have a different meaning when used in reference to God, though, as also indicated, they clearly have some significant reference. A somewhat similar case appears with a pet. It does make good sense to speak of "love," "good," "faithful," and so on, in connection with a dog; and yet in each case the meaning of the word is significantly different from what it is when we use it about a human being. To try to gauge *how* different these words are in this new usage, and thus what they might mean in the new context, is the task, respectively, of animal biology and psychology and of theology. Our discussion of the symbols of creation and preservation has been an example of that effort to understand through analogical language.

Thus I say that our words about God are not literal, direct, or univocal (that is, used in precisely the same way) in relation to God because of the divine transcendence; also that they are not empty, meaningless or "equivocal" because of the essential and recognizable activity of God in the world of our experience. Rather, our words are analogical or symbolic—words which in some respects apply and in others do not, in which, as Tillich says, the characteristics of finitude are affirmed and negated at the same time.

To speak directly or literally of God is to imply that God is an object or entity in the universe and essentially (metaphysically), therefore, similar to other entities. In such a case God ceases to be "God" as a transcendent and yet related creator and preserver, which were the very grounds on which the concept was first broached. To be unable to speak at all of God in terms of our words, on the other hand, is to imply either that he/she is not at all real or else that the divine is so transcendent to us and so out of relation with us as to be irrelevant to life within our world. It is the continuing and intelligible *immanence* of God in the world, in general and in special experiences alike, that gives meaning to the *new* uses that words such as "being," "act," "intend" undergo, that anchors, so to speak, the analogical use of these words in speaking of God. It is the transcendence involved in each case of that immanence, the special "role" of God at each point, that makes these usages new, that gives "being," "act," and "intend" the *new* senses which it is the task of theology to explore and explain. The difficulties of theological language are, there-fore, merely the difficulties of theology itself set now into linguistic form. Insofar as theology faithfully uses its sources to talk through Christian symbols intelligibly and perceptively of our experience in its relation to God, the intelligibility of its language will appear and remain defen-sible because it is in that application already defended.

In this part our finitude and then its relation to God have been discussed. A new vision of our experienced creatureliness in the midst of our temporality, transience, and conditionedness has been put forth: finite temporality is given a destiny from the past which can be creatively shaped, a present in which freedom has room to constitute itself, and a future full of possibilities of enlargement. And, as was shown, the temporal structure of finitude so understood pointed beyond itself to its divine source, ground, and principle of unity. As cultural and religious experience alike witness, this divine ground is, on the one hand, continually "experienced," however dimly, in human existence; while on the other the requirements of a rational or coherent understanding of finitude imply this same ground. Given the pervasiveness of the religious di-mension in human existence and the persuasiveness of these arguments of "rational theology," theism seems as obvious empirically and as indubitable intellectually as it is essential to any form of Christian belief and life.

As is evident in our actual life, however, theism has, to say the least, no such unchallenged and invulnerable status. The religious dimension of existence remains largely unrecognized, the divine rarely experienced, and the arguments of natural theology continually questioned by unbeliever and believer alike. The historical world as we frequently experience it seems anything but the crea-tion of a divine ground and a sovereign providence. The past seems to smother and not encourage freedom and new possibilities; the present seems closed to genuine self-creation; and the future looms before us barren of real possibilities. Thus even the essential structure of finitude—destiny, freedom, and new possibilities—seems obscured and so dubious; and, a fortiori, the God who constitutes this threefold structure appears in *this* situation as an "opiate" against an awareness of radical evil and thus as a justification of an unjust world. That this essential structure of creative finitude and creative ground is "there," both experience and argument confirm. That it is deeply *obscured* and consequently dubious is also continually confirmed. Not only is our existence strangely not what it essentially or "really" is, and what, therefore, it "ought" to be; also, it is estranged from itself, its roots and its possibilities; and thus both its creative structure as good as well as its divine ground, are obscured, questionable, and denied.

This dialectic of an essential structure—our "nature" as God's creatures and so blessed with possibilities in our life—and of "fallen actuality" or "estranged actuality" constitutes a difficult set of notions to put together intelligibly. Perhaps an image or analogy will help. On a clear blue day the entire seascape is visible to the sailor in a small boat: familiar islands with their treasured landmarks dot foreground and horizon alike, and helpful buoys are evident a mile or two away. Thus is the *structure* of the scene visible to every eye; and since it is easy to find one's way, so to speak, "by sight," no special means are necessary or even thought of. Let us suppose, however, that now a fog covers the whole bay, shutting out everything except fifty yards of gray water around the small boat. The structure of the bay has quite vanished: islands, landmarks, and buoys are as if they were not there at all, and a general direction, much less a particular course, is anything but evident. The structure, of course, is still there. But now it is unseen and unknown; its rocks and shoals can appear as a menace rather than as a blessing. Special means of "knowing" it come immediately into relevance, for only through those means—compass, radar, depth soundings, and so on—can that structure now be known at all.

So it is apparently in our existence. The temporality and finitude characteristic of our existence and history is that of creative destiny, freedom, and new possibilities; it is "good," and it manifests a divine creative ground. However, there is a reality of estrangement or of fallenness to that existence which has obscured not only the divine ground but also the creative nature of our creatureliness in time. To a further discussion of this strange fog we now turn.

NOTES

1. For a more detailed account of the influence of science on theology and so on theological meanings, see the author's *Religion and the Scientific Future* (New York: Harper & Row, 1970), especially chaps. 1 and 4.

2. For a description of the historical consciousness, its rise, character and influence on modern theology, see Langdon Gilkey, *Reaping the Whirlwind: A Christian Interpretation of History* (New York: Seabury Press, 1977), chaps. 8–11.

3. As I have argued in *Reaping the Whirlwind* (chap. 3), it is one of the ironies of our intellectual history that the fact and the promise of science, as experienced by the members of its own community, has been the basic cause of all *three* of these characteristics of modern culture: its sense of relativity, of autonomy, and of new possibilities for the future. This is an irony because in our cultural life science likes to "stand for" the reign of universal and inexorable law and for an emphasis on the objective rather than the subjective—and so for anything *but* the significance of the autonomous or the novel in our existence. See *Religion and the Scientific Future*, chap. 3, and *Reaping the Whirlwind*, chap. 3.

4. Sören Kierkegaard (perhaps first) stated explicitly this notion of the self-limitation of Absolute Being by which a relatively independent creature is set into being "over against" its creator. See Kierkegaard, *Concluding Unscientific Postscript*, translated by David Swenson and Walter Lowrie (Princeton University Press, 1944), pp. 217–21; and Kier-

kegaard, *Works of Love*, translated by David Swenson (Princeton University Press, 1949), pp. 218–22

5. The central characteristic or attribute of God for the great theologian Karl Barth is the divine freedom; that God, despite his absoluteness, universality, and utter righteousness, wills to love us, to redeem or elect us all, to come as a man, in this man, in this place and time, in order to bring us to Himself—all of this quite unpredictable, seemingly in fact impossible, and totally unmerited action is evidence of the utter "freedom" of God to be Himself.

SUGGESTED READINGS

Recent Classics

Aulen, G. *The Faith of the Christian Church*. Muhlenberg Press, 1948.

Brunner, H. E. *The Divine-Human Encounter*. Westminster, 1943.

———. *The Christian Doctrine of God*. Westminster, 1950.

———. *The Christian Doctrine of Creation and Redemption*. Lutterworth, 1952.

Collins, J. *God in Modern Philosophy*. Gateway Books, 1959.

Hartshorne, C. *Man's Vision of God*. Harper & Bros., 1941.

———. *Reality as Social Process*. Free Press, 1953.

Niebuhr, H. R. *Radical Monotheism and Western Culture*. Harper & Row, 1960.

Temple, W. *Nature, Man and God*. Macmillan, 1935.

Tillich, P. *Systematic Theology, Vol* 1. Univ. of Chicago Press, 1951.

———. *Biblical Religion and the Quest for Ultimate Reality*. Univ. of Chicago Press, 1955.

Whitehead, A. N. *Religion in the Making*. Macmillan, 1926.

———. *Science and the Modern World*. Macmillan, 1925.

Current Discussion

Altizer, T. *The Gospel of Christian Atheism*. Westminster, 1966.

Braaten, C. *The Future of God*. Harper & Row, 1969.

Cobb, J. B. Jr. *A Christian Natural Theology*. Westminster, 1965.

———. *God and the World*. Westminster, 1969.

Farley, E. *The Transcendence of God*. Westminster, 1968.

Gilkey, L. *Maker of Heaven and Earth*. Doubleday, 1959.

———. *Naming the Whirlwind: The Renewal of God-Language*. Bobbs-Merrill, 1969.

———. *Reaping the Whirlwind*. Seabury, 1977.

Hamilton, W. *The New Essence of Christianity*. Association Press, 1961.

Hick, J. *Evil and the God of Love*. Harper & Row, 1966.

Kaufman, G. *God the Problem*. Harvard Univ. Press, 1972.

Ogden, S. *The Reality of God*. Harper & Row, 1964.

Pannenberg, W. *Theology and the Kingdom of God*. Westminster, 1969.

———. *The Idea of God and Human Freedom*. Westminster, 1969.

Rahner, K. *The Trinity*. Herder & Herder, 1970.

———. *Foundations of Christian Faith*. Seabury, 1978.

Rubenstein, R. *After Auschwitz*. Bobbs-Merrill, 1966.

Schillebeeckx, E. *God the Future of Man*. Sheed & Ward, 1968.

Van Buren, P. *The Secular Meaning of the Gospel*. Macmillan, 1963.

PART THREE

"...and in Jesus Christ His Only Son Our Lord..."

6

THE HUMAN PREDICAMENT: ESTRANGEMENT AND SIN

IN the last part I considered the human as creaturely, or, in the terms of my creedal theme, I viewed our
common nature as it is reflected in the Christian confession
of belief in God the Parent Almighty. There I emphasized, on the one hand, the contingent, precariously
"risky" character of our temporal being—its boundedness,
its limits, its dependence, its mortality, and consequently
its essential anxiety. But I also stressed, on the other hand,
its vast and exciting possibilities, or as our tradition, both
biblical and theological, has put it: its "goodness."
Finitude, I concluded—when viewed in faith—is placed in
a world whose ultimate reality, and thus whose ground is
creative love, and where renewed order continually overcomes and replaces disorder. As a consequence the past is
given to us replete with creative opportunities and powers,
each present is the locus of a freedom to shape ourselves
and our world with intelligence and foresight, and each
future is open to continuing advance. This view of the
essential nature and the real possibilities of being human
represents a contemporary interpretation of what the tradition has termed the "goodness" of our "natural" or
"created" state of existence, its original purpose, or God's
intention at creation, symbolized by the paradise briefly
present according to Genesis before the fall.

To the eighteenth and nineteenth centuries—or to many articulate persons in the privileged classes of those epochs—this picture of the human condition as "good," full of exciting possibilities and the power to realize them, was not at all a utopian dream, but the way human existence and history were, or soon would be. To them what Christianity had said through its faith in God about the possibilities of the human estate seemed to be the direct, obvious, empirical truth about our universal situation and its possibilities. For the last few decades, however, human existence has worn a different, a grimmer, a less promising, even a menacing hue. Thus this optimistic picture of what we really are has seemed strange, unreal, out of touch to us in the mid-twentieth century. Correspondingly, even the Christian view with its insistence on human possibilities in an essentially good world has probably appeared far too sanguine. And surely compared to the grim, hopeless worlds of Lagerquist, Kafka, Golding, Pinter, and Beckett, not to mention Heilbronner, this judgment that Christianity is basically optimistic is true.

Nevertheless, the Christian tradition has been well aware of the evil as well as the good possibilities of human being. In fact, probably the main claim to intelligibility and to credibility the Christian faith has had in this century has been less its arguments for theism than the powerful interpretation of human evil it has offered, an interpretation that, unlike many forms of humanism, is neither simply optimistic nor pessimistic, idealistic or cynical, but a subtle appreciation of both elements in our nature and of the dialectical relation between our good possibilities and our wayward actuality. At the beginning of this part, then, I shall discuss the Christian view of the darker side of the human, and in the next chapter I shall set this understanding of our estrangement and sin in correlation with Christology, an explication of the Christian witness to Jesus Christ and his meaning for ourselves and our history.

The reasons for this traditional correlation of apparent opposites are twofold. First of all, it has been usually accepted in the tradition that "it was because of our sin and for our salvation" that Jesus Christ appeared among us and that he lived and died as he did. His essential role has been held to be that of the redeemer from sin, fate, and death; to comprehend the meaning of that witness, therefore, we must first understand how Christians have understood the evil from which we are rescued.

Second, Jesus has been for Christians the revealer, the uncoverer—as well as the redeemer—of the depths of their predicament. I do not share with Karl Barth the view that it is only in the reflection of Jesus Christ that we can know anything about the estranged situation of the human. Evidence of that estrangement, and clues to its structure and consequences, are all about us and can be seen in part by anyone strong and open enough to look. There is, however, little doubt that the final interpretation of that condition is understood only in the light of the perfection of Jesus' humanity and of the character of the divine love manifest in and through him. As before, I shall begin in this chapter with the evidences of our estrangement as they appear in our ordinary experience, continue with an analysis in terms of Christian symbols of that estrangement, and then in the next chapter relate this predicament, so understood, to God and to God's response in Jesus Christ. These evidences of the human problem—whatever that problem may turn out to be—are multiple and varied. There are as many explanations or interpretations of this problem as there are forms of it: political, social, psychological, philosophical, and theological. As I shall try to show, most of these explanations fall by the wayside as the evidences mount.

The first evidence of the depth and seriousness of the human problem is its obvious but often forgotten universality. On a very simple level, whenever we hear people—whoever or wherever they are—talking about human events, political, economic, social, we hear them saying "shocking," "awful," "How dare they?" If something good happens, we say "What a relief" indicating a normal or steady-state situation of unrelief, of gnawing worry about events and the course they may take. Each past year has been a year "full of crises"; each present an "unprecedented crisis"; each future year full of seemingly unresolvable threats.

Yet despite this, frequently the universality of the human problem is obscured to us. We tend to blame the particular people, leaders, groups, or forces involved in these unwanted events, as if, were they only not the way they are at the moment, the problem would recede or vanish.[1] Obviously, however, if everyone is saying and feeling this about everyone else—which seems to be the case in family conflicts, in small-town squabbles, in a corporation or city government, among classes, races, and nations—the theory that the problem is all the fault of one group is hardly credible. The cause cannot lie uniquely in this or that group when all share the same symptoms: the capitalists, the unions, the communists, the unenlightened and irrational public, the politicians, the priests and kings (to use the eighteenth century's favorite "fomenters of evil"), the older generation (to use our own). Rather, it is *all* of us, even we: American, white, Christian, educated, clergy, male—or, alternatively, young, female, and black!

Modern culture tended to agree that even if it were universal—all of *them*—it would not always be so. The real extent of human evil lay in the past; the problem then deeper and more widespread than now. With the passage of time, the development of civilization, and especially the growth of science, of labor-saving inventions, of education and moral ideals, the brutality, violence, injustice, and untold suffering characteristic, say, of Roman or Medieval life, are receding. Whether we are better than they were remains, perhaps, a moot point; in any case, relations are gentler, people more lawful, government power less harsh, laws more equal and just, and customs less onerous on the weak. This improvement was regarded as a fixed law of history—as certain, because analogous, as was the biological law of the progressive development of species.

I am old enough to remember intelligent (that is to say, academic!) people saying in 1934–35 when the persecution of the Jews in Germany began: "How *could* this happen in the twentieth century?" Clearly, to them, manifest evil such as this seemed more natural, "at home," in the uncivilized past than in an advanced modernity. As we in the 1970s know well, events since then have almost completely overturned this view of the relation of human evil to the passage of historical time. The developed science and technology, the nearly universal education, and the refined moral and social ideals of modern culture have neither eradicated nor substantially lessened the human problem. Although unquestionably significant advances have been made in special area after area, violence, oppression, conflict, fatedness, lostness, and despair stalk the hearths, the streets, and the public places—and haunt the inward souls—of contemporary life as almost never before. Though many particular symptoms of evil have been drained off, so to speak, the pot of human evil seems to be bottomless, an infinite witch's brew sending off poisonous vapors in every generation and always threatening to boil over in universal catastrophe.

Empirically, then, the problem is universal in space and time. But where does this infinite brew come from? Why *are* we all this way; why is social life—not to mention family life—so full of conflict, and why is history so brutal, lethal, terrifying? Here there has been significant disagreement. Some (mostly American intellectuals) have felt the problem to have its ultimate source in damage to the psyche. If only our neuroses could be straightened out and we could become real, individual selves again, wrote a leading analyst, our social problems would disappear. For then we could be the rational and moral persons we cannot now seem to become by ourselves. It is the "authoritarian personality" that creates authoritarian society; denature through psychological wisdom and techniques that kind of personality, and you resolve the corresponding outward social manifestation of it. A less expensive form of this emphasis on the inward self was embodied in existentialist philosophy: the problem lies in inner emptiness and outer conformity, the answer in personal decision, self-affirmation, and self-direction. Believing firmly in their own open, individualist, and fluid society, and in the democratic process created to resolve its continuing problems, Americans tend to regard society and its institutions as relatively healthy because malleable to that democratic process. Consequently, they have been apt to locate the source of the deeper problems of life in the inward psyche and the answers to these problems in education, therapy, and moral (or religious) conversion.

For another large group—mostly European intellectuals—society molds individuals, not the reverse, and so the deeper levels of the problem lie in the objective social sphere, in the injust and unequal forms of social institutions. These institutions, inherited from a long, stable, consolidated past, and perpetuating an age-old class structure, have seemingly stubbornly refused transformation whatever individuals have felt or done or whatever political processes were instituted. From this perspective—and one can see how persuasive Marxism is to such an established traditional society—the American emphasis on the psyche appears not only naive but self-serving, a typical bourgeois "cop-out," a theory, therefore, that more illustrates the human problem than clarifies or resolves it. Any Marxist would expect a bourgeoisie well-fed by American institutions to insist that our basic problems are private and inward—and not institutional—and that the only cure lies in individual therapy. By means of this "ideology," the bourgeoisie relieve their guilt for the sufferings of others by locating the problem elsewhere and by coping with it through psychology (though Karma is more effective for that end), and at the same time they clearly avoid eradicating the *real* cause of that suffering, namely our anachronistic capitalistic institutions. For this view psychotherapy in a secular culture has replaced religion as the most effective rationalization of injustice and an unparalleled (and profitable) "opiate of the people." Since, furthermore, for this view the problem lies in the character of the objective social order, not within the soul, only a radical political, economic, and social, that is to say, structural or institutional, change in that order will effect a resolution of the human problem.

Despite the obvious correctness of much of this view of America and of many of the problems of social life generally, this view does have obvious difficulties as a full-scale exposition of the scope and depth of the human predicament. Although changes in the social structure can undoubtedly improve the situation (for example, the introduction of democratic self-government into the American colonies) and thus are very important, they do not eradicate the human problem. For that problem reappears, as it did in our own American case and as it has done in Russia, within the new structure, possibly in new forms and often undiluted in intensity. There is a polarity of individual and society, each mutually influencing and each mutually corrupting, as well as mutually improving, the other. Each of these two views I have briefly rehearsed has a firm grasp on one end of this polarity and ignores the other—with unfortunate results, both intellectually and socially.

Another polarity has throughout human reflection appeared as responsible for human disorder and evil. Granted, say many who have thought about it, that the human problem is universal, is it not clear that in every case of violence, conflict, injustice, egotism, etc., it is our unchecked impulses that are at fault? Have not blind desire or greed, or powerful feelings and emotions, been allowed free reign; has not the lower self ruled the higher rational self rather than the reverse? Wherever impulse rules, there occurs a reappearance of primal chaos; wherever intelligence, and a will submissive to intelligence, governs, there order, harmony and so humanity appear.

One may remark that it is no surprise that academics, who, so to speak, live off the mind as fishermen live off the sea, should regard intelligence—of which they presume themselves to represent the main contemporary embodiment or, better, "caretakers"—as the highest of human attributes; and correspondingly that they view impulse, which they have successfully repressed to a feeble flame indeed, as incredibly dangerous. As a distinguished physicist once remarked to me, the human problem arises because most people are uneducated, unintelligent, and thus irrational, guided solely by their passions. Few, at best, of the public have learned to be rational enough to be objective about life's problems, and those few of us who have developed their intelligence have, alas, no say in the course of the world's events. As a consequence, he continued, politics is irrational, government self-interested and stupid, and history replete with oppression and conflict. Social evil and historical chaos represent not the fault of reason but merely the triumph of unreason, and until the elite become the crowd or the crowd the elite, this state will continue. A few decades ago this faith in informed intelligence embodied in the scientific community was optimistic and egalitarian, as, for example, in the thought of the great John Dewey. In our more pessimistic day the same faith takes on the aristocratic, resigned, and not-to-be-blamed passivity of my laureate friend just quoted.

The problem with this rationalism, whether platonic, stoic, or modern scientific, does not of course lie with its encouragement of intelligence; for clearly, like impulse, intelligence is basic to all forms of human creativity and fulfillment. It is that it views refined intelligence as "pure," as in itself free of taint, prejudice, bias, self-interest, and the will to power—even when threatened or anxious. Thus it is confident that a fully developed intelligence, because it understands universally, is able to *be* universal, capable of transcending and controlling the local and particular interests of the self or of its group. The fact, of course, is that a highly developed intelligence—in the executive, the statesman, the scientist, or the professor—can, despite its "universal" understanding, be in concrete life situations itself the instrument of the particular self and its will to power. Then, harnessing a sharp intelligence to serve its own interests, that will to power is more dangerous than is a merely impulsive, arbitrary, and inconsistent will. Correspondingly, a fully educated, highly developed scientific and technological culture—"intelligence" in this case socially embodied—can be just as nationalistic and imperialistic—and thus more dangerous—than can a less educated, less scientific culture, as Germany and as we ourselves have shown. We do not fear Russia less but more if education increases among its people, if the number of Soviet scientists grows, and if their technical expertise expands and prospers—and they feel the same about us. Since intelligence can, like impulse, become the tool of the self, the problem lies deeper than the polarity represented by these two ancient antagonists.

I have skipped quickly over most of the purported "causes" of the human problem and found each of them wanting. It cannot be due to certain kinds of groups of people or to certain people's views; it cannot be the past only or our animal ancestry; it is not just psychological maladjustment or even our faulty social institutions. Nor is it a lack of knowledge, of hard or of clear thinking, of correct theory about ourselves and the world. In and through all of these symptoms of the problem, a wayward *self*, the self-interested, closed, prejudiced, ego-tripping self (or community of selves) seems always to appear, using impulses—that might be generous—using intelligence—that might give excellent guidance—to cause conflict without and despair within.

Viewed thus deeply, below the level of this or that fault, this or that national, cultural, racial, or sexual weakness, it might appear that the finite self itself, *as* finite and particular—as *this* self and no other, as "me" or "us," is to blame. And no wonder! As noted in the last chapter, the self is a conditioned, often threatened, exceedingly finite, and particular little fragment of life. It is in time; it loses itself continually as each moment slips by; it faces a new and thus fearsome world in each instant; it is dependent on all sorts of conditions and forces out of its own control, bound to certain groups, hemmed in by certain perspectives, and governed by certain partial aims. The self seems *determined* in being what it is and doing what it does, driven by internal and external forces it cannot hope to master. Its finitude or creatureliness is thus precisely its problem, not its opportunity; to be dependent on and conditioned by others is a cause of suffering rather than a potential blessing; it is a victim and not a perpetuator of evil in the world. Consequently, its only hope is resignation and then escape, to cut its ties of attachment to itself and its world, to cease to desire to be and to be in the world, and thus at last to know peace until it vanishes altogether.

This understanding of the problem and its answer—put most powerfully probably by Buddhism—introduces a quite new and subtle vision of the human. Here true humanity appears at last almost when the human itself ceases or vanishes or, surely, when attachment to it and veneration of its value die down. To be in time, to share inwardly in that passage, and to seek to understand it, plan for it, direct it; to use impulse, intelligence, and will in order to take one's part in creaturely life and creatively to transform it; to develop creative relations to other persons, to a community, and to humanity as a whole—the humanist aim, whether Christian or secularist—these, whether in noble or trivial form, are all "desire," and they lead only to more suffering. It is being a self in the world among other selves, and it is attachment to the self, to others, and to its world that together constitutes the human problem. Finitude, creatureliness, and the love of both are at fault.

As shall be shown, although this is close to the Christian view, it is not the same. The attraction of this vision is obvious for a contemporary world suffused with potentially mortal conflicts and frequently with an acute sense of the emptiness and vanity of worldly attachments. The power of its insight—as well as the power of the experience of divine reality it offers—is shown in the recent rise of Yogic and of Zen groups. Although this vision is radically different on every level from Western views of the self, when one considers what the affirmation of the ego by the West has meant historically, culturally, and militarily in imperialism and conflict, the intelligibility of the Buddhist diagnosis is indubitable. We had forgotten our own parallel understanding that the self must die if it would live. Instead, we took that ultimate affirmation of the self and its life involved in the Christian dialectic as the undialectical affirmation of the self, of the sanctified, the intelligent, or the well-intentioned (and well-armed!) self—and thus in the ecstacy of those affirmations, spread gunboats and crosses all across the globe.

One significant evidence, however, against the final

truth of this profound understanding of the human problem—as caused by our finitude, not our freedom; by the fact we are particular, temporal selves, not what we do with that condition—is the persistent appearance and reappearance, again both in others and in ourselves, of moral blame or moral condemnation whenever estrangement manifests itself. On both a personal and a political level, none of us, religious or secular, determinist or free-will advocate, can escape blaming others. We find ourselves "naturally" doing it as if they were responsible for what they are and do.

Interestingly, we invariably consider others responsible and so free—and so at fault, blamable—if we do *not* like them; thus we insist that they have willfully chosen their path and were not mere victims of it, pushed into it innocently. Correspondingly, we excuse our friends, our selves, or our group (say, our nation) as "determined" by the inescapable situation to do unwillingly what they did or we did. Paradoxically, in personal and political arguments alike, we tend to assign freedom to our enemies so as to judge them morally, and we assign being determined or being fated to ourselves so as to escape moral blame.

Also on an existential level, we know that we too are responsible—and thus blameworthy—however we may tell ourselves or be told otherwise. Only for this reason do we so heatedly deny that we are to blame. The sense of guilt, or the fear of its presence, is all-pervasive in human experience.[2] No one likes to be a fool or to be seen as one, but we all prefer the picture of ourselves as a noble being, led astray into foolishness by our virtue, rather than as a preditory scoundrel paying only for his intellectual miscalculations.

This frantic effort at moral self-justification bespeaks an awareness both of our freedom and of our estrangement. As anxiety was the inner echo of our temporality, so guilt is the inner echo of our estrangement and of our responsibility for it. Religion has always and in various ways sought to deal with this experience of the uneasy or the guilty conscience. It did not create the experience or the reality it reflects any more than it created our sense of dependence—or anymore than Marxism created injustice or psychoanalysis neuroses in order to have something useful and profitable to do.

Thus, the human predicament is not something that has just "happened to us" from the outside. It is not a part of the given, necessary human condition in itself as are our finitude, our dependence, our temporality, and our mortality. As is shown by this universal experience, which everyone in real relations with others knows and assumes, our predicament is something our freedom has done and does. If this be so, then this general condition of our existence in some strange way is *like* a particular action that we decided at some moment to do and then proceeded to carry out and thus something for which we feel responsible and blameworthy—though we may well deny both. The aptness of the Genesis story of Adam's fall, blaming the general human condition on a particular act of Adam and Eve, stems from this queer correlation in universal experience of an awareness of guilt and responsibility, on the one hand, and an awareness of a general condition from which we all suffer, on the other—as if that general condition were the consequence of some bygone, almost forgotten act of someone representing us. Clearly, even more apt to this experienced duality are the symbols of transmigration and Karma; for them it is our own responsible soul or self which in its acts in our past lives has created the general situation of ignorance, desire, and selfishness from which we now suffer.

One of the problems of talking intelligibly and empirically about the human predicament has now been uncovered. On the one hand, this predicament appears in experience to be quite a universal *state*, nearly inevitable, seemingly a *necessity* and a given like the human condition itself, almost as if we were tragically fated to it. Thus half of the usual explanations proffer a *necessitating* cause of our predicament and thus deny the responsibility that is also an aspect of it. On the other hand, we experience our own part in the human predicament (and especially that of our antagonists) as personal, individual, and free, as something for which we are responsible and so blameworthy and, consequently, similar to an *action* which is not at all necessary and determined but willed and chosen. Here arise the two types of language that one meets on this theme in sociology, psychology, philosophy, and theology alike: the language of inevitability, necessity, and universality, and the language of choice, will, and freedom. The symbol of Karma unites these two forms of language by assigning the language of freedom, of free choice and responsibility, to one's own *past* existence and the language of necessity to the conditions of the *present* existence. In the Christian tradition these two types of language are illustrated by theological reflection on the story of the fall and its consequences. The language about Eve and Adam in the garden has represented the language of freedom, choice, act, and responsibility; the language about our common inheritance from that act has represented that of necessity, fate, and so of universality and inevitability. We may be sure that any explanation, sociological, psychological, philosophical or theological, that ignores or explains away either side—the fateful and tragic or the free and responsible side—will in the end prove both unempirical and inconsistent.

The other relevant evidence against a view of our human problem as a necessary aspect of our nature as finite, and thus inescapable as long as we are in human life at all, stems from specifically Christian rather than from general experience. As noted in Chapter 2, it is an aspect of the Christian awareness of ourselves in relation to God that we experience directly the goodness and possibility of our creaturely finitude: the richness and creative opportunities latent in our destiny, the shaping power of our freedom, and the new possibilities within our future. To experience God as the unifying ground of our actuality and our possibility is to experience the goodness of creaturely being. It is, therefore, to know that the human problem is not a necessity to our condition but that in relation to God it can be transformed. And to experience that possibility of being "a new creature" (or what Tillich called "the new being") is to know that estrangement, although universal, is a *warping* of the human situation and not its essence, that to be finite is not necessarily to be estranged. For the Christian tradition, therefore, the essential structure of our humanity, its self-transcending finitude, its conditionedness, its dependence, and its relations to the world and to others, are good because created and upheld by God. How, then, has this tradition understood the actuality of evil in life and in ourselves? Is this understanding more intelligible in relation to our experience of existence than are the ones just reviewed?

Almost everyone in the West is familiar with the orthodox understanding of evil in the Christian tradition—and with its difficulties within modern times. Based upon what was regarded as a clear affirmation of scripture (Genesis 2–3; Romans 5:14ff.), this understanding traced the entire human experience of evil to Eve and to Adam's sin in the Garden of Eden. Because of that sin of disobedience, of unbelief or untrust ("of course you will not die"), and of pride ("ye shall be as gods")—not, it should be noted, an act connected with sexuality—God punishes (as he/she had promised) this original pair and their posterity with exclusion from the garden, with the curse of hard work and bodily suffering, and with death (Romans 5:14). And as the unfolding scriptural story made plain (cf. Cain and Abel, the Tower of Babel, the sins leading up to the flood, and the tragic and sinful history of Israel itself) included in the effects of that original act was a loss by subsequent generations of their original or natural innocence and goodness and a strange propensity to evil and conflict. This loss of goodness and this strange propensity to evil and conflict Augustine "explained" by the doctrine of the transmission of concupiscence (of inordinate desire) by means of the lust of the sexual act by which all of us are conceived. This ever-recurring situation was regarded as so serious that, on the one hand, it merited over and over again acts of the severest divine judgment and even of the divine condemnation to eternal punishment of Adam's posterity; and, on the other, as so hopeless that if there was to be relief at all, it called for divine rescue from these effects of sin. The obviously tragic character of historical experience in each generation—including catastrophes, disease, and death itself—were in this way "understood," not in terms of the structure of human finitude, but in terms of an act of freedom at the beginning of historical time, an act in which both the creative freedom to do the good and the possibilities of eternal life were lost. In their place came the fallen character of historical experience, with its pervasive conflict, brutality, and injustice and its ever-recurrent want and misery, its diseases and its certain death. The good creation, condemned and helpless, now under the control of demonic powers, is warped, waiting in groaning pain, and yet in expectation for a rescue from its deep predicament (Romans 8:18ff.).

This realistic and/or grim (if one agrees with it, it is "realistic"; if one does not, it is "pessimistic" or "gloomy")

picture of human existence in history is, or course, associated with the symbols of sin and especially of original
sin. Perhaps its main feature is to account for what we call
natural evil (floods, droughts, sickness, death) by means of
human evil, an act of sin. The first symbol, "sin," expressed the fact that, whatever the worldly consequences
of that first act, its central quality was that of a willful and
rebellious *defiance* of God and of his/her will, an act which,
therefore, broke the relation to God and so incurred his/
her wrath, on the one hand, and an act for which the
perpetuators were personally responsible, uneasy in their
conscience, and thus guilty, on the other. The symbol,
"original sin," referred to two facets of this picture: to the
original defiance of God (the original sin) by Eve and by
Adam that caused the deplorable human condition, and to
the correlated doctrine of *transmission* which explained how
each generation came to share in that condition and its
grim consequences by inheritance.

Despite what to us are the mildly bizarre, and even
perverse, aspects of this doctrine, it had many aspects,
besides its authority as the apparent dictum of Scripture,
which obviously made it a convincing account to generations of Christians. After all, the entire picture seemed to
have ample warrant in experience itself, experience both
personal and sociohistorical (as Augustine's *Confessions* and
The City of God illustrate). The situation which original sin
sought to explain was no fantasy of a sick imagination, to
be explained away in terms of the neuroses or prejudices of
the explainers. Human life seemed in fact to be universally
caught in endless rounds of evil; no one, bad or good,
seemed free of this taint or its consequences, and catastrophe after catastrophe—most of them clearly the results
of someone's propensity to evil—characterized the human
lot. Moreover, this condition, or predicament, while as a
whole obviously the direct fault neither of any one person

nor of any particular group and while clearly inescapable for all, was nevertheless also interlaced with aspects of freedom and of responsibility—and as a consequence the general feeling of an uneasy conscience and of guilt that accompanied it seemed appropriate and thus valid. *What* the story and its correlate, the chain of inheritance, sought to explain was, therefore, real enough indeed.

The story and its correlate had, moreover, a certain profundity that seemed to fit the experienced paradoxes of the human condition and to provide an appropriate and reasonable explanation for it. Evil as we experience it does seem a grim, unalterable, and thus tragic condition or state of existence and ourselves its victims; and yet we are also aware of being ourselves continuing perpetuators of this same evil and thus responsible ourselves in a strange way for it. The story, with its inheritance which we each proceed to actualize, fitted this experience. While, moreover, the mark of evil pervades every aspect and region of existence, and its odor permeates every sacred as well as every profane place, still there remain—in nature, in history, in communities, in institutions, in personal relations, and in individual people—dramatic facets of creativity and of goodness, undeniable possibilities of virtue, and the continual and unabated relevance and claim of the ideal. If evil were *natural*, a simple necessity of our nature, these positive moral and ideal aspects would be sheer illusion, a cruel hoax; and cynical consciousness dominated only by the claim of self-interest would be the only rational option. But this obviously is itself a misreading of the facts of any concrete situation, and such cynicism is as destructive of its adherent as is a naive and foolish idealism. It remains a *good* world; humans are moral beings despite their waywardness; and life has possibilities despite its evident tragedy and irrationality. Thus the traditional symbolism of "a good thing spoiled," a good history that has fallen, of

a race condemned by its own act to be untrue to itself—
and yet claimed for the ideal it really is—also makes sense
in experience as against either a cynical or an idealistic
reading of the facts.

Finally, in pointing to a universal propensity to sin, as
well as to each person's "sins," this symbolism seemed on
two counts to be accurate. We do experience that propensity; even when we intend the good, something propels us
to spoil it—with hostility, with defensiveness, with pride or
insecurity. And clearly those who on the level of their acts
are without reproach (that is "responsible," "good" citi-
zens) are yet seen to be—when, like their butlers, we
"know them well enough"—subject to the same propen-
sities as are we. Good people, intelligent people, mighty
people, proud people, educated people, and saints are also
caught, as we are. This truth, so evident in experience and
yet so vigorously denied by most alternative explanations,
seems to validate and revalidate the story of an entire race
"fallen" in an act of freedom and thereby condemned to
reenact, each in his or her own unique and creative style,
the story of sin all over again. Thus the validity of the
doctrine of original sin continued to be accepted and powerfully defended in ages where little (except what the Bible
implied) was known of the prehistory of nature or of the
race, where the reality of human weakness, suffering and
death were for a variety of reasons particularly apparent to
all, and where, of course, the authority of this story was
unquestioned as a significant aspect of the religious beliefs
that dominated the ethos of the entire culture.

With the coming of the modern world, replete with new
scientific and historical knowledge and dominated by quite
new attitudes towards the possibilities of life and of history, this traditional picture of the human condition, and
even more this orthodox explanation of it, seemed increasingly grotesque and irrational. In the later eighteenth and

early nineteenth centuries, through geology and paleontology, the knowledge of the long, slowly developing history of the earth increased, and through anthropological and historical studies, knowledge of the early periods of the human race developed. As a result of this new and vastly extended vision of the past, suddenly the picture of an original pair, acting out this drama some six thousand years ago in a Near Eastern garden, seemed not only bizarre and childish, but clearly contradicted by innumerable well-established facts. Moreover, the new biological knowledge of the evolutionary development of Homo sapiens as one among the whole family of animal species made incredible the orthodox theory that human weakness, disease, and death, not to mention its precarious accommodation to its environment, resulted from an act of human sin and not from the conditions of all finite life which we share with all other animals. As a factual account of the origin of evil, both natural and human evil, the Genesis story seemed, therefore, simply false, and thus any theological symbols based upon it way wide of the mark.

Equally significant, however, in the "demise of original sin" were the new attitudes towards life and its possibilities and towards individuality and autonomy characteristic of modern culture generally. With the development of the new science and its tested methods of inquiry in the sixteenth and seventeenth centuries, the steady advance of knowledge and thus of understanding seemed now a virtual certainty, and with this certainty a new confidence in the growth of reason's control appeared. What had been dark mystery might now be enlightened by understanding. And with understanding, especially empirical understanding of the causes of things, will inevitably flow, said Francis Bacon, the power to manipulate, to control these causes for human welfare. Correspondingly, forces that had once been beyond our control, whether we refer to nature's forces or to human social arrangements, might now be brought under our purposive direction—and a new era of human well-being will arrive. Thus far from "fallen," human history represents a steady progress towards betterment; far from being a realm of frustration, guilt and punishment for weakness and failures we cannot escape and for sins we cannot avoid, life in space and time can in the near future become at last free of disease, free of want, free of oppression, free of injustice, free of fear. With the coming of the theory of evolution (and of the Marxist ideology as well) in the nineteenth century, this faith in human progress appeared to receive the status of a cosmic law. As the biologist George Gaylord Simpson, speaking as a scientist about what he regarded simply as scientific truth, said: "Man has risen, not fallen."[3]

The symbol of original sin now seemed, in other words, not only to be incredible scientifically but, even worse, to be simply an error about the quality and the possibilities of human existence. Suffering from natural evils and participating in moral evils may, to be sure, have characterized our primitive, ignorant past when this dogma was developed; but the conquest of natural evil through science and technology, and of moral evil through the growth of idealism, of education, and of social reform is now in sight. We suffer from no problems our own capacities cannot resolve as we and they become mature. We need no rescue that our own developing powers cannot effect. Thus are religion's gloomy diagnoses of the human condition and religion's promises of salvation not only incredible but irrelevant, and not only irrelevant but destructive of our confidence and our energy.

Along with its optimism, modern culture also developed—as has been noted—a keen sense of the reality and value of human autonomy, of our own thinking, judging, and deciding, our own initiating action, our own experiencing. Thus nothing should be true for us unless *we* have established its validity: nothing should be good for us unless we judge it so; no act of ours is moral unless we have decided and initiated it ourselves; no act immoral or sinful unless our personal responsibility for it is clear. Needless to say, such an emphasis on personal and individual autonomy rendered the doctrine of original sin morally and religiously incoherent. How can *we* be justly blamed for a religious revolt against God which we neither initiated nor carried out; how can we be punished and, worse, eternally so, for a sinful act we did not ourselves commit? Thus to sensitive liberal Christians—even had they never made contact with the new studies of geology, anthropology, ancient history, and biology—the dogma of Adam's original sin, of the transmission of a sinful propensity and its associated guilt, and the threat of divine judgment for both, seemed primitive and barbaric in the extreme. To such liberal Christians, religion might not thereby be irrelevant or untrue; but to them its relevance would no longer be conceived as a rescue from the effects of the original sin by the long-deceased progenitors of our race. In tune with their optimistic age, they insisted that it was the essence of Christianity to affirm the value of each person, not his or her guilt; to emphasize the possibility of virtue, not its impossibility; and to encourage our own building of the Kingdom, rather than to "wait patiently on God." For a host of reasons, therefore, each one fundamental to the modern culture that was developing, the traditional Christian understanding of natural and moral evil, represented by the doctrines of original sin, of the fall and of the effects of both on historical life, suffered an eclipse, not only in the rising humanism, but also in the dominant liberal religion of the later eighteenth, the nineteenth and the early twentieth centuries.

As frequently noted, however, the wind has significantly shifted in the middle decades of the twentieth century. With successive world wars, the vast ideological struggles, the revolt toward liberation of the Third World, and finally the menacing ecological crisis, a vivid sense of the pervasive, continuing, and even dominant presence of evil in historical life has appeared—or reappeared. The idea that cruelty, oppression, exploitation, inequality, injustice, and the tragedy and suffering they bring have receded and will gradually be eliminated as time passes has become itself an incredible and barely comprehensible "myth." The proud conviction that with modern civilization humanity has become mature, capable of resolving its major problems, and, consequently, capable of rescuing itself from them now seems, on the one hand, to be itself radically unrealistic and immature and, on the other, to be in fact ideological, the sly justification for the advance to further hegemony of the dominant economic and political interests of our epoch—and thus itself evidence against the growing innocence of modern liberal culture. It is now the underdeveloped countries that are the victims of evil, the "advanced" countries that are its major perpetuators. In such a scenario what has happened to the confidence that with the move from primitive to civilized one moves towards moral innocence—and away from evil? The sharp contemporary awareness of the injustice, the exploitation, the inordinate self-concern, and thus the ultimate self-destruction of *even* modern, liberal scientific culture—the culture that was to eradicate precisely those characteristics of historical life—has, therefore, directly refuted the dream of progress and validated in a quite new way the traditional sense of a fallen, or at least a deeply troubled, history. An awareness of the poignant relevance (if not the truth) of the ancient symbolism of original sin—and of the need for rescue from *somewhere* or other—are very much a part of contemporary sensibility.

For this reason a significant number of recent theologians have looked at this old doctrine with entirely different eyes than did their optimistic predecessors. The complicating factor, however, has been that, although they did not share with the liberal generations their faith in the innate goodness and reasonableness of men and women nor their confidence in progress, still they *did* share their acceptance of the validity, albeit the approximating or relative validity, of the results of scientific and historical inquiry. Thus they, too, have subscribed to those factual objections based on geology, biology, anthropology, and ancient history to the conception of an actual original pair of progenitors some few thousand years ago, created near the beginning of things, initially innocent of lustful, oppressive, or self-serving motives, potentially immortal and cavorting in a Near Eastern paradise free of want, of disease, and of the scourge of iniquity and death. Being children of a post-Freudian culture, these theologians also shared the critique that a transmission of "desire" (*cupiditas*) through the lustful character of all sexual acts is not only a lame explanation at best, but even more an "uptight" slander at the entire realm of organic and pleasurable feelings. They agree, moreover, that a divine punishment, especially an eternal punishment, for the sin of another or for sins committed because of the sin of another, is an injustice unworthy of God. And finally they object that such an explanation of our situation in terms of Adam's defiance and our inheritance blames Adam alone for sin, absolves into necessity the freedom with which *we* in turn sin, and thus drains off our personal responsibility for our situation and our own actions. Contemporary theology has, in other words, sought to reject the literal, historical Adam and the theory of causal transmission and yet to retain the symbolic Adam and the symbolic fall. Or, as the distinguished historian of science John M. Greene put this in the concluding sentence of his extraordinary volume, *The Death of Adam*, on the development and impact of the concept of evolution: "The historical Adam is now dead, a casualty of scientific progress, but the Adam in whom all men die lives on, the creature and the creator of history, a moral being whose every intellectual triumph is at once a temptation to evil and a power for good."[4]

This effort to reject the literal, historical, "ontic" referent to a theological doctrine or concept and to retain or even develop its symbolic meaning will by now be familiar to readers of this volume. It has appeared already with regard to the concepts of revelation, of the good creation, and of God's action in historical process. It will reappear in a significantly different form in relation to the interpretation and comprehension of Jesus as the Christ; for there the historical reference of theological symbolism is unavoidable and unexpendable.

In fact, the way modern theology has dealt with the symbols of original sin and the fall has been paradigmatic of its major problems and, correspondingly, of its most significant triumphs. In no other case has the structure of contemporary theological revision or reinterpretation been so clear. Here the *literal* truth of the symbol and thus the explanatory power of the doctrine (that is, explanatory of our situation of evil)—the historical Adam, the actuality of his unfortunate act, and the theory of generational transmission—all have been sacrificed. In their place has come the *symbolic* Adam, Adam as symbol rather than as fact and explanation (Ricoeur), the fall as "permanent myth" (Niebuhr), or as "broken myth," the transition from essence to existence (Tillich).[5] This "symbolic" Adam, his act, and the fall thus refer not to an actual Adam at all but to the human situation generally and thus to our own situation. These symbols thus become heuristic (illuminating) concepts that uncover and expose the hidden, complex, and mysterious actuality of our human existence generally and of the actual existential situation of each one of us individually. There is still, it should be noted, a quite concrete referent, namely, every particular case of human existence in time and space. In this changed reference to all facts rather than to a special fact, the symbols of sin and of original sin are similar to those of creation and of providence which in a parallel way refer to all events.

Most fundamentally, the role of the religious or theological symbol has changed. Its role is no longer to inform us of a particular fact or a particular series of facts unknowable except through revelational information: about the first pair, or about the beginning of time and of the world, how the animals were created, how evil came into the world, and so on. Rather, the function of a religious or theological symbol is to uncover the deeper or *religious* dimension of all facts, specifically (as theological symbols) the dimension in which facts are related to their eternal ground, to God. Theology, through its symbols of creation and fall, does not know and cannot say when the world began, who the first humans were, what they were like and did, or precisely how evil first appeared in history. What it can say through this symbolic structure is how any humans anywhere—and so how each of us—is originally related to God, how we each break this relation in coming to be, what the structure of that break is, and what its effects on us and on our history are. In other words, theological symbolism can relate experienced facts, the present situation of our inward and outward experience, to their ground in God and thus illumine their deepest problems and their most significant possibilities.

Granted, then, the relevance and intelligibility of religious or theological symbolism even in a modern scientific culture—at least in one where the menace of human evil and so the problem of its understanding still press heavily on us—what is the justification for *this* symbolism, for the story of Adam and Eve and their fall—whatever "story" and "fall" may now mean? Put another way, what more specifically does that story of the fall mean when thus made symbolic, and how is that meaning illuminative of our universal predicament or situation—or, as Reinhold Niebuhr used to say, how does it help to make sense of the baffling facts of our common experience?[6]

It is, first of all, important both to the coherence and to the meaning of Christian witness and for the understanding of our own experience to retain the symbolism enshrined both in the "story" form and in the story of a "fall." To interpret a universal situation, as this one is, in terms of universal *structure,* or specifically of metaphysical or ontological structure, is to render that situation necessary and essential and thus an intrinsic result of our being finite and of our being human at all. Such a form of interpretation consequently dissolves the role of freedom in our predicament and, thus, any shred of responsibility for it—which, as was noted, contradicts both our common experience of human evil and the essential implications of Christian belief. To state that history is intrinsically and directly good, or getting better and better—and thus to understand evil as a mere accident or "sport"—is directly unempirical, a remaining remnant of a lost humanistic faith. To state that history is essentially evil and unredeemably lost, void of hope for meaning and fulfillment is to deny other aspects of experience and certainly to run counter to every fundamental Christian promise. To affirm that our human being is essentially good but fallen, warped away from its true nature, and, consequently, separated from its possible fulfillment, is both empirical and Christian; it is to describe a universal situation or predicament but to do so in such a way as to make room for freedom and thus for responsibility in that situation—

which is much closer to the quality of actual experience. However such responsibility for our common situation may be denied in theory, it is, as I noted, always affirmed in our common personal and social practice.

What is important to see in this connection is that the story form, and the story of a fall, is analogically, not literally, a story. A literal story about an actual event is univocal or literal historical language; it portrays the divine as *simply* an actor in space and time; such language about a divine event, or the relation of men and women to the divine, is *historical* language about *deity*. This is "primitive" myth, profound but ultimately representing a category mistake and ultimately leading to confusion.[7] To reject on this account *all* story language is to be forced, if one speaks of our universal situation, into ontological or metaphysical language; this is the language of mystical pantheism and pessimistic naturalism about evil, namely, that it is "built into" the structure of our finitude and utterly inescapable. The only recourse, then, if one is to speak seriously, and yet without despair, of the reality of evil is to use the form of story or myth, and yet analogically as referent not to an actual human event or act, but to the *becoming* of all human events in their destiny and their freedom. In coming to be, all human events "fall" from their own deepest and most essential relations and thus from their own essential possibilities. As noted, only a mythical or symbolic understanding of human history as fallen can escape the two errors of idealism or of cynicism.

Second, the story of the fall goes on to speak of Adam and Eve's rebellion and of their unbelief or, better, their distrust in God and their defiance of God's will. If this was not an actual event in primal history, to what, then, does this story refer? What does it mean, and has it any relevance at all to our experience? First of all, it is clear that here evil arises out of the pretentions of spirit ("ye shall be as gods") rather than from the lusts of the flesh. It is because Eve and Adam were *human*, that is, free to disobey, capable of seeking divine status on their own, able to become their own source of security and meaning, not because they were "animal" or "ignorant" or "primitive," that they sinned. Here it is the spirit in humanity that makes us human beings, and that is also the source both of our creativity and of the possibility of our evil.

Specifically by "spirit" I refer to the self-transcending and thus self-constituting power of human existence—its power to unite past, present and future, to survey its world and itself and consider both—that is, its self-transcending power; and, consequently, its power to know, to judge, to decide, and to act on the basis of itself, its judgments, and its decisions; that is, its self-constituting power. Here, then, in spirit lies the seat of human creativity; here also lies the seat, the locus, of human estrangement and sin.

The first and most obvious role of spirit in estrangement and sin is that spirit is one of the parents of anxiety; the other parent is our finitude, our conditionedness, our mortality. Spirit—the freedom compounded of alternatives, of choice, and of committed decisions—opens up infinite possibilities for the self in becoming itself. But because of our particularity and finitude, choice must be made and some of these possibilities rejected if the self is to be at all, to be *this* self and, thus, real; yet possibly these rejected alternatives are better! One particular person must be chosen if any person is to be loved—and there are always alternatives. Making its appearance here is the anxiety of possibility, a "dizziness" that threatens and unsettles the self. As it inwardly becomes itself in relation to its destiny and its possibilities, the self is tempted by the infinity in which it shares into estrangement, either to forgetting its concrete destiny—and seeking to be *all* of its possibilities—or to forgetting its real possibilities—and so to cease to be a real self, a *unique* self at all.

In its outward life in the world, as in its self-becoming, the self is tempted by anxiety into estrangement or, in this context, into sin. It is through the same spiritual self-transcendence, our ability to survey the world and envision the future and to set them both in relation to the self—as intellectual, practical, planning beings—that we are anxious about the future and ourselves in that future: about our food supply, about our enemies or potential enemies, about our land, our power, position and status, and so on. It is, then, out of this anxiety that we are "driven," as we say, to secure ourselves at the expense of others. How can I help stealing from my neighbor when my children must continually be fed? How can I help accumulating money when all the bills for education are going to arrive? How can we help annexing new territory and building new bases when our enemies might attack us from just over there? Anxiety about the future drives the self to secure itself; since spirit surveys an infinite future and an infinite space, the anxiety of each finite creature is never satisfied. Hence, precisely out of spirit arises the infinite extent of imperial aggression, of the drive for wealth and power, of the urge for domination over others. Anxiety is the precondition of estrangement and of sin in the sense that it tempts us to act for ourselves and against others, to do what we would not wish to do.

Anxiety arises out of our finitude in conjunction with our spiritual self-transcendence or freedom; it is, as Tillich says, finitude "felt from the inside." It is *temptation* to sin, not sin itself (if it were the latter, estrangement would be necessary); it represents only the temptation, and not the necessity, to secure the self against all others because there is the ideal or essential possibility that our life be centered on God, the ground of our being and meaning, rather than on ourselves. Were *that* the case, then the anxieties of our condition would be—as they also often are—the occasion for creative cultural, historical, and personal achievement rather than that of the vicious and infinite domination over, agression against, and exploitation of the neighbor and the environment. But instead of centering ourselves on God and his/her purposes, we center our life on ourselves and our own, and depend entirely on our power—or that of our group—to provide security and meaning to all we are and love. Then, in *that* situation, anxiety is not only the temptation to aggression; now it leads to aggression. It is, then, as the story reminds us, the prior "sin" of unbelief, of lack of trust, the rebellion against God by making the self the center of its world, that is the root of sin.

It is, therefore, in freedom and so in spirit that sin arises, when the finite self ceases to depend on its creator and sovereign and depends entirely on itself. In that estrangement from God arising out of freedom, the self becomes estranged from its own ultimate security and meaning and is therefore driven into estragement from itself, its community, and its world. The rebellious act of Adam and Eve is, therefore, the rebellion of each self in centering its world about itself, its lack of trust in God, its estrangement from the ground of its being and meaning. Although these are different theological modes of interpreting this primal symbol, each points to that ultimate root in human existence where evil enters, that is, where in fact the break in the relation to God appears. The rebellious act once upon a time in history has thus, in modern theology, become the symbol for a rebellion or an estrangement (both vocabularies are appropriate analogies) that occurs in our own *depths*, at the center of our existence, where the self constitutes itself. This deep estrangement is encouraged by our common, historical destiny, by the historical tradition of estrangement in which each community lives out its life, and which is thus passed on to each generation. However, as our experience of responsibility indicates, we each enact anew this fundamental centering of the world around ourselves, which constitutes this original rebellion. As Schleiermacher felicitously put it, "In each the work of all, in all the work of each." The story of the fall is now the story of the coming to be in history of each self and each community, and of the responsibility and freedom of each self for the estrangement and self-centered character of its actuality.

Third, as traditional theology realized, the story of the fall, as the interpretation of our situation, presupposes not only a rebellious act once upon a time by Eve and by Adam, but also the *transmission* of the effects of that act from them to us. How, in the modern world, is *that* aspect of this symbolic structure to be interpreted? First, there is, as noted, the historical transmission of estrangement passed on communally. We absorb more than our cultural ethos—language, concept, norms, and so on—from our own heritage; we also absorb that community's "fallen" character—its centering of its world about itself, its inordinate self-love and love of its own. This is the *inner* side of the Kingdom of evil, which is an aspect of history; the outer side is composed of warped and unjust institutions and trends which I shall term "fate" and which I shall speak of later.

Thus there is a historical dimension to sin; it is passed on, but passed on communally, not sexually, as the deepest level of the destiny that is ours. However, as in all cases of destiny, what is given must be appropriated, reenacted, and reshaped by freedom. The historical destiny of estrangement is also appropriated, reenacted, and reshaped by *our* rebellion, our centering the world about ourselves as we become ourselves. Thus, in coming to be, we each reenact the Adamic story and, in helping to create a community of self-concern, we each aid in the transmission of that fated and faulted destiny—as every parent, passing on their defensiveness, hostility, and self-concern (as well as their neuroses)—comes sadly to realize.

Also presupposed in this theological understanding of the human predicament is the distinction between the *root* of estrangement in the depths of our existence and its *effects* or fruits in our conscious attitudes and intentions and our explicit acts—symbolized traditionally in the distinction between the inherited original sin of Adam and the particular sins of each generation of men and women. Most liberal interpretations of human evil do not accept such a distinction: sin, say they, lies only in the conscious intentions of the author of sin and in his/her explicit acts—otherwise, how are they responsible? Thus only when they intend evil and consciously act out of that selfish and hostile intention is there sin—and they point to the criminals, the bully, the mobster, the tyrant as examples of sin. The problem with this view is that experience clearly indicates that almost all real sins—acts of cruel, ruthless aggression, exploitation, injustice against a neighbor—are done under the delusion that they are good and, consequently, with the intention of being creative rather than destructive. And, what is more, they are done by the "respectable" as well as (or perhaps more than) by the "criminal" members of society. Certainly colonialism was justified by good as well as shady people as "helpful to the natives." Certainly wars were similarly justified and continue to be so. Certainly upper and "moral" classes oppress other classes "for the order of society." Certainly the rich gouge the poor "for the sake of the economic well-being of all"—even slavery was defended as religiously and morally sound. Sin, if it be sin, arises at a deeper level than that of our conscious intentions and our explicit choices; it arises on the level, as Augustine said, of what we *really* love, in the character of our love and our willing, in what he called "the gravity of the soul." It is for this reason that we find it so hard to change or reshape, to conquer this propensity, for this is for the self to try to change or re-shape the self itself. Sin has affected that deep center of our being that shapes all we are and do, including any process of self-transformation we may embark upon. Our problem is not only that we continually make wrong choices, speak hostile words to others, do selfish deeds that hurt others, and so on. Our problem is that those explicit symptoms of our estrangement arise from a depth in our being that is itself falsely centered, inordinately attached to itself, at odds or estranged from itself. In this sense, then, there is an "original sin"—or a deeper level of estrangement—that generates our specific sins.

The view that our human predicament arises from a psychic or spiritual depth below our conscious attitudes, thoughts, intentions, and deliberate acts—and thus below our entire *explicit* cultural ethos and social structure—is not unfamiliar to the dominant modern interpretations of the human predicament. In Marxist theory, the thoughts, norms, intentions, and actions of the bourgeoisie are twisted and refashioned by just such a prior, hidden, de-termining situation, namely, the relations of production characteristic of capitalist society. In classical psychotherapeutic theory, a hidden, yet all-determining situation of neurosis lies in back of the concrete thoughts, attitudes, ideals, aims, judgments, and acts of each neuro-tic patient, twisting the latter's total being, powers, and acts in unintended, unapproved, and yet destructive ways. In each case, however, there is little if any contribution of freedom or of self-constitution to this hidden, determining situation. We are, here, victims respectively of the class-consciousness that we have inherited or of our parents—though few Marxists feel that way about the bourgeoisie.

But this is in fact to find *no* one responsible, and so to locate the problem no where at all—for the false consciousness that creates class and the domination of the parents that creates neurosis must themselves be understood, unless, as neither Marx nor Freud believed, we are fated by necessity to reenact these warped forms of humanity. In the parallel Christian view, there is a *re*appropriation and *re*enactment by freedom or by self-constitution, even at this most fundamental level. Thus, both as bourgeois or proletariat, and as child or parent, are we in part victim, in part perpetuators, of the self-centering that characterizes our common existence.

In the Christian understanding of evil, then, like these other two, there is a "double-level" understanding. There is, on the one hand, an originating depth where estrangement gestates and, on the other, a surface where intentions appear in consciousness, judgments are made, thoughts formed and expressed, decisions taken, and actions enacted. And each culture (and society) reflects, as I have noted, both levels: it is characterized by an inordinate self-love, by centering its world about itself, its ethos, its norms, and its ways; its institutions in turn reflect also that determining and pervasive self-concern; and its actions manifest the same fundamental estrangement. Here the creativity and the estrangement of spirit, intertwined in personal existence, are likewise intertwined in historical life. This means that the ethical or moral, and certainly the legal, distinctions characteristic of all cultural life—and necessary to it—are not *final* determinants or *ultimate* criteria for moral or political judgments. Good and bad, respectable and unrespectable alike are characterized by estrangement; and their society and its norms—which define good and bad in a given culture—are likewise so characterized. In this sense all of history—primitive and civilized, underdeveloped and developed, aggressive and peace-loving, communist and democratic—is "fallen," and despite their significant differences, all illustrate both estrangement and its consequences, both sin (original sin) and sins. The universality of the problem is, here, classically uncovered and explicated, and an ultimate equality of us all in this predicament, and in responsibility for it, deeply affirmed. Not only is this true: are there differences in the *ultimate* self-love between groups, classes, and races? It is also significant in praxis; for the point is not that those dubious characters over there are also sinners (that I already believe), but that even *we* illustrate it as well.

In such a double-level understanding, clearly it is the root or depth situation that determines the forms on the surface—as Marx and Freud agree. Thus do our views, attitudes, standards, judgments, and decisions reflect (for Marx were epiphenomena of the class structure) the inordinate self-love, the estrangement, at the center. Or, as Freud put it, they are rationalizations of our neurosis. In the Christian view, this influence of our deep estrangement on our conscious, and, so, on our cultural and moral, life is not understood as merely a causal process, the one inexorably determining the other. As Reinhold Niebuhr put it, the self is not simply a victim of its estrangement; rather it "deceives itself" that its actions are just or right, that it is itself "not at all hostile," and that it "was only seeking to help others," and so on. Each self is far from ignorant of these depths; we are all dimly conscious of our selfish aims, our insecurity, our aggressive hostility, our desire to dominate and to be glorified by others. But this dim consciousness of the reality of our selves is frightening, productive of a new and deeper level of anxiety—as any psychoanalysis reveals. This is something we do not want to know if we can help it. Thus the structure of the rationalization grows higher and more complex, the effort of justification more energetic, the voice louder and louder—as any argument in marriage or diplomatic conflict can testify. The last thing the sinner wishes to admit is that he is a sinner; the most unacceptable reality about us is our own estrangement. Clearly here the self is transcendent enough over itself to sense the reality of itself, and thus, because it longs to be good, then to deny that reality. The hypocrisy of the self and of any group thus testifies to the innate virtue and the irrepressible freedom of the self, as well as to the depth of its estrangement.

Fourth, another symbol in the original story of our estrangement from God is the demonic. Originally the demonic was referrent to the legions of satanic powers, who themselves represented both principles of evil and agents of evil. In contemporary theology, however, this symbol refers to a dimension of human existence crucial to the latter's understanding in both its individual and its social forms and thereby central to any interpretation of history in its blind fanaticism, its unlimited destruction, its infinite cruelty. One central aspect of our predicament is the striving on the part of both individuals and groups to elevate themselves to the level of the divine, to replace God, to *be* God—that is, the unrestricted striving to become the center of their world and of its meaning.

The symbol of the demonic is "theological" in that it reflects negatively our relation to God: without security in the divine power and love, we experience a radical and unbearable insecurity. Without meaning and significance grounded in the divine purposes, our precarious worldly meanings and significance are fundamentally threatened. Without acceptance by the divine love, we are unable to accept and affirm ourselves and, consequently, are bereft of identity. The centrality of the divine through our being, our meaning, and our selfhood means that estrangement from the divine creates an infinite void we cannot bear;

and all our empirical behavior reflects our efforts to fill that void, to replace through our own powers the divine center, the divine security, and the divine meaning now absent from our existence. This effort to become the absolute and unconditioned principle of being and of meaning in our existence is expressed in the symbol of the demonic.

Because it is finite, each self and each group finds itself inescapably the perceiving and acting center of its surrounding world. Because, moreover, it is dependent, each self and each group can be itself only in relation to other creatures, and in these relations each must affirm its uniqueness, its life, and its powers in order to be at all. It is, then, neither to this natural centering of the world around each perceiving, knowing, and acting self, nor to this natural affirmation of the self and its life that the symbol of the demonic refers. It is, rather, that in being itself among others, each self claims to be the *center* of all significance in its world; and, as a consequence, in its relation to others it affirms itself as *more* significant than they and, thus, as *against* them. The demonic represents, then, an inordinate and infinite self-love or self-concern, a "turning in towards itself," an elevation of the creature to the level of the divine ultimacy, absoluteness, and sacrality. It appears both in the inward relation of the self to itself and in relation of the self—or the community—to its world, to nature, and to others.

For most of us this inordinate, all-encompassing love of the self is redirected towards our group, our nation, our race, our cause, our career, or profession. We find—when pressed by others, as we shall inevitably be—that we are willing to use our intelligence, our virtue, all our powers to further this ultimate concern at the sacrifice of others and, ultimately, of ourselves. Obscured in the life histories of ordinary people to all but those who live with them, this drive to claim ultimacy for all our powers, ideals, and aims, to give universal and thus sacred status to our local meanings, to make our own security the be-all and end-all of existence, breaks out into the "open" only in the behavior of "world-historical" individuals, of large families, of nations, and of races. Each finite center becoming ultimate and absolute, each comes, therefore, into inevitable conflict with the self, the group, the ideals, and the purposes of others. Thus arise the imperialisms, the injustices, the oppression, and the resulting chaos of history. The demonic is the central symbol of the *curse* of historical life, validated continually in any epoch and every region; it cannot be made intelligible without theological interpretation.

As the original satanic referent of the symbol implies, the demonic points to the negative possibilities latent in what is most creative in creaturely life. It can appear in the life of the intelligence, in examples of moral goodness, and in the life of the spirit, in religion. Perhaps the unique insight of a Christian interpretation of the human predicament is, first, that only God is God, and, second, as a consequence, all else, even the most creative aspects of our human existence, are not absolutely good, good in themselves, but possess the possibility of the demonic if they are made self-sufficient and central. Our technological, industrial culture, potentially the servant of the well-being of all, elegantly illustrates this dialectic characteristic of creaturely creativity. In this culture, intelligence and techne, human ingenuity and skill, devoted in so many ways to the worthy aim of human well-being, is nevertheless running amok. Its science made into the exclusive form of knowledge, its technical advance unrestricted, it is now a threat not only to civilization but to the Nature on which civilization is dependent. Despite their evident creativity, science, technology, and industrialism together can become *negative* forces in history, a demonic fate bringing even the highest of cultures to self-destruction. In the absence of God, the first moment is the effort to replace God, and the first result is the destruction of the other creatures with whom we share our world.

Fifth, a central aspect of the traditional symbolism of sin and the fall was, of course, "desire," "lust," or, officially, concupiscence. To a postromantic, post-Freudian, and moralistically relaxed world—with its new and positive assessment of both sexual libido and of sexual relations—this aspect of the symbol seemed anachronistic and unredeemable. Surely it was simply an ascetical or puritanical error (inherited from Hellenism) to regard sexual passion as *the* sign of sin; to condemn desires of all sorts as instruments of self-destruction; and thus to consider vice as almost synonymous with sin. Are not the spiritual sins—for power, wealth, prestige, domination, personal glory, personal holiness—infinitely more selfish, infinitely more subtle, and infinitely more destructive? Are not the mighty and the proud, the economically, intellectually, and spiritually privileged infinitely more culpable of society's wrongs and of its sufferings than the poor wino, the glutton, the prostitute, the pervert? Who do they harm but themselves? Thus in much recent theology did pride replace concupiscence as the central symbol for sin, and the harm we do to others (injustice) edged out the destruction we wreak upon ourselves (vice) as the primary examples in behavior of the immorality that followed upon sin. That this important shift represents a gain in the profundity and validity of theological analysis, I do not question—as this whole volume shows. It seems clear, however, that inordinate desire, lust, or concupiscence do constitute (as the tradition insisted) a major and not a minor aspect of estrangement and that, in fact, concupiscence, rather than the demonic, may represent the central symptom or moment of sin in our own time.

Concupiscence is not to be understood as "ordered" desire, desire or passion directed at a particular object, say, sexual desire directed at a loved person. The latter is, of course, vastly creative, of communion and community, of self, of joy and ecstasy in life. Concupiscence is *infinite* desire, desire, as Tillich says, for the whole world, for more and more goods, more and more money, more and more women or men. Such inordinate or infinite desire is *felt* as desire—hence, it is blamed on the flesh and its so-called instincts, and hence it finds its major examples in instinctive life. But it is no more merely "instinctive" than is pride; for it is possible only to a being with spirit since it reflects a dislocation in the self, in the relation of the self to its ground, and thus to itself and to the world. Only a creature that by its essential nature participates in infinity can be driven by an infinity of desire.

Human being is created and preserved by its participation in the divine power, and it is given meaning by its participation in the divine purposes. Its security and its meaning are, therefore, by nature dependent on an infinity of power and an infinity of meaning, which are, accordingly, essential components of the human, reflected in the dimension of ultimacy and of sacrality apparent in all aspects of human existence. When an estrangement or separation—a break—occurs between the self and God, when the center of the self is in itself rather than in God, then the self still requires, needs, and yearns for an infinity of security and of meaning to be itself. Thus arises the demonic, as has been shown: the refusal to be content with a relative security, or relative truth and relative value. Therewith also arises concupiscence: the impatience and dissatisfaction with merely this or that object, person, amount, and the consequent drive to possess and devour ever more objects, persons, amounts, an infinity of finite beings to replace the unconditioned being and the unconditioned meaning that have become absent. This interpretation of concupiscence and its relation to sin was first seen and formulated by Augustine: "Thou hast made us for thyself, and our hearts are restless until they rest in thee." It has now become the main clue to the predicament of an industrial consumer culture.

As with most aspects of estrangement, concupiscence can be seen most clearly on the macroscopic or social scale, though it appears also in each of us individually. There we see an ever-expanding industrial culture devouring an ever-increasing (in fact, exponentially increasing) amount of natural resources in order to supply an apparently infinite demand for consumer goods. These goods are, of course, required for the legitimate needs of an expanding population; and part of the reason for the apparent infinity of demand is anxiety's drive for more and more security against hunger, poverty, want. Nevertheless, there can be little doubt that the central dynamic of this infinite demand is not anxiety about security but desire, lust for more and more, and impatience and dissatisfaction with what is now possessed, a sense of yearning emptiness if more is not gained, of felt conviction that meaning, be it excitement or satisfaction, comes only with continual accession. The ever-increasing scale of demands, the incitement to "more," to the new, to the "better," characteristics of all advertising; the principles of rapid obsolescence and of expendability—all these point to a *subjective* fever of desire for consumption correlated with, and ultimately responsible for, the driving *objective* expansion of the industrial consumption of resources. For it is also a lust or concupiscence for power and wealth that drives the industrial leaders, as well as a lust for goods that animates their clients, the consumers.

The theme, familiar especially to our own American culture (which consumes 54 percent of all natural resources used up each year), of a whole society seeking to cram the whole world into its mouth and devour it seems drawn from Dante or Heironymus Bosch—and yet it is true. It can only be explained theologically as reflecting the loss of an infinity of security and of meaning now sorely missed and so desperately sought. Its menacing results are evident: the consumption of available resources, the despoliation of nature, the disintegration of community—a possible *dénouement* to both history and a nature hospitable to history. The ultimate judgment on sin, in quite concrete historical terms, is here clear, even clearer than in the case of the demonic. The bondage to sin, despite the certainty of that judgment, is also clear. For no community wishes to stop that infinity of consumption (except by others), nor apparently will any community tolerate leaders who wish to do so, if they knew how! The reality and destructive character of estrangement in history, as both hubris and as concupiscence, are here vividly manifest.

Sixth, the final aspect of the symbolism of the fall, the third moment of estrangement from God, is represented by the associated symbols of divine condemnation and of human self-destruction, of the curse, of fate, of death, and of an ultimate non-being, which estranged men and women have brought upon themselves. In the absence of God, the first moment, following anxiety, is the demonic, and the second, concupiscence; but the third moment is the disintegration of time and the loss of self, the loss of world, of identity, and of being, an emptiness, an absence of direction inside, and an experience of fate outside. This has been described in modern experience many times in novels, plays, films, and perhaps most powerfully in recent theology by Paul Tillich. I shall refer to it only briefly in terms of our earlier discussion of the temporality of our creaturely being and then reintroduce the important category of fate in the final chapter.

In relation to God, our temporality is an aspect of the

created goodness of all creaturely existence. It can be experienced first as creative destiny, a given with many possibilities. In such relation to God, the present is also experienced as electric with freedom and with vital self-affirmation, as suffused with a sense of our own reality, power, and meaning because of the real choices latent in our time; and of an open future whose alternatives are real. Here time is united by its relation to God: the past is destiny, the present is replete with decisions and creative freedom, and the future is full of real possibilities. With this union of historical process and through its relation to God, self and world become correlated, if not united. The self is creative, strong, and purposive, full of vitality and intentionality; the world reflects both an order and an openness to creative work. Creation is good, and time is filled with meaning.

To be in time can, however, be experienced in an entirely different manner: as emptiness, as fate, as self-destruction and despair, or merely as a journey towards death. The given from the past is oppressive with no creative but only with destructive possibilities and, thus, alienated from our present and our future aims. The present is thereby empty of real choices and, consequently, void of freedom, self-affirmation, and identity, and the self experiences itself as an empty, directionless, listless, and driven entity or non-entity. What future there is is only a repetition of this fated, empty present. This is also an experience of the human, and a recurrent character of history. Here the weakness, dependence, and helplessness of the finite creature is experienced inwardly as unreality and despair, as devoid of security and meaning, as condemned merely to share a crowded present with hostile inmates, as destined only for death in the end. The opposite of the demonic, where the self and its group are elevated to the status—and privileges—of deity, this self-destructive aspect of estrangement reduces the self and its community to fated, empty objects, to virtual non-being. Politically and historically, the twentieth century has manifested the demonic; but *inwardly* it has felt more the stark chill of creaturely unreality and condemnation.

The demonic and the self-destructive are, of course, intimately interrelated in history. Socially and historically, the experience of fatedness is a result of the demonic ambitions of others which create unjust and oppressive institutions. The social and historical "fate" that crushes the lives of countless people has been caused by the sin of their fathers—or more likely the fathers of others—who helped to create unjust and oppressive social institutions that remain in time and cause untold suffering. On the other hand, "fate" in the form of unjust and oppressive institutions is a cause of future demonic eruption, the breeding ground for the self-elevation of that now empty group into the center of all history. The dialectical cycle of ambitious pride, inglorious fall, ravaging emptiness and despair, followed by even more extravagant pride and even more total destruction—illustrated clearly in recent German and Japanese history—appears and reappears, not as much in myth as in historical actuality. And each step on the cycle repeats itself, as in a mirror image, in the inner inflation vacillating with an inner emptiness characteristic of our individual life. It is from this characteristic of objective history and of private existence alike, leading to objective destruction, inner non-being and death, that we need rescue. In the absence of God, our self-transcending finitude, our temporal creatureliness manifests itself as demonic, lustful, and self-destructive, as a self-elevation that oppresses others, as a desire that devours all else, and as a non-being oppressed by fate and lacerated with emptiness.

It is to both the demonic and the self-destructive aspects of estrangement that the redemptive action of God in

Christ addresses itself, namely, to redeem us from sin and the demonic consequences of sin and to rescue us from self-destruction and fate. Confidence in the reality of that redemption and rescue forms, therefore, the substance of the witness: "I believe in Jesus Christ, His only Son Our Lord." In the next chapter of this part, I shall explore the meanings involved in that affirmation.

NOTES

1. One evening in a Munich cafe in 1960 I had a long talk with an Algerian student. Impressed (and rightly so) with the suffering that imperial France had brought to his country, this patriot spent our whole conversation assuring me that Algeria's troubles would all be over when the French had left, when the Algerians were at last alone to constitute their own community in their own way. "Do you mean," I asked him, "that *all* possible evil in your country has come via the French, that they represent the *sole* source of your difficulties, so that when they are gone there will be no one—except lingering Frenchmen—to cause you difficulties?" "Yes," he said, "*all* our troubles come from the French, and when they are gone, *then* we shall be free of evil." Lest this seem naive and bizarre, the result of the beer in München, let us note the similarity of this view in principle to the Marxist belief that resurgent evils are solely the result of lingering "bourgois" influences and that a society without conflict will inexorably result when these reactionary influences are at last quite gone. The same principle appears among Americans whenever we assure ourselves that *any* opinion critical of American action or influence is the result of "Communist influence."

2. I can recall how frantically Nixon denied the presence of guilt. What he feared, plainly, was the accusation of moral, not of intellectual, weakness: "I made mistakes, sure; but my motives were pure. I may have been a fool, but I was no knave; I was the victim of my own good intentions and of my unconditioned loyalty to my colleagues and friends."

3. George Gaylord Simpson, *The Meaning of Evolution* (New York: Mentor Books, 1955), pp. 155–56.

4. John M. Greene, *The Death of Adam* (Ames, Iowa: Iowa State University Press, 1959), p. 338.

5. See as great examples of this discussion in modern theology: Paul Ricoeur, *The Symbolism of Evil* (New York, Harper & Row, 1967);

Reinhold Niebuhr, "The Truth in Myths" in *The Nature of Religious Experience*, ed. J. S. Bixler (New York: Harper and Brothers, 1937); idem, *Beyond Tragedy* (New York: Charles Scribner's Sons, 1937), chaps. I, II, VII; idem, *The Nature and Destiny of Man* (New York: Charles Scribner's Son's, 1941), vol. I, chaps. V–X; Paul Tillich, *Systematic Theology*, (Chicago: University of Chicago Press, 1957), vol. II, part III, I. For the author's most extensive discussion of the relevance, meaning and validity of this symbol, so interpreted, see *Shantung Compound* (New York: Harper & Row, 1966), chaps. V–VIII.

6. For Niebuhr's discussion of the available ways of "validating" such symbols as that of "original sin" in relation to the "facts of experience," see Reinhold Niebuhr, *Faith and History* (New York: Charles Scribner's Sons, 1949), Chap. X.

7. It may also be pointed out that "Progress," the ruling "myth" of modern intellectual culture, represented also *literal* and *historical* language about meaning or value (modern stand-ins for deity) and thus *also* bred confusion.

SUGGESTED READINGS

Recent Classics

Brunner, H. E. *Man in Revolt*. Westminster, 1947.
Camus, A. *The Fall*. Knopf, 1957.
Kierkegaard, S. *Sickness unto Death*. Princeton Univ. Press, 1946.
———. *The Concept of Dread*. Princeton Univ. Press, 1946.
Niebuhr, Reinhold. *The Nature and Destiny of Man*. Vol. 1. Scribners, 1941.
———. *Beyond Tragedy*. Scribners, 1937.
Tillich, P. *Systematic Theology*. Vol. 2. Univ. of Chicago Press, 1957.
———. *The Courage to Be*. Yale Univ. Press, 1952.

Current Discussion

Becker, E. *The Denial of Death*. Free Press, 1973.
———. *The Structure of Evil*. G. Braziller, 1968.
Gilkey, L. *Shantung Compound*. Harper & Row, 1966.
Miller, A. *The Renewal of Man*. Doubleday, 1955.
Ricoeur, P. *The Symbolism of Evil*. Harper & Row, 1967.

7

JESUS AS THE CHRIST

W E come now to the center of Christian
witness and understanding, of the Christian community's
life, and thus of all Christian theology. This center is Jesus
of Nazareth, he who is affirmed by the Christian community to be "the Christ," or as I described it in Chapter 3, is
said to represent the definitive and decisive event of revelation in which God's power, will, and ultimate purposes
are manifested in a unique way to human beings. As I
have argued, much of what Christians believe can be
sporadically seen and dimly known in general experience:
the potential goodness of finitude, the supreme glory of
love, the estrangement of human existence, and even the
presence of a divine ground—and all of this can be shown
in the end to be intelligible or to make sense in relation to
general experience. Nevertheless, each fundamental Christian symbol—about God; about human nature, its alienation and its redemption; about historical communities and
their possibilities; and about our ultimate hopes—receives
its final certainty and its definitive shape only through this
center: the life, teachings, and fate of Jesus who is the
Christ. If there be any uniqueness to Christian belief and
existence or any criterion of what is or what is not Christian, it is this: while it is not necessary that every form of
action or belief be derived from this center, still each mode
of life and obligation, each rite and each institutional form,

and each pattern of thought and hope must be justified and molded by reference to this figure.

This figure—Jesus of Nazareth—is a historical figure: a particular man in a particular time and living within a particular religion and culture. Yet he is given this transcendent, universal, and ultimately significant revelatory and redemptive role: he is called the Christ. Thus, strangely, for Christians the most general and important truths about ultimate reality and about our existence are finally tested and shaped in relation not, as reason might expect, to all persons, cultures, and events—to "general laws" discoverable in the widest experience; nor, as much religion might expect, in relation to our most compelling spiritual experiences, even our meditative or mystical experiences. Rather, it is one historical event, or series of events, that is taken to be the determinative or normative channel or medium through which both truth and grace, illumination and healing appear.

As a consequence, Christianity has sustained a uniquely creative and uniquely disturbing relation to history. To believe that the ultimate truth, the ultimate norm, and the ultimate promise of existence are entailed in a particular human, and thus historical, figure is, of course, to affirm unequivocally the reality, the significance, and the potential goodness of natural and human finitude, of human individuality, of historical events, and, finally, of the space-time matrix itself. The celebrated positive affirmation of the Christian West of the material, the human, and the historical has its deepest root here.

To center in this way on a particular historical event is, however, also to put oneself in a disturbingly vulnerable position. In the Hellenistic age, which distrusted matter, abhorred history, and thus was committed to a "spiritual" interpretation of truth, such a concentration on a particular example of history appeared naive, primitive, materialistic, unspiritual, in a word, "gauche." To the modern age, taught by Christian tutelage the potential intelligibility of natural and historical events, and thus committed to an empirical interpretation of truth, this same concentration on one actual past event has ironically, and for opposite reasons, also seemed unscientific, irrational, and infinitely precarious. Quite understandably, modern Christian people have experienced a new requirement: if this event is to make the claim to be a real event—and if it was not, how can *it* be revelatory or of ultimate significance—then it must stand the test required of all other past events, namely, the test of unbiased, "scientific" historical inquiry. But suppose historical inquiry certifies that it did not happen, or happened really differently (as we used to ask Tillich: suppose he died in bed?)—then what can be left of a religious faith built on this event? As natural science and new views of history forced a rethinking of older concepts of God, and as anthropology and evolution have forced changes in the interpretation of Christian symbols about human existence, so historical science has, on an even deeper level, raised apparently mortal questions for Christian belief in Jesus the Christ and thus for Christian reflection upon that belief.

Difficult as these historical questions are, they are unavoidable. Christian witness cannot proclaim the significance of Jesus, nor can Christian theology reflect on that significance (Christology), without dealing with historical questions about the event each claims to be central. Thus we must start with what historical sources we have, begin "from below," and at the beginning ask, what can we know on the basis of historical evidence about Jesus of Nazareth?—although as we shall see, Christian belief as a whole is dependent, and for intelligible reasons, on much more than the bare results of historical inquiry. Historical inquiry, and the relative certainty it brings, is a necessary, but by no means the sufficient, basis for Christian confidence in or certainty about God's revelation in Jesus of Nazareth.

As with many of the problems besetting contemporary theology, this question about "the historical Jesus" is a new question for Christian faith and theology. Before the modern period, the New Testament was believed to be true from beginning to end, true in all of its propositions. Thus, for any Christian, the Jesus of history was readily available in four different, and equally infallible and authoritative, biographies (the Gospels). What these four quite different accounts told us about his life and his historical person might be hard to bring into coherent unity, to be sure. But that together they provided an utterly reliable historical picture of his birth, of the course and development of his life, of his teaching, of his deeds, of his death and final ascent to Glory, this no one doubted. It was only when the Scriptures began to be regarded as human documents, and so the absolute infallibility of each proposition of the Old and New Testaments began to be questioned, that the historical validity of these historical descriptions came into question. As a consequence, the issue of our knowledge of the historical Jesus became a problem for Christian faith and for theology. There arose the distinction, crucial for modern theology, between the "Jesus of history"—the actual human Jesus as historical inquiry can discover him—and the "Christ of faith," the divine Christ or Lord of the apostolic preaching and witness in the New Testament, of the creeds and preaching of the churches, and of the faithful in every age. Unsatisfactory as this duality between the Jesus of history and the Christ of faith may in the end be, it has become, and continues to be, an unavoidable distinction: aside from all that Church and faith may wish to say about Jesus the Christ, what can we know about him that is historically reliable?

As is well known, answers to these historical questions about Jesus are not easy to come by. In the first place, almost the only sources for historical knowledge of him are the documents of the New Testament. And, in the second place, these documents, being witnesses to the faith of the early Christian communities, are understandably more concerned to proclaim, express, and define the significance of Jesus the Christ for those communities than they are to provide detailed facts about his life. As scholarship has slowly uncovered, the picture of Jesus in the Gospels reflects as much the developing beliefs of the Christian communities in the face of new and difficult crises as it does actual episodes in his life or the authentic teachings of his ministry. Thus, no biography of Jesus tracing his life's development, exploring his inner consciousness, or even outlining systematically his philosophical and ethical teachings, is possible. Are the unavoidable historical questions about him, therefore, moot, shipwrecked on the rock of futility? Fortunately the answer, according to most contemporary inquirers, is no. Although our historical knowledge about Jesus is in the above ways limited, it is, as Hans Küng says, "relatively reliable," and enough can be known to provide an authentic "picture" which, as I shall argue, represents a firm basis for Christian faith and for adequate Christology.

Although no one saying or episode is in all respects certain (in the sense that anything in past history can be certain), what can be specified with that sort of certainty are the following: the time, place, and surroundings of his life; the general contours and character of his proclamation and teachings; the typical mode or style of his life's pattern, his actions, and of his relations to others and to his social world; and his "fate" at the hands of the Jewish and Roman authorities. In filling out this historical picture, I shall seek to show how these authentic contours of the historical figure of Jesus point to, imply, and even require for their intelligibility a further theological symbolization;[1] in other words, how the historical Jesus is to be understood as being fulfilled in the Christ of faith and how this particular history can be called the decisive event of divine revelation.

The role of Jesus in his world is not easy to categorize. Both his actions and his words continually criticized, challenged, almost deliberately provoked, and so set him against, the various establishment groups of his time: the political rulers of Palestine, the religious leaders of his people, the intellectual scholars, the rich, and the successful. The main thrust of his teaching concerns a radical change in the political, social and religious orders that is about to take place; and every proclamation of his ethic challenges the sacred norms and laws of his social community. He appears as a prophetic, rebellious figure, alienated inwardly from every established form of power, social, political and religious. On the other hand, he is just as clearly not a political or social rebel in the usual sense. His critiques are leveled at the spiritual sins of leaders and dominant classes rather than the iniquity or injustice of institutional forms. He outlines neither a criticism of the social system, nor a positive social program; and he seeks to establish neither a political nor a military base from which to operate. On the contrary, he deliberately renounces economic, political, and military power; he warns continually against any use of force; and he insists that only nonresistance and even love of one's enemies is acceptable in the kingdom of which he speaks. No ethic for rulers, for rulers' advisors, or for rulers' adversaries, no scheme of political behavior—wise, moderate, reformist, or revolutionary—could be drawn directly from anything he said or did. Above all, for him both the ultimate condemnation of his social world and the establishment of a new order will be by means of acts of God, not of men and women, and thus transcendent to the dynamics of human political action, good or bad. All that he says and does has, to be sure, vast political relevance and inexhaustible political consequences. But he was himself not at all a political revolutionary; nor was his cause directly a political or a social cause. In fact, except in his close identification with the lowly and the outcast, he seemed almost equally estranged from political rulers and from political rebels, from defenders of established order and rebels against it. *If*, in other words, he is to be taken as a final norm, the "fallen" character of our *entire* social world, both established and disestablished, a viewpoint later theologized by Augustine, begins immediately to become evident.

It is, of course, not strange for moral and religious leaders—prophets, saints, and holy men—to disassociate themselves inwardly and outwardly from political and military action of all sorts. An emphasis on the moral law, and thus on the highest modes of moral conduct, or an ascetic withdrawal from worldly life represent universal forms of human spirituality and were widely illustrated in his own social world. However, he represented neither, and, in fact, his words and deeds defied the requirements and precepts of each as much as they subverted the rules of political action. Although his life was totally pure in its devotion to his own cause or calling, he seemed almost deliberately nonascetic. He enjoyed a reputation for feasting and drinking; he abjured all the common rules about fasting; he made no attempt to withdraw himself into a holy, religious community. He continually defied in act and in word many important moral and religious laws of his community: the law of the Sabbath, of clean and unclean foods, the laws against association with immoral or sinful people. And he criticized, morally and religiously, "respectable" people for their pride, their hypocrisy, and their spiritual emptiness. He deliberately identified himself not only with the economically poor and politically inept and rejected but, even more, with the morally dubious characters of his world: swindlers, cheats, and tax-collectors ("the contemporary quislings," as Norman Perrin calls them), on the one hand, and "fallen" women, on the other. Morality and religion, as they appeared in that actual world, seemed as much under his concrete judgment as were his world's social and political institutions and parties. His own actual relations, like his authentic parables (for example, the Prodigal Son) thus embodied and manifested a totally new perspective on morals, religion, and human renewal, later theologized in Paul's letters. It is not a righteousness gained through observance of the law that heals or renews—for none of us is righteous in and of ourselves. Rather, it is a new righteousness given in grace that is grounded in loving forgiveness and a new attitude of trust and commitment arising out of that acceptance.

From whence does all this proceed? What is the basis for this radical critique, this inner distance, and these new perspectives on all of life; on its political and economic institutions; on its moral and religious foundations? If nothing around us—ordinary existence in family and community, conservative or radical politics, sacred law, religious ritual, and even mystical withdrawal—can provide a center, what can? What does Jesus proclaim? On these questions there is little disagreement: Jesus proclaimed the coming of God's Kingdom. Correspondingly, the coming rule of God provided the unswerving center for his actions, his words, and message and for the ultimate direction which he gave to his life.

By the Kingdom of God, or the reign of God, Jesus referred not to a place—surely not to a place above—but to the concrete ruling of God in the world, the actual or fulfilled sovereignty of God's will and purposes, and thus of the divine power among God's creatures. In a real, and yet hidden, way God, as creator and preserver, has also "ruled" in the past and "rules" in the present, as I sought to make intelligible in Chapter 3. Jesus is reported unequivocally to have affirmed this rule of divine providence, even amidst the chaotic ambiguity of ordinary events (Matt. 5:44–46; 6:26–33; 7:11; 10:29–31; Luke 1:50–53; 12:6–7, 28–29). Nevertheless, the coming Kingdom to which he refers is different from this hidden providence in the past and the present; it is distinguished as the complete, and so manifest, rule of God as opposed to his/her partial and hidden rule in the chaotic evil world. The main thrust of Jesus' message was that this actual, full, and manifest sovereignty of God was now coming: it is in our midst, already on its way, "at hand" (Mark 1:1–15), "has come upon you" (Luke 11:20), "in the midst of you" (Luke 17:20). Whereas his predecessor, John, had proclaimed a coming judgment, Jesus spoke of a coming age of grace: of healing for the sick, restitution for the outcast and the poor, new life for the burdened, the guilty and the lost; a new age for the weary and the suffering world: "Thy kingdom come, thy will be done, on earth as it is in heaven." Finally, this "coming" is the decisive, all-transforming act of God on behalf of his people. It represents not just a single episode in history, however significant, nor merely one portion of time's full cycle. It is, rather, the thus far hidden, yet real, goal of God's creation, that promised salvation time towards which all of history has moved. Jesus' coming is thus the center of history, and as the center it points to the final end time to come.

As is clear from all of the "authentic" sayings of Jesus about the Kingdom, there are two distinguishable polarities central to this image, symbol, or concept. First of all, it had clearly a future reference: it was coming, about to come, beginning to dawn—and it soon would be fully manifest (Luke 11:2; 22:18; Mark 14:25; Matt. 6:10; Luke 11:2; Matt. 8:11; Luke 3:28–29). On the other hand, in Jesus' deeds and words it was beginning already to be present, "in your midst," already under way (Mark 3:27; Luke 7:22; 10:18; 23; 11:20; Matt. 11:12; 12:28; Luke 17:20). A great deal of scholarly argument has taken place whether the Kingdom is simply future or whether it is "realized," already there, so to speak, with Jesus' appearance in history. At present, representatives of the two sides appear to agree that both emphases are present in the authentic words and parables of Jesus: the Kingdom is now beginning or about to come; its full manifestation lies in the near future, but with Jesus' life, action, and preaching, it is starting, "in your midst." As Reginald Fuller sums this up: "The message of Jesus proclaims the proleptic presence of the future Kingdom of God"[2]

In any case, in the midst of these imagistic or symbolic words and parables, and signaled by his extraordinary deeds of power, lies hidden a radically new vision of history: the power of God has now entered history in a new way, manifesting itself increasingly in a myriad of saving events and deeds, a power aimed at the realization of the final purposes of God: restitution, reconciliation, healing, and reunion. History is thus now on the move, headed towards its ultimate goal; all present life, all sacred and secular institutions, all sacred and secular norms, all actions and hopes are to be illumined, reevaluated, and reshaped by response to the future that God is beginning to establish. The present is at last the locus of God's new redemptive activity; the future represents its fulfillment. Present and future, therefore, if held in creative tension, take on a new dynamic meaning unknown before.

The second polarity—around which major arguments have also swirled—is that between the objective social and historical locus of the Kingdom (the rule of God), on the one hand, and an inward, spiritual, private, and thus individual locus, on the other. Is God's final sovereignty to be manifest in objective history? Is the Kingdom a new and final age appearing in the global time scheme itself, and thus inclusive in its effects of social communities, their institutional structures, and the events and relations that constitute objective history? Certainly all apocalyptic made this assumption; the age to come—almost as an ice age might—would transform and end the historical process as a whole, engulfing in that transformation all that characterizes social history. As our references to the Kingdom to come and our remarks about a new view of history make clear, in Jesus' proclamation this objective, historical aspect is noticeably present (Matt. 8:11; Luke 13:28–9; the Lord's Prayer, Luke 11:2 and Matt. 6:10): this is a new age characteristic of all of history, namely, God's rule there, and thus events, institutions, and the persons within them will enjoy a qualitative change at its inception. It is this note in the apocalyptic and eschatological traditions that has been so powerfully sounded in the contemporary political theologies, who see Jesus' Kingdom (like the Marxist utopia) as the promise of a new social and historical future for the communities of mankind.

On the other hand, there is little doubt that the Kingdom Jesus proclaims also comes inwardly, in the hearts and minds of women and men, as a radical qualification of their most fundamental personal and inward attitudes, commitments, and trust, and as a result of their own personal decision in the face of the challenge of its appearance—themes represented powerfully in our time by the Bultmannian tradition. Thus, despite the reality of the new age with its amazing new powers, its dynamic movement towards culmination, and its general possibilities for all, the Kingdom is not externally visible, re-

plete with objective "signs" connected with natural catastrophes or world events (Luke 17:20). Rather, it comes
silently, hiddenly, in the responses of men and women and
in the total transformations of their lives that result. Parables and words alike stress the necessity for decision *now* in
the face of the Kingdom (Luke 14:16–24) for being open to
quite new attitudes, aims, and goals with regard to others,
to oneself, and to God (Matt. 20:1–16; Luke 18:9–14); for
becoming willing to give everything up in the light of the
Kingdom (Mark 10:23, 25, 31; Luke 9:60, 62), to become
as a child (Mark 10:15), to serve others rather than oneself
and one's honor (Matt. 5:39–41), to love one's enemies
rather than defend oneself (Matt. 5:44–48). In each case a
radical *inward* change of attitude, commitment, love, and
trust—is called for as characteristic of the new Kingdom
(Mark 10:29; Matt 5:21–48; 6:19–24). As a result, the
Kingdom represents a quite different mode of relations
among persons in marriage, in social contacts and attitudes, in the kind of caring service each does for the
other, enacted and symbolized by the "table fellowship"
Jesus encouraged with all sorts and conditions of human
begins and by the messianic banquet imaged in his parables (the Prodigal Son; the Good Samaritan, etc.). In each
case, the ground for the new attitude and the new sorts of
relations in community—of forgiveness, of love, of self-
sacrifice, of openness to and service of all—is that this is
the way God relates himself/herself to us in the Kingdom.

Clearly, although it represents an objective change in
public history and promises to usher in a new quality for
communal existence, the Kingdom makes its appearance
on an inward level, at the deepest personal center of
human beings in their relation to God, to themselves and
to others. Because participation in the Kingdom involved
this deep inward conversion—to a new love of God and of
neighbor—the external law, objective religious obser-

vances, moral and social rectitude, all are relativized; all these miss the mark, are insufficient, compared to the need for inner singleness of commitment, purity of heart, and freedom for radical self-giving. Yet, when such qualitative inwardness expresses itself in existence and in action, objective social relations change and are transformed, new forms of communal fellowship are possible, and outward history itself takes on new contours. Thus Jesus' proclamation contained latent within it, not only a new understanding of and promise for history and its movement, but also a new understanding of the interdependence and interwovenness of individual and community, an interdependence of inward attitude and self-constitution, on the one hand, and of social relations, institutional forms, and public events on the other. In word, and perhaps especially in deed, Jesus dealt with the deepest and most intractable of human problems: the issues of inward sin and of death. Yet the very depth of his treatment of inward sin meant also that his message opened up the promise that historical fate—the objective social lot of the oppressed and the outcast—will also be conquered. In the end, then, as Jesus proclaims it, the Kingdom stands for the final conquest by the coming action of God of sin, of fate, and of death; in his appearance it already has begun; his message is that in the future, its coming will be completed and God will reign.

The Kingdom, then, is both future and present, both objective, historical and inward, personal. The subsequent task of theology is to find ways of keeping these two sets of polarities in creative tension. The Kingdom, as Jesus proclaimed and portrayed it, had, moreover, a particular and quite unique content. It represents in imagery a particular *kind* of human existence, and thus a particular kind of human world—all, as I noted, in imitation or reflection of the character of the God who is establishing it (Matt. 5:48;

Luke 6:35–6). It is above all clear that when God's will and purposes reign, human existence becomes recreated, rescued, and fulfilled. God's deepest will is, therefore, for the total well-being, the completion of the fullness of joy in human life. Thus is the divine law *for* men and women, not men and women for the law (Mark 2:27–28); thus is the central relation or bond of God to those in his/her Kingdom that of loving care; and thus is the characteristic action of God in establishing his/her Kingdom that of searching, of reaching out, with the ultimate aim of rescuing what was lost and reuniting with it.

Two aspects, therefore, are utterly essential and unique to Jesus' view of the Kingdom. First, God is its absolute center, his/her will is regnant, and his/her purposes fulfilled; so all loyalty, trust, commitment are there directed towards him/her. Second, for this reason it is a *human* kingdom, the locus of the rescue, the fulfillment and the completion of individuals and community alike. Thus both theocratic (theonomous) and humanist (autonomous) impulses (united appropriately in the summation of the law) stem legitimately from the Kingdom as Jesus proclaimed it, and as he acted that proclamation out in his life. Again, the task of theology is the preservation and continual recreation of their unity.

Central to this new attitude characteristic of God and of those who share his/her Kingdom, is forgiveness. This is, above all, God's attitude towards all of us who are unworthy; it thus extends particularly to those who are most visibly and deeply caught in sin, and thus who are most conscious of their wretchedness. And it is the crucial and continuing basis for our presence in the Kingdom itself. In parables (Prodigal Son, Lost Sheep, Lost Coin, and the Laborers in the Vineyard) Jesus teaches that this is God's attitude towards the sinner and the explanation or ground for God's outreach towards all, even the most unworthy.

Jesus declares this as God's attitude by his bold declaration of forgiveness to the most obvious sinners (Mark 2:5–12; Matt. 9:2f.; 12:31; Luke 15:1–10; 7:36–50); and in his life he enacted it over and over again in his own close relations and fellowship with obvious, and even notorious, sinners.

Clearly related to forgiveness is self-giving. This does not involve a self-hatred or even a lack of self-affirmation or of self-esteem. Jesus himself and his apostles were strong individuals, conscious of their unique task, and filled with courage and confidence in its enactment. Rather, it involves such a relation to the self that the needs of the other, and of the Kingdom, are given priority: a willingness to be, as Barth says, "for others," to give the self, even its security and certainly its honor and status, for the sake of the neighbor—and for the task of God. Continually, Jesus makes clear that our normal desire to be first is fatal and that to be willing to be last, to lose one's life, is the only way to find oneself (Matt. 10:3, 24f.; 20:26). Here the self is removed utterly from the spiritual center of its world, and God's Kingdom set in its place (the first commandment), with the result that service of the neighbor is now possible (the second commandment)—thus are the theocratic and the humanistic elements reconciled.

These two radically new inner attitudes—forgiveness of sins against us and a willingness to give the self for the other—result in radically different relations among people, relations that are to characterize the life of the Kingdom. The "neighbor"—he or she whom I am now to relate to and help—ceases to be exclusively kinsfolk, countrymen, those who in family, class and advantage are like ourselves. The neighbor becomes simply he or she who is there and in need. As the obviously authentic parable of the Good Samaritan makes plain, our responsibility as neighbors in the Kingdom is both quite universal and quite concrete. It knows no artificial social, racial, class, or national bounds, and it directs itself at actual situations of need. Further, and most radical of all, this concrete inward obligation also includes those on the other side of the highest fence of all: our enemies, those who revile and persecute us, those who seek to do us harm (Matt. 5:43f.; Luke 6:27f.). The implications of forgiveness and of self-giving, of a life directed entirely to God's will and not to our own security and well-being, are here drawn fully out. Again, the ground of this requirement for our humanity is the forgiving love of God who not only preserves and fosters through his providential action his enemies, that is, the unjust, but even more who with the redemptive appearance of his Kingdom seeks out the sinner.

In Jesus' life and teachings alike, therefore, the Old Testament concept of God's love for an unworthy Israel is expanded and deepened into God's forgiving and redemptive love for all of God's enemies, the unjust and sinful wherever they are. This strange love of God thus becomes (as agape) the central new character of God, a characteristic more basic than and transcendent to even his/her power, his/her rage for order, or his/her devotion to moral righteousness. The association with sinners characteristic of Jesus' life, and these words and acts representative of divine forgiveness, formed the historical root and the historical paradigm for the theological symbols of God's grace and of God as love. Finally, as is evident, it is through the parables and teachings of Jesus, on the one hand, and perhaps even more through the quality of his relations with others—of forgiveness, love, patience, service, and persevering care—that the character of the Kingdom as a loving community, and thus the character of the ultimate goal and end of history, receive their definition. Both God and the historical destiny of time are here revealed.

The most indubitable element in the tradition of the historical Jesus is his violent and demeaning death. This event occurred perhaps four years before Paul's conversion (34 A.D.), is central to Paul's letters, written about fifteen to twenty-five years later (49–58 A.D.), and forms the core of each Gospel narrative probably written two decades, or so, further on. It is also this event that is reported in the few "secular" sources about Jesus that are extant.[3] Crucifixion was not only a cruel and painful form of execution; it also was explicitly degrading, reserved by the Romans alone for criminals—and thus unthinkable for a Roman citizen—and "cursed" in the eyes of Jews. To be crucified was thus to be identified by all relevant human, and even divine, authority as a law-breaker, an outcast, one rightly rejected alike by God and by men and women.

Those of us living in a Christian civilization find it hard to take this moral and religious rejection seriously. Even if we do not consider him to be God incarnate, we know full well that Jesus was at least one of history's "greatest religious and moral geniuses." Also, because of our long tradition of inner distance and even rebellion against stated political, legal, moral, and religious authorities (owed in no small part to this figure's—and Socrates'—end), it is hard for us to feel the weight of that condemnation by the Jewish Sanhedrin and the Roman courts as it would have been felt in the ancient world. Those political and religious authorities that unequivocally thus judged him represented the divine order and the divine law—and what else was the divine except sacred order and sacred law? And considering Jesus' explicit claim to ultimate authority, his scorn for the rules of the sacred law, his willingness to associate with sordid and despicable traitors, was he not in fact demonstrably a heretic, a blasphemer, insanely presumptuous and immoral—a dangerous, possibly insane, fool? At that dark moment, because he was condemned by legal and religious authority, he was in truth the epitome of disgrace and of guilt, a paradigm of sinful rebellion against God and his deputies on earth; as Paul said, "made one with sin" (2 Cor. 5:11).

Nor with our irrepressible awareness of the victorious future-to-be of Jesus' cause, can we feel the weight of failure, even of fakery and charlatanism that accompanied that fate. We *know* God was *really* on his side. Would we have known that then, without the two thousand years of Christian triumph? But the stigmata of failure and repudiation were surely there: he who had claimed an authority over the sacred law, who had certainly—whatever title he may have used—considered himself an instrument of God's decisive activity on earth, and who had promised the appearance of God's earthly rule—he was now left condemned to perish, and no help, or even voice, intervened with or abrogated that final judgment. Surely, then, he was a fake, his claims, his message, and his cause repudiated or ignored by God; he was a deluded, hopeless failure.

This mood of total rejection and deep failure must have hung heavily over the disciples, as it apparently did over him at the end. For another indubitable fact in the story was the disciples' quick desertion of him at his condemnation. There has been human courage aplenty in history for any cause that is intelligible and credible. Such immediate desertion by those closest to him, therefore, bespeaks deep unbelief, radical uncertainty, dark disillusionment—the emptiness, despair, and thus weakness of utter failure. God had forsaken him, and so did his followers; the world was, after all, right and he a fool. As Hans Küng has pointed out,[4] no other founder of a religion has died so rejected by the world, in such moral disgrace, and with such obvious religious, and even cosmic, failure—an irony surely when we consider that Christianity has in its development been history's most successful and powerful religion, unequaled in its aggressive conquest of territories and of peoples, and thoroughly "established" in whatever world it succeeded in dominating.

It is important to note that this mortal conflict with the world was no accidental or tragic mistake. It represented—again with Küng—"the logical conclusion of his life and teaching." He had, as I noted, first of all distanced himself from the world's political and social rulers; further, he had deliberately and openly challenged and even provoked the moral and religious authorities and the sacred beliefs and norms they upheld. Above all, he denied the ultimate sanctity and authority of the sacred law by every aspect of his teaching and action, and he seemed to ignore the welfare of his own people by associating with those traitors who served the Roman occupation. According to every relevant contemporary standard, he was religiously a heretic, blasphemer, and false prophet, directly dangerous to established religion, indirectly dangerous, in a world seething with religious tensions, to established political rule. A watershed becomes apparent here that forces on each onlooker a decision; as his teaching and his life confronted men and women with a decision, so even more does his death. Either he was in mortal error, a fool and a fake, and the world right about him; or the world, even at the highest levels of its legal, moral, and religious life, is estranged and fallen, in need of new insight and new powers of healing. Implicit in his proclamation, his ethics, and his lifestyle, this new understanding of history's universal and all-inclusive estrangement becomes incontestable with his condemnation and death—*if*, that is, he is taken, even on a purely humanistic level, as a paradigm and norm of human excellence. This is the historical root of the later theological affirmation that in the cross the depths and universality of the sin of the whole world are revealed.

Obviously, to place the blame exclusively on the par-

ticular actors in this drama—the Jews or the Romans, as if
it were only *their* pride, blindness, and insecurity that were
revealed there—is to miss entirely the essential moral and
religious point. It is to assume that we who now look back
on the cross would all then have—or could have—had the
insight to counter and challenge the judgments of the
Jewish and Roman authorities or had the faith heedlessly
to scorn the flabby skepticism of the fleeing disciples. The
Church's continual failure to experience any judgment on
itself in the cross it proclaimed, and for which it insisted on
blaming the Jews (why not the Romans?), is a further
testimony to the depths and universality of sin, even
among the redeemed. No, the cross is and continues to be
the unequivocal revelation of the world's estrangement—
or, if not *that*, it can manifest only Jesus' error in witnessing to a God of history, of love, of the forgiveness of sin,
and of a coming Kingdom. The paradoxical tension in this
historical drama is unresolvable: the teacher of God's immediate and parental loving care, of the closeness of God's
rule, of God's outreach in power and grace to the outcast
is, for that very teaching, judged heretical by the world
and an outcast, and is left abandoned by the very God
who, he proclaimed, abandoned no one. The strangest
episode in the history of theology is how many "liberal"
churchmen and churchwomen could believe, and still believe, that it is possible, even rational, to hold to the radi-
cality of that teaching, and of the values associated with it,
and yet to confine their interest only to the historical Jesus
and their language only to the contours of historic fact,
when on the level exclusively of the historical that very
teacher died forsaken and rejected, and so, ipso facto,
wrong in all he taught. It was, one may hazard, only because they really believed in the deity of historical
progress—that what history *then* did to Jesus, history will
not continue to do to its saints—that they were able to

regard his life and death as the vindication, rather than the falsification, of his teachings.

The life, the teachings, the community, and the élan of the movement associated with the historical Jesus thus, quite literally, reached a dead end. And yet, historically, this was not at all the case. Christianity began anew, and it began precisely after this apparent demise. The scattered and panicked disciples regrouped and proceeded with courage and confidence to spread a new word; the teachings, once contradicted by history, became the basis of a new gospel of hope; the life which ended in disgrace was now regarded as the revelation, even the incarnation, of God himself/herself; and the death, so recently a stumbling block to all intelligibility and all belief, the very cornerstone of a new understanding of God, his/her purposes and his/her activity in the world. In short, in Bultmann's phrase, the proclaimer—who seemed once to end in futility—became him who was triumphantly proclaimed, the center of "good news" about God, history, and human destiny. How was this radical change—a kind of historical resurrection of a religious movement out of its own death—possible?

There is neither point nor purpose, I believe, in endeavoring from this admittedly unexpected and extraordinary development to prove the objective reality of the resurrection. As Hume wisely warned, the apparent lack, even the apparent impossibility, of purely historical causes as explanatory for an actual occurrence does not establish the rational necessity for invoking a divine cause for that occurrence. In fact, he insists, what is rational is to continue indefinitely to search for those elusive historical or natural causes. Thus is historical science, like physical and social science, for better or for worse, essentially, that is methodologically, confined to finite or empirical causes as

explanatory of events, and so essentially (methodologically) "secular" in its conclusions. This does not
mean that the divine has no part in this or any other historical event. It merely means that that presence cannot be
historically or *scientifically* established without defying the
methodological canons, and so the moral commitments, of
scientific and historical inquiry.

Although for these reasons it may not be possible to
demonstrate rationally or "historically" that the resurrection of Jesus was the real "cause" of the disciples' experiences of the risen Jesus, of their startling new belief in the
resurrection, or of the subsequent rescue of the Christian
movement itself, still it is historically undeniable that that
new movement, that is, the Christian community or
ecclesia, based *its* new life and confidence on its certainty
that God had raised Jesus from the dead. In turn, that
belief was, so we are told, founded on reports by innumerable disciples of experiences of Jesus alive in their midst.
These reports, as they are recorded in the New Testament,
are by no means later legendary editions. Rather, as Fuller
remarks, they represent "one of the very earliest post-
Easter traditions in the New Testament, possibly going
back to the year 33, that is, within three years of the actual
events reported."[5]

If, in other words, there is anything "authentic" at all in
the tradition, it is these reports. Further, if there is to be
any intelligible accounting for this amazing rebirth, and
for the power and validity of the message subsequently
proclaimed, it is, I believe, solely to be achieved by means
of these experiences and this reported event. However, let
me be clear: to accept that "explanation"—as I do—of the
rebirth of the Christian community is to accept *their* subsequent interpretation of this strange history; in effect, it is
to accept what they call the "gospel" or the kerygma. That

is to say, inescapably it is to view God as at work here, to see the life, death, and subsequent presence of Jesus of Nazareth as that total event in which God is decisively present revealing his power, purposes, and will to men and women, and in so doing being active in new ways within the course of history. Insofar as the entire "fact" of Jesus the Christ manifests to us in this way the presence and power of God, the event which we term the resurrection becomes the intelligible center of that unique and decisive total event, from which all other modes of intelligibility, including historical intelligibility, stem. This is, however, precisely to be a Christian, at least in belief, namely, to center one's understanding and existence on this total event (of Jesus as the Christ) as uniquely revelatory of God's power and love. In short, it is to accept the kerygma, to "have faith." For theological reflection this means that the resurrection is an aspect, not of our description of what historical inquiry can establish and confirm—as has all that has here preceded—but an aspect of "Christology," of the Christian witness to God's presence and activity in and through the event of Jesus. This is not at all to say that it is not "real"—unless we are content to leave out all talk of God whatsoever, and, so, in this case, to be left with only a barren and forsaken Golgotha to ponder and to explicate.

That the resurrection experiences, and thus the event of the resurrection that they implied, represented not the *result* but the originary *basis* for the disciples' faith and witness there is no doubt. For us, on the contrary, this sequence or relation is reversed: faith in *their* total witness, experience of its healing and illuminating power, and acknowledgment of the word spoken to us through that witness is the basis for *our* understanding of and assent to these reports and the event to which they witness. As Jesus is reported to have reminded his questioners (Matt. 22:29), belief in the possibility and intelligibility of the resurrec-

tion is dependent on belief in the power of God; consequently, our belief in the actuality of his resurrection is
dependent on trust in the unique and effective presence of
that divine power in and through the life, the death, and
the subsequent destiny of Jesus.

The resurrection was, then, both a real occurrence as
the ground of the faith of the community and the work of
God as the sign of God's presence within Jesus' life and
destiny. Since it was the work of God and not a "natural"
or ordinary event, it possesses dimensions, and thus mystery, in a way that the historical events of his life, for
example, Jesus' preaching or death, do not. It represents
that which culminates and transcends the substances and
the processes of life and of history: our bodies, our movements and actions, our identity in space and time. Thus, in
describing it, all language, even all apostolic language, is
markedly symbolic, using images from our ordinary
experience—of seeing, touching, hearing, of "glorified
bodies" and transcendent light—to describe an event that
participates in our ordinary existence but culminates and
transcends it. It is, therefore, impossible for us to say *how*
this event took place, or precisely *what* happened, or to
explicate the mystery of this event in literal, spatial terms,
as with the later stories of the empty tomb and of a bodily
ascension to upper space. If, as I noted, we acknowledge in
faith and experience the creative and redemptive presence
of God in and through the whole life and destiny of Jesus,
it is then only *that* there was a resurrection that can be
affirmed, that is, that through the divine power and love,
the non-being of death was conquered and that Jesus the
Christ received a new, transcendent mode of being in and
with God. More than this we cannot say either about his
ultimate destiny or about ours.

Throughout this volume, possibly as its single major
theme, a fundamental dialectic has appeared that practi-

cally defines the unique form of Christian symbolism. This is a dialectic of affirmation, of negation, and then a higher reaffirmation that, in overcoming the negative, also transmutes the originating positive. This dialectic was beginning to appear, first of all, in the affirmative symbols of creation and of a good finitude, moving thence to the deep negation of both in estrangement (for both the goodness of life and the reality of God were obscured in sin), and implying a further movement of redemption. The originating affirmation of goodness is true, but, taken undialectically, it is false; the negative represented by estrangement is also true, but, taken undialectically, it too is false.

In this chapter, this dialectic both culminates and reappears in a new, more historical, form. It culminates now in the promise entailed in this event of the redemption of the history that has been estranged and in the coming rule of God that was so powerfully proclaimed. In turn, the dialectic also appears or reappears in the form of Jesus' historical life and his teaching. As he constantly reiterated, if one would be first, one must be last; if one would lead, one must serve; if one would live, one must first die. Now the dialectic has burst forth concretely, explicitly, and historically as the central motif of the total event of his life and destiny and of the apostolic witness to its meaning: his life and person were unique, decisive, and utterly extraordinary, an unequivocal, though hidden, manifestation of God. Nevertheless, this life was not just a life of triumph; it terminated precisely in its own death, apparently negating all that had preceded in that life. Correspondingly, his death was not mere negation, but precisely the condition for the entrance into a fuller, eternal life with God.

To receive him undialectically as Messiah (whether as teacher, religious genius, prophet, or Lord) was, as Paul said, to falsify the real human situation, the ultimate nature and purposes of God, the meaning of his messiahship, and the conditions of human renewal and salvation. He is Messiah only as the weak, the vulnerable, the suffering, the disgraced, and the forsaken one; he is lord only as he who was crucified; he is savior and giver of life only as he who was not saved and who died. In his teaching he affirmed, lived and gave hope to the world, humanity, and history; in his death he judged each of them; in his resurrection both his life and death are manifest again as instruments of the world's salvation. As his life led inexorably to his death, so, too, resurrection is here united, though not identified, with death, salvation with renunciation and self-negation, redemption and new life with judgment and repentence. The dialectic must be held together if either his message or his destiny are to be understood. Correspondingly, God the creative power of being and of life appears in existence as weakness, powerlessness, suffering, and even as sin in order precisely to effect on a new level a new creation and a new being beyond negation. Finally, in the apostolic reflection on the meaning of Jesus' life, death, and resurrection, the same motif reappears: the self is affirmed and not denied, but it must deeply die to itself in repetence and trust, depend solely on grace and the spirit, and rise only in Christ—if it is to be a "new creature." Being and non-being, affirmation and negation, life and death are here united, and yet differentiated, held together dialectically so that each, in participating in the other, transcends its own limitations.

This dialectic persists, I would suggest, as the fundamental formal structure of Christian symbolism, what it is that is unique to the Christian understanding of reality and of existence. As I have shown, it has its inception and paradigm in the life, death, and resurrection of Jesus, and it unfolds in reflection on that center in each significant theological, ethical, and political—and ecclesiastical— dimension. This means that there are elements of affirma-

tion of the world, of space, of time, and of human existence (of "being") in Christian faith that have been both
creative *and* dangerous—as Christian and western history
show. It means also that there are elements of renunciation, negation, and denial (of "non-being") in Christian
faith which historically have also been part of its creativity
and its difficulties. To reinterpret creatively this fundamental dialectic in and for each age is the major task of
theology. I suspect that it is more crucial for a theology, or
for preaching, that it is faithful to this dialectic than that it
adopt any particular philosophical scheme.

Returning to the theme of the resurrection and the
community's reflection on it, it is evident why "proclaimer
became proclaimed," that is, why Jesus as the Christ,
crucified and risen, rather than the future Kingdom Jesus
himself preached became the center of the Christian message. To put it in terms of the dialectic outlined above, the
teachings of Jesus, even of the Kingdom, underwent a
stark negation at his sordid death. The proclaimer apparently ended in futility and error, his message of the Kingdom and the future thoroughly contradicted by reality.
Only with his resurrection was that message of confidence
in God, in God's future, and, thus, in the reality of the
Kingdom "justified" again, and thus reinstated. But now
it was reinstated—or reinterpreted—in a new form in the
new context of his death and subsequent resurrection.
This new context was characterized by two new factors
relevant to theology that were implicit in, but not a part
of, the original message: first, the deeper realization of the
estrangement, or darkness, of the world (John); and, second, the realization of the revelatory and redemptive significance of the total event itself of Jesus as the Christ or
Lord, of his coming, his life and teachings, his death, his
resurrection—and now (not before) his coming again. The
resurrection justified, in other words, both Jesus himself

and his message of the Kingdom, and justified them both together, in unity, so that proclaimer and proclaimed, teachings and person, crucified Messiah and Kingdom were now indissoluably mixed, and in being mixed, each was transformed.

At the earliest stage of this transformation, we find prominent the identification of Jesus as Messiah or Son of God with the expected eschatological Kingdom, namely in the apostolic preaching of the immanent Parousia of the Son of Man. But then, slowly, other elements implied in the dialectic became prominent: (1) because of the cross, there occurs a new development of the symbols of fall, of sin, of estrangement, a deepening of the sense of the predicament of human existence—although, as noted, this was continually there and evident enough in both the teachings and the life of Jesus. (2) Even more significant, this new context meant that new, transcendent, holy, even divine titles from the Jewish and the Hellenistic environments are now applied by the community to Jesus crucified and risen: Christology begins. (3) This new context meant that a theological interpretation of the cross as a redemptive, as well as a negative event, begins to appear: the atonement. (4) It meant that concepts and symbols of "grace" in present as well as in future experience become significant, centered about the work of the Holy Spirit and of the risen Christ. The apostolic witness, in letters and gospels alike, represents this reuniting in new forms of message, person, event, and expectation. That total witness is filled with a wide variety of incipient Christologies, untried concepts of sin and grace, and even changing ideas of what or who is to be expected in future history and when. Theology begins with, not after, these earliest New Testament documents—and, ever since, has sought to interpret our existence and our history in the light of this baffling mixture of elements which together make up Christology:

what Jesus said, what he did, his fate and death, his resurrection—and so who he really was, and, above all, what it was that God was doing and revealing about himself/herself, and, so, about existence, history, and the ultimate future through Jesus' life, teachings, death, and resurrection. As noted at the beginning of this chapter, Christology is thus the center of Christian symbolism, redefining and reshaping every other symbol (God, human being, sin, the end, etc.) because Christology directly represents the community's reflective response to the event on which the community and its relation to God is founded.

In an introduction, I can only briefly discuss the specific symbols and issues generally associated with Christology. In classical theology, reflection on Jesus as the Christ has been divided into: (1) Jesus' "person": his divine and his human natures—what each might mean and how they are related. Here the symbols of the pre-existent Son of God, of the Logos, and of the incarnation have, of course, been central. (2) Jesus' "work": his redemptive activity in "atoning for our sins," "rescuing us from the devil," or in "making a propitiary sacrifice" through his death on the cross. (3) Jesus' coming again as judge and savior and the relation of that return to history, to the Kingdom of God and to eternal life. As is evident to anyone familiar with the classical interpretation of these symbols, the orthodox Christologies based on a divine person, completing a saving work and returning at the end of time have, in modern life especially, faced two seemingly insurmountable difficulties.

First, they tend, taken literally, to express a picture of God's action in Jesus that reminds one of pagan mythology and so one that is hardly credible: of an individual but vast divine being (not unlike Superman) descending, acting out its role, ascending again, and then returning at the end. Such "mythology," picturing God as a large being acting in space and time, represents invalid speech about God and the way God acts in history—if it is speech at all about *God* and not about an individual divine being or pagan deity. Second, and correspondingly, they invariably seem to engulf the human, and so the historical, referent of all valid Christological statements (that is, about *Jesus* as the Christ). The actual human person named Jesus of Nazareth is here transmuted into a mythical divine being, and his history into myth. Such Christological speech represents invalid speech about Jesus of Nazareth and about history itself. In classical terms, therefore, these "orthodox" categories tend, almost despite themselves, to create Christologies that are Arian (salvation comes from a demi-god), or Docetic (salvation comes from a god-figure who is really not human at all). Thus the critique of orthodox interpretations of the "Christ of faith" stems not only from the grounds established by the modern historical consciousness and by the issues of historical inquiry into the New Testament. It stems on an even deeper level from a *theological* criticism of orthodoxy as in its Christology inadequately representing both God and the human Jesus.

In recent theology, since roughly 1800, there have been several of ways of reinterpreting Christology so as to avoid these two difficulties. I have suggested the category of "event" as possibly one of the most helpful. The whole history of Jesus of Nazareth—his life, teachings, actions, death, and resurrection—represent a unique and decisive "event" in and through which God has manifested his/her power, purposes, and love—his/her grace—for the illumination and the redemption of men and women and of the historical process in which they live. This mode of interpretation makes possible an emphasis on the dynamic and initiating activity of God without compromising Jesus' humanity and creative role, on the one hand, and an emphasis on the complete humanity and historicity of Jesus without compromising the centrality of divine action, on the other. It avoids both a supranaturalist, and thus mythological, picture of Jesus and a humanistic, "religious hero" picture. Because the constituent elements of this event are the total history of Jesus, there is a component of Christology based on and dependent on historical enquiry. This historical element roughly corresponds to the "human nature" of orthodox theology. Because, however, this history participates in and represents a *divine* event, there is a theological component witnessing to and describing the divine activity in and through that history. This corresponds to the "divine nature" of orthodoxy and, of course, as has been shown, presupposes faith as the basis for this religious witness and this theological reflection. In conclusion, I will explore a little further a few of the central themes or symbols of Christology within this framework of the decisive event whose constituent elements are the life, words, death, and resurrection of Jesus of Nazareth.

It has always been assumed that Christian understanding provided illumination on human nature, on God, and on the character and goal of history and of human destiny. It has also been assumed that this knowledge, while possibly fed by many other sources, nevertheless is given its final certainty and definitive shape in Jesus Christ as the decisive revelation for Christians of the nature of God, of human being, and of the world. It is, therefore, the major responsibility of any Christology to express and make intelligible what illumination on these ultimate questions Christian faith finds in the event of Jesus Christ. In briefly dealing with this responsibility, I should note that—as this discussion has already implicitly shown—*both* the life and teachings of the historical Jesus *and* the wider theological implications of his death and resurrection ("the Christ of faith") contribute—often in baffling and surprising mixtures—to a Christian understanding of God, of human being, and of our historical and ultimate destiny.

Who we really are, what are the requirements and possibilities of being really human, and what we should or could be are questioned and debated, answered and unanswered throughout history. It is not as if anyone knew definitively or could take answers for granted. Yet an answer of some sort is, on the one hand, inescapable—both as individuals and as communities we each live *out* some answer. On the other hand, that answer we live out is in large part determined by the accidents of cultural and religious inheritance—most of us, for example, merely reenact the contemporary American answer. In Jesus, for Christians, an answer, a model, a paradigm of authentic humanity has appeared: the possibilities of human existence are here defined and enacted, and thus the requirements of being fully human for the first time are made plain. Here is a life lived under the same conditions of finitude we experience; of time and of space; of need and of weakness; of identity and yet of relation with others; of an uncertain and precarious vocation or task; of suffering, danger, and death. Yet it was lived in devotion to God; in courage, serenity and inner integrity; in utter self-giving and sacrifice to others (as Barth says, "He was a man for others"); and in transcendent devotion of self to a cause, the cause of God's Kingdom. The really human has appeared, characterized—and this was not known before—by faith, love, and hope, ennacting, therefore, the two commandments that summarize the law. The older categories of the "perfection of his human nature" and his "sinlessness" mean, in other words, that Jesus presented to us not only the fulfillment of human possibilities, but the definitive definition of those possibilities—and its requirements.

Thus he replaced, in fulfilling it, the sacred law as manifesting to us what the uncomfortable, and yet inescapable, requirements of our own fulfillment are.

As has also been made clear, his life, teachings, and especially his death uncovered, as a light uncovers both the deep darkness of a basement and the cracks in walls and floor—not to mention the crawling things lurking there—the depth, universality, and structure of the human predicament, revealing its presence, even among the mighty, the intelligent, and the spiritual, exposing its character as a love of self rather than of God and of neighbor, a love of self that loses both self, other and world, and underlining the need of all of us—whoever we are—for divine mercy and divine grace if we are to be whole again. The character of Jesus' historical existence revealed both the real possibilities and the radical estrangement of human existence; as Irenaeus said, "He presented *man* to man in a new light."

The revelation in Christ, and so the wisdom pointed to in any adequate expression of Christian faith, is not and cannot, however, be confined to the "*re*-presentation" to us of human possibilities, that is, the manifestation of the perfection and requirements of being human, important as that issue and its revelation may be. To confine Christian revelation to this is (1) to assume (as did Pelagius) that we can, by our own power, enact these possibilities (i.e., fulfill the law); (2) to assume that we already, by other means, know all that there is to be known about God; and so (3) to omit from our understanding of God what is uniquely revealed of him/her precisely through the event of Jesus who is the Christ. The first denies the relevance of the symbols of sin or estrangement and our universal need of grace; the second denies that the event of Jesus Christ is a revelation of God as well as of human being; and the third simply ignores those central aspects of the divine character and the divine love which were unique to Jesus' teaching and uniquely embodied in his life and destiny. After all, although admittedly human nature and the destiny of history are mysteries in need of uncovering, the deepest mystery of existence and our most important question is the nature, character, and purposes of God—that is, of the ultimate reality with which we have finally to deal. Is that reality inwardly cold and dead, void of experience, feelings, purposes, thus blind and heartless, ignorant of suffering and evil, deaf to value, heedless of life, content with ultimate death—as a naturalistic or materialistic view has it? Is there any value that does not pass, any life in the universe that is not subject to death, any eternity that is not swallowed up in the maw of time? Such "theistic" questions about God are not merely theoretical but existentially significant. With deep passion they explore the ultimate horizon of our existence, asking about the connection of value and meaning to reality itself.

Granting the theistic answers to these basic questions, however, we may still have other deeply existential questions about God. Is the divine in reality, which we now assent to, *only* inclusive of order and so of value—and thus "righteous," the holy defender of virtue and value, but, by the same token, mortally threatening to vice—as most ancient and modern mythologies about the divine (from the Timaeus to Whitehead) have suggested? Is there hope, in that case, for those who find the good inescapably significant, an ultimate claim on themselves, but know also that they are estranged from it, that history itself is "fallen," and, therefore, that without redemption they have no access to that good? Is salvation possible for those of us who defy, reject, and even destroy—however good our intentions—an ultimate order, a final beauty, a lasting value, a reuniting love? Is there, then, hope for history, for the meaning of the human communal story—both in time

and transcendent to time—if all are, like ourselves, un-
righteous, hostile, incapable of creating the Kingdom? If
these latter "post-theistic" queries also be real questions—
and they seem to me to be at the heart of both the Gospel
and the secret longings of the human—then it is a revelation of the nature of *God*, even more than of the possibilities of human being, that is essential for trust and for
hope, either for hope for our own fulfillment or for the
fulfillment of the human story.

What is it, then, that is revealed of God in and through
this event, for nature, history, and human experience give
us ambiguous clues to these questions. What does Christology say about *God?* Again the coming or happening of
the event itself, and Jesus' teachings and life, his death and
resurrection, unite together to answer this question. Central to this new understanding of God is, first, the divine
"going forth," "coming," "reaching out" to rescue the lost.
This is, of course, a theme vividly portrayed in Jesus'
teaching through his parables about God. It is also a motif
borne especially by the symbol of the incarnation, "God so
loved the world, that he sent his only begotten Son" (John
3:16), and expressed in and through the category of God's
initiation of and participation in the event of Jesus the
Christ.

This central motif of the divine outreach, of the divine
coming in love, is, second, deepened by two more elements which together define this new conception of the
divine love: the participation in the suffering of his creatures and the forgiveness of their sins. Both of these appear, of course, initially and most vividly in the life and
words of Jesus. They find their main locus, however, in
the event of the cross, where not only is human sin uncovered and human fidelity and courage manifested, but
where—as a revelation of God—the participation of God
in our suffering and his/her mercy to all, even to sinners,

are revealed. The symbol of the Atonement has, in various ways, expressed these two themes of the divine suffering for us and the divine forgiveness of us. Both are essential if the depth of the divine agape, the love of God for the unworthy and the identification of God with the suffering and the lost, are to be expressed. It is here, in the manifestation both of the divine judgment and the divine mercy, and of the participation of God in the suffering resulting from sin—and not through the representation of human possibilities—that the problematic of sin, both as the demonic and as the self-destructive, is countered and resolved.

Third, in Jesus' proclamation of the coming Kingdom in new union with his death and resurrection, the final *victory* of God over sin, fate, and death is revealed and thereby the ultimate basis for faith, hope, and love for God given. Implied in the unconditional *power* of God expressed in the symbols of creation and providence, a power united with the *love* of God taught by prophets, priests, and Jesus alike, this confidence in the final efficacy of the divine saving will, both for individuals and for history, is vindicated—and symbolized—by the victory over fate and death in the event of Jesus' resurrection. The goodness of God—known in many ways—is for Christians not merely a struggling and possibly ineffective goodness. God's love is a *victorious* love—a point taken for granted by all of us but, when we consider it in relation to the apparent character of reality, by no means as obvious as we like to think. "Of course," we say, "God is love, God forgives, God rescues the lost, God is victorious—of course." But where does that "of course" come from?—an "of course" assumed throughout the modern mythologies from evolutionism and process thought to Marxism and humanism. Ordinary life experience? *Time* magazine? the six o'clock news? "reason"? a well equipped laboratory? This is the question I have tried to answer in explicating the revelation of *God* in the total event of Jesus Christ. As Irenaeus, again, said: "Also he presented *God* to man in a new light."

Finally, the revelation in Jesus who is the Christ uncovered in a new way the problem, the resolution, and the ultimate goal of historical process. The fallenness of the world, the depth of the problem of sin, the outrageous dislocation of institutions, and the waywardness of their leaders—all of this was revealed in Jesus' teachings, life, and death in a depth and clarity unknown before. But most important, in his proclamation of the Kingdom and of the reality of God's future, the mystery of the "whither," of the purpose, goal, and direction of history's processes, was unveiled. How his life, teachings, and resurrection combined to give a new content and a new role to this crucial category of the Kingdom or Reign of God I shall elaborate further in the final chapters. Then my subject will be the Holy Spirit, the presence of God in the ongoing stuff of historical life, creating new forms of community, and thus realizing, despite sin and fate, what had been both represented and promised in Jesus of Nazareth.

NOTES

1. For the following discussion I am particularly and gratefully indebted to two New Testament scholars and one theologian. First, to my recent and much-beloved colleague and friend, Norman Perrin, in his *The New Testament: An Introduction* (New York: Harcourt Brace Jovanovich, 1974), chap. 12; and his *Rediscovering the Teachings of Jesus* (New York: Harper & Row, 1967). Second, to Reginald Fuller in his *A Critical Introduction to the New Testament* (London: Duckworth, 1966), pp. (102–3;) and his *The Foundations of New Testament Christology* (New York: Charles Scribner's Sons, 1965), chap. V, especially pp. 103–8. For much of the argument as well as the content of this chapter, I am very much in Hans Küng's debt; see his excellent volume, *On Being a Christian*, trans. Edward Quinn (New York: Pocket Books, 1978), pp. 145–342.

2. Fuller, *Foundations of New Testament Christology*, p. 104.

3. See Perrin, *The New Testament: An Introduction*, p. 283, for an account of these scant extra-biblical sources.

4. Hans Küng, *On Being a Christian*, p. 142.

5. Fuller, *Foundations of New Testament Christology*, p. 142.

SUGGESTED READINGS

Recent Classics

Aulen, G. *Christus Victor*. Macmillan, 1954.

Baillie, D. M. *God Was in Christ*. Scribners, 1948.

Barth, K. *The Humanity of God*. John Knox, 1960.

Brunner, H. E. *The Mediator*. Westminster, 1947.

Bultmann, R. *New Testament Theology*. Vols. 1 and 2. SCM, 1952.

————. *Jesus Christ and Mythology*. Scribners, 1958.

Cullman, O. *Christ and Time*. Westminster, 1960.

Dodd, C. H. *History and the Gospel*. Nisbet & Co., 1928.

————. *The Apostolic Preaching*. Willet, Clark & Co., 1937.

Forsyth, P. T. *The Person and Place of Jesus Christ*. Independent Press, 1951.

Knox, J. *The Man Christ Jesus*. Willet, Clark & Co., 1945.

————. *On the Meaning of Christ*. Scribners, 1947.

————. *The Death of Christ*. Abingdon, 1958.

Tillich, P. *Systematic Theology*. Vol. 2. Univ. of Chicago Press, 1957.

Current Discussion

Cobb, J. B. Jr. *Christ in a Pluralistic Age*. Westminster, 1975.

Fuller, R. *Foundations of New Testament Christology*. Scribners. 1965.

————. *A Critical Introduction to the New Testament*. Duckworth, 1966.

Griffen, D. *A Process Christology*. Westminster, 1973.

Harvey, V. *The Historian and the Believer*. Macmillan, 1966.

Kümmel, G. K. *The Theology of the New Testament*. Abingdon, 1973.

Küng, H. *On Being a Christian*. Pocket Books, 1968.

Moltmann, J. *The Crucified God*. Harper & Row, 1974.

Niebuhr, R. R. *Resurrection and Historical Reason*. Scribners, 1957.

Ogden, S. *Christ without Myth*. Harper & Row, 1961.

Pannenberg, W. *Jesus: God and Man*. Westminster. 1968.

Perrin, N. *Jesus and the Language of the Kingdom*. Fortress, 1976.

————. *Rediscovering the Teachings of Jesus*. Harper & Row, 1967.

Rahner, K. *Foundations of Christian Faith*. Seabury, 1978.

Schillebeeckx, E. *Christ, the Sacrament of the Encounter with God*. Sheed & Ward, 1963.

PART FOUR

"... and in the Holy Spirit ..."

8

HUMAN EXISTENCE AS COMMUNAL

WHEN most of us in the West consider reflectively the human, we immediately think about the individual: as creaturely and temporal, as free, intelligent, moral, personal, and so, "of infinite value," or, alternatively, as sinful, proud, lost, or lonely—as existentialist philosophy and theology describe each of us. This emphasis on individuality, personal uniqueness, and freedom or self-actualization is both creative and Christian. It probably will be of increasing relevance and value in the collective world towards which technology and industrialism are driving us.

Nevertheless, this emphasis is one-sided, both empirically and philosophically and biblically. We are also as humans communal beings, participants in one another if we are to be ourselves at all. Our reality and fulfillment lie as much here, in ourselves as parts of societies, of communities, small or large, beyond ourselves, as it does in our own individual powers and our particular uniqueness. And because this is so, uncovering, emphasizing, and valuing the communal pole of our being is not to encourage the on-rush of an unwanted collective. Rather, an overly individualistic culture—economically, politically, psychologically, and religiously—will inexorably generate its own polar opposite. Isolated, lost, and fated individuals "by nature" long for community, and they will give themselves to any collective structure if only they too can "belong." Thus, as Tillich reminded us, as the achievement of genuine community depends on the presence in it of real and unique individuals, so the preservation of individual uniqueness and freedom depends entirely on real participation in and with others, both in immediate personal relations and in a strong wider society, in an emphasis on the *common* as well as on the individual good.

In explicating a Christian view of the human as communal, it is evident that that aspect of the creed, and that person of the godhead, that is relevant is the Holy Spirit. For in our tradition, the Holy Spirit, the divine as it dwells and works within us, is the principle of union, of reunion, and of communion. According to classical theology, the Holy Spirit is in God himself/herself the bond of love between parent and son; and in the New Testament and the tradition, the Holy Spirit is the principle of reunion with God in faith and love and of communion with the neighbor in love. It is the Holy Spirit that "sheds the love abroad in our hearts" that fashions the new community of those who are "neighbors" to one another and thus fashions as well the new community of those who love one another, the ecclesia. And it is the Holy Spirit dwelling in each creature that reunites the separated and thus creates out of a disrupted and inharmonious creation the divine harmony that was creation's goal. As in previous parts I shall begin with our common experience as communal and then, in unraveling that experience, shall show how we are led inexorably to a divine dimension; that is, we are led to the Holy Spirit.

When we speak of our being as communal, we naturally think at once only of communities of people: of family, tribe, local community, small town, and so on. Interestingly, neither primitive people nor the most recent scientific understanding of ourselves would start there. As both primitive life and modern biology would tell us, our *first* community is the community of nature, the natural communal process of mineral existence, of vegetable and of animal life out of which we arise, on which we depend, and with which we are and must be in continual interaction in each moment. This sense of *community* with nature, our participation in nature as one of its children, has long been forgotten in the West—and we are paying dearly for that lapse. It was not so when each tribe had a totemic animal as its sacred ancestor and guardian; nor is it so in the religions of Karma where you and I pass in and out of vegetable, animal, and human existence on the one seamless wheel of life; nor is it so in the theory of post-Darwinian naturalism according to which we are products of nature and thus dependent parts of its ecological system. In all of these—and each expresses one aspect of the whole truth—we are dependent *through* nature for our being. Our ultimate dependence on God the Parent is mediated to us from moment to moment through nature and our embeddedness in nature. Unless we participate in and respect and nurture nature's systematic order of interrelations, we vanish.

Although a sophisticated understanding of this dependence on nature has only recently come through our new biological knowledge, humans have always felt it whenever they have made personal contact with nature. The infinity and eternity symbolized in sea and mountain, the astounding order of its interrelations, the beauty and artistry in its least aspect, the vitality and power within the human body itself—these are signs at once of our dependence on nature, of our intimate embeddedness in it, and of the infinite power and order on which it in turn depends and so to which, in all its glory, it points. Humans *are* only as intrinsic parts of nature, not as incarnate angels sent arbitrarily into a nature that is an alien kingdom. Our religion, and so our culture, have forgotten this in their discovery of and wonder at what is peculiarly human and in their emphasis on the transcendence and dominance of human intelligence and skill over nature. In this way, ironically, even the truth of Western humanism, and even the treasured symbol of a humanity made in the image of God, each one raising through its emphasis the human above nature, can become vehicles of the demonic human drive to devour the whole earth and so in the end can lead to self-destruction. Here, note, a biblical symbol itself becomes demonic and thus, quite unintentionally, illustrates the truth of the message of which it is a part.

The other community on which we are dependent, from which our own reality arises and in which alone it prospers, is the human community: our family, our local community, and the cultural whole in which we come to be. Together with nature this human community makes up the "world" from which we come and in which we live. It, too, is a medium of the divine power of being and the divine order out of which all creaturely life arises. Consequently, its security, its institutions, its ethos, and its leaders alike enjoy the aura of sacrality and make, even if they do not deserve it, an ultimate claim on us. As I noted in Chapter 2, even our individual uniqueness is branded with the mark of our communal origins: in language, perspective, habits and manners we reflect to the end the particular and local human world in which we came to be. This is "natural," a part of our creaturely finiteness, a crucial aspect of our dependence. The individuals we *are* are at the same time communal in their origins, their characteristics, and their fulfillment. As anxiety is the inner echo of our temporality, and an uneasy conscience the inner echo of our estrangement, so loneliness, the pained despair of isolation, is the inner echo of our natural state of union with others and of our drive for reunion.

Since it is in dependence on community that we become unique selves, it is no surprise that it is in participation in community that we fulfill or realize ourselves, even our uniqueness. Our creative labors in our vocation, a crucial aspect of our individuality, become real and objective, and receive worth, as Marx notes, in a community of shared meanings and values to which that work contributes. If we find no such community in which to participate through our work, our creative talents, and our sense of our own reality and worth, wither. This participation in the creative work of the world has, incidentally, in the past been rigorously denied to many groups: to "lower" classes and to blacks, who have been allowed to work for but not with the world, and to women who have worked only at home. As each of these groups has progressively realized, such a denial of creative participation in the wider community, in objective labor in the world, and thus in the judgments of worth by one's peers effects a truncation of one's humanity, a refusal of full dignity, and a lessening of the reality and uniqueness of the individual self.

Even more important, our individual selves become themselves and so are fulfilled only if they are enabled to love, and so again to be, but in a different sense, participants in community. To be enabled to love is the greatest gift that can be given to us, even more enhancing of the strengths of the self, of the depths of its joys, and thus of its reality and uniqueness than being loved. Thus it is the parent who is really blessed by the presence of the child, not the reverse, because of the incredible gift of another being whom one can hardly help but love. Modern technological and professional culture tends to value participation in the world's work (a career) above participation in an intimate community of love and, when pressed, to sacrifice the depth and richness of the latter to success in the former.

It is because of this essential need to love as well as to be loved that Niebuhr was right when he said, "Love is the law of life"; love is that participation in one another through which we find and come to be ourselves and in the absence of which we destroy each other and ourselves. Love, therefore, expresses quintessentially that union of individuality and community that is precisely the human; for to love is an act of a unique individual towards another unique individual, and yet it forges and expresses the deepest bonds of community and of participation in community. As the self becomes a self in encounter with other persons, so it fulfills itself in loving union with them; both the "archeology" (origin) and the telos (completion) of the self lie in loving community with others. The "moral" arises here in the midst of this spectrum moving from the origin of our personal reality to its fulfillment. We experience obligation towards others—and the moral rules of every community reflect some such forms of obligation—because it is our nature to be in creative community with them. And that form of obligation comes as an "ought" because we are estranged from that nature, called by it to embody it, and thus having to be *told* to do so and how to do it as if from the outside. Because to be human is to be in community, to be human is to be morally obligated to others, and to be fully human is to fulfill that obligation in love.

Every level of our being reflects this drive toward communion: as "animals" (the organic level), as parents, as workers, as creative artists. And on every level we *know* this need: our bodily instincts, our emotional feelings and longings, our personal spirits. Yet, strangely, this component and requirement, essential from top to toe of our human being, is the most difficult, even the most impossible, of all things for us. Though we are lost without it, we cannot will it; and if we try, it will not come. When it árrives, as when "she" or "he" finally appears, or a child comes into our life, and suddenly community is formed, it is as a sheer gift, unexpected, unwilled, undeserved. Love, which is a necessity to our being if the latter is to be human, which is our "nature" in that sense, always appears as sheer grace—and is our first "secular" sign of grace.

As my previous remarks have indicated, empirically considered, the human is a baffling matter vis-à-vis community. Clearly as our feelings, as our history, and as the life and social sciences tell us, we are by nature communal beings. We depend on each other for all we are, the natural impulses in us drive us toward each other, and our psyches are neither renewed nor fulfilled in alienation from each other. We cannot be human without each other. Yet what is "nature" at the level of what we "really" are (what we "originally" are), seems *unnatural*, impossible, a mere dream or ideal, a painful longing, in terms of what we *actually* are. For us, in fact, community is elusive and evasive (what we all look for), on the one hand, and demonic and destructive (what we use to destroy), on the other. What is on every level more natural than the family? Yet what is more elusive and rare than a real family, more insubstantial and precarious than most families, or more destructive than all too many actual families? Whàt has happened that what is natural has become unnatural, a difficult task at best, and a frustrating impossibility at worst? And what grounds are there for hope that what is most natural and real about us, namely real community, may finally be established?

Our finitude, I said, was a self-transcending finitude, a creatureliness compounded of bodily, organic, psychical, and spiritual levels or powers. Thus while it is dependent, temporal, contingent, and mortal—as is all creaturely life—it is self-actualizing and self-creative as well, and thus creative also of its world. Because we are dependent, temporal, and contingent, the need for participation in community remains. We cannot, even if we would, "go it alone," be separated from and independent of nature and of others. But because we are self-transcending, made in the divine image and therefore free to create new forms of life, that dependence on community—and on nature—can take innummerable and novel forms: the infinitely varied forms of human societies and cultures and thus of relations to nature. As spiritual, and thus creative of the new, humans create new and varied forms of community, the wide spectrum of cultures, rather than representing over and over the same predetermined patterns of communal life. For the same reason, namely, that there is a spiritual, creative dimension to human existence, human communities are lived in through shared meanings, principles, values, norms, and aims. Each human community manifests a spiritual side, what I have called an ethos. Human community is not just an interacting and interdependent set of social, economic, and political relations necessary for bodily security. It is also of necessity a "culture," a systematic network of meanings, norms, and goals that structure, guide, and justify those social relations. We live not only by instinct in a world of nature and of other human beings. We live also by intelligence and spirit in a world of common knowings, of meanings, of norms, of plans, and of projects for the future. Such is our freedom to transcend nature, others, and self—but not to leave any of them behind.

Spirit, then, represents the freedom and the power to transcend and thus to re-create, reshape, refashion the given, what is "natural," and thus also the communities we are and need. Freedom also involves, unhappily, the power to divert and warp the natural in some fatal way and thus to make what is natural unnatural. And nothing

(except perhaps sexuality) illustrates these dual capacities
of spirit to create both value and the demonic more vividly
than our relation to community; for it is in and through
spirit and its capacity for freedom that we are estranged
from ourselves and thus from our most crucial communal
relations: to nature, to family, to other persons, to the
wider communities in which we live, and to history itself.
Thus does our nature as love become elusive for us and
have to be revealed to us—a strange phenomenon for a
communal being! And thus does the Kingdom, the normative community for historical beings, have to be proclaimed; thus is it ever "coming," and thus is it in the end
eschatological.

The deep estrangement in our common relation to nature has only recently made itself manifest. Even generations who believed in the fall did not see *that* consequence
of our fallenness. Yet this is, one may say, the prototype,
the paradigm of estrangement. It is not that we are now
either less dependent on nature or even out of relation to it;
we need constantly, moment by moment, what nature
supplies. The point is that that essential dependence and
that continuous relatedness has taken on a warped,
twisted, grotesque form: the form of domination, manipu-
lation, use, and exploitation. Nature has become a mere
object for our use, in fact, strangely enough, the primary
example of "an object," of the manipulable, of mere "raw
material" for our consumption, and thus the primal case of
the disposable and the expendable. Our human alienation
is well shown by the fact that while such usage and exploitation of human lives has for centuries been challenged—
fortunately with some success here and there—it is only
now that the estrangement inherent in our callous exploitation of nature has dawned on us—and only because that
exploitation now threatens our own security!

Ironically, the powers and the means by which this

exploitation was made increasingly possible represented the very glory of the human: the self-transcendence of human being, the language by which nature has become an "object" for us, the science by which the dynamic forces of nature are understood, the technology by which those forces are manipulated and nature refashioned and used, and the industrialism that required the ever-expanding consumption of nature's goods. These magnificent powers have become the instruments of exploitation of our natural environment rather than of our participation in, communion with, and preservation of that environment. Even our own spiritual and religious traditions share in this fall: *imago dei*, dominion and stewardship, have expressed a superiority over nature, and the right to its dominion, and thereby seemed to sanction a ruthless use and exploitation of it. Through the very creativity of the human, what is natural has become unnatural, that is, demonic and self-destructive.

Such is the vast extent of the contemporary power of human technological creativity that it actually threatens nature itself. The creativity of human ingenuity, and so of history, long a threat to other civilizations that the ingenuity of others had created, has now reached the point where it can engulf nature itself, as well as civilization, in the ambiguity of our common estrangement. The ancient religious myth that nature fell, and thus suffered because of the human fall, has now, to our surprise and horror, begun to be historically fulfilled to its end through the advances of a scientific and technological culture and its destructive potentialities—precisely when that culture's wisdom had prepared the obituary of such myths and of the religious perspectives they represented. The final irony is that it is a naturalistic, scientistic culture, insisting on a theoretical level that men and women are "only" products and, consequently, parts of nature, that has itself represented the quintessence of this estrangement, this superiority, this separation, and this exploitation. For that culture, having no norms beyond usefulness, no aim beyond the pleasures of consumption, and aware of no knowledge but manipulative knowledge, has, in both its capitalistic and its communist forms, ravaged nature as never before.

More familiar to us because as old as human self-awareness, and even older, is the universal estrangement of human being from human community or, alternatively, within human community. Of necessity we live in groups—families, circles of friends, local communities, tribes, cities, states—and in various sorts of vocational, economic and social groups, and various, and changing racial groups. This particularity and diversity among us all—being this person in this group rather than another in another group—is a part of our given creatureliness and by no means necessarily a cause of conflict. It could, or might, contribute richness to our common life rather than chaos. Nevertheless, it is evident that however natural it is for us to participate in particular groups, we do so "unnaturally"—at least in the sense that much of the tragedy, injustice, and suffering of history, themselves the central, pervasive evidences of the human predicament, of history's "out of jointness"—appear in our group behavior. The group we need by nature, that we live in and cling to, becomes the main expression and instrument of the demonic in history: the claimant on our ultimate loyalty, the main actor in our conflicts, the oppressors in injustice, the "gods" of a fallen and suffering history. Although human community represents the essence of our humanity, the locus of our creativity, the place of our deepest love, the embryonic kingdom, community appears in history also under the devil's sign as the instrument and servant of hell, the lords of the kingdom of evil. The principle and source of the moral, our intrinsic and primordial relatedness to others, becomes the main sign of the immoral, of the cruelty, violence, and injustice of history. To participate with others in particular communities is natural; but unless, in some strange way, that participation is universal—unless, that is, we can also transcend that particularity—it quickly becomes demonic. The search for a universal, and thus transcendent, community, for the Kingdom, is therefore itself universal; and it is so because it is in a paradoxical way the search at once for the natural and the primordial and for what is yet to come—for the eschatological. No wonder profound religion has spoken in symbols of ideal community, the object or referent of this search, pointing in one moment to an *initial*, but lost, paradise, to the originary locus of our nature, and in the next to the *future* culmination and hope, to the "Kingdom," to a reunion with nature and with one another in a transcendent community, to the restoration and fulfillment of what we are and what we will finally be.

The natural and also the unnatural or estranged state of our human existence as communal is clear enough. But how is the transcendent, a divine principle, involved in this dialectic? How are communion with nature and with one another religious issues calling for a religious ground or resolution? Why must human community, like temporality and estrangement, also be seen, if it is to be understood aright, in the reflected light of our knowledge of God, this time as the Holy Spirit, the bond of love, and of community?

We cannot prove the Holy Spirit any more than we can prove Parent and Son. Perhaps we can, however, show that the various forms of human community, both as essential to our being and fulfillment and as unnatural and estranged, reveal a transcendent dimension and call for a transcendent grace—which, when experienced in faith and shaped by the Christian witness, is what we mean by the work of the Holy Spirit.

There are two communal worlds from which we arise and in which we live: the community of natural beings and the community of human selves. Our present problem is their estrangement and the domination and exploitation of the former by the latter. This split lies in ourselves, in the subordination of ourselves as dependent participants in nature to ourselves as consuming participants in a technological and industrial community. Some principle transcendent both to ourselves and to these two wider communities is, therefore, necessary if a redeeming reunion is to become possible. Some principle creative of both communities and normative for both is called for. No contemporary society can return to a simple, undialectical participation in nature, as in the primitive forms of cultural life where the human is subordinate to, even submerged by, the power, order, and mystery of nature. With the advent of the historical dimension, of the institutions and arts of civilization, with a consciousness of spirit, intellectual and moral, as transcendent to unconscious nature, and with the advent of technical control over—and exploitation of—nature, such an undialectical return is impossible unless this complex civilization is itself abandoned or destroyed. On the other hand, a continuation of an exclusive emphasis on the historical dimension, on the improvement of the institutions of society, on the furtherance of the intellectual and moral dimensions of the human, and on technological advance and expansion—in fact, on all the facets of *humanism*—can spell our common doom. In both its religious and its secular forms, the emphasis on human capacities, human value, and thus humanistic aims has consistently separated us from nature, objectified it, and so led to her heedless use and lethal exploitation. The modern existential antithesis between the human and its natural

What is gileep's view of human nature?

environment, denied by modern scientific theory, but exacerbated by modern technological praxis, points to and calls for a divine bond uniting both: the Holy Spirit as the divine creative principle.

Primary human community—in our culture the circles of family and friends—is built on organic needs and impulses, on a mutuality of significant interests, and on emotional bonds of love, affection, and respect. It is also continually threatened and, again, in our culture dismembered and destroyed. This destruction may be effected simply by incompatibility on the sexual level, on the personal, temperamental level, or on the level of social habits and background, of vocational interests, and of spiritual perspectives and aims in life. More often, such differences become destructive because of self-concern, egoism, tendencies to aggression or withdrawal, and by inordinate authority and corresponding rebellion. In such cases where deep rifts appear out of the conflict of anxious and separated egos, the organic impulses, the mutuality of interests, and the love and affection that created the community are *themselves* rendered precarious. As often as not, in such situations, these very factors—especially sexual needs and mutual interests—can more easily impel us outward from the family towards other possible partners than they can re-create that now-precarious community. Mutuality, in sex, in interest and in affection, presupposes a deep, often unbidden community; it can hardly thus either preserve or renew the community if that community begins to disintegrate into warring, hurt, and angry selves.

Only if the incessant conflict between the selves that make up primary community is tempered by some principle transcendent to both, and thus transcendent to what they share in common, can community be maintained—for what they share sexually, in interests and in felt affection, is as ephemeral as is their threatened community itself, often more ephemeral than is their persistent self-concern, pride, and insatiable search for personal happiness. A common commitment beyond the needs, interests, and feelings of the moment; a tolerance of the temptations, failures, and even wanderings of the other; a sense of the fallibility, self-concern, and even sin of oneself; a willingness to subordinate even my own happiness or, at least, my self-interest—in other words, a principle of repentance, of self-sacrifice, of commitment and trust in new possibilities—these are essential. These virtues are the staples of all communal existence, whatever its form; they come to life, endure, and are creative in many situations. But they do so most effectively when they emerge in relation to a transcendent divine principle of judgment, of forgiveness, and of the grace of ever-renewed possibilities. Thus can inescapable breeches in natural community, so destructive in our era because so out in the open—between husband and wife, parent and child, friend and friend—be re-created from moment to moment, as they are threatened day by day. A transcendent principle of judgment and of love (agape), breaking in on our precarious communities of mutuality and of self-concern, is necessary if community is to survive: the Holy Spirit as the bond of love between us.

Each wider community is held together by common commitment to shared convictions, values, and goals—bound, as Augustine said, by "a common love"; in our case by the "American way of life" and our loyalty to it. This ethos and our commitment to it share an unconditional character. This ethos is the ground of the proximate meanings resident in our cultural life that energize and motivate our individual, and thus conditioned, lives. If the sense of meaning, value, and purpose that animates the whole culture becomes to people in that culture *itself* relative and dubious, tasteless and barren, or oppressive and evil—as, for example, it was to many in the generation of the late sixties, as it is to many radicals presently in Europe, or to dissidents in Communist Russia—these proximate meanings of the culture's life, its vocations and roles, become themselves meaningless, and the culture as a whole is in danger of disintegration. But by the same token, if this ethos is made explicitly unconditioned, an ultimate center of life's security and meaning, an "ultimate concern," then it becomes, or can become, demonic, a threat to its members and to other communities. Community inescapably has a religious substance, but that substance can be at once creative and infinitely destructive, the source of the danger of each community to the peace, security, and well-being of other communities.

Again, only if the religious principle within cultural life is *also* under a critical principle, if the community in relating itself to an unconditioned meaning also knows the divine judgment on that meaning and the divine calling to refashion that meaning, can historical communities be creative and redemptive rather than destructive and unredemptive. In other words, the religious dimension of communal life must transcend the community's existence as well as empower and guide it; it must participate in and reflect the Holy Spirit as the source of repentance and grace if natural communities are to be creative and not destructive in history.

Throughout these chapters, and explicitly in the last two, a fundamental dialectic has appeared. The first moment or thesis of the dialectic is our essential nature as communal beings, a "nature" viewable, in part, in ordinary experience, witnessed to in history, in culture, and in religion, and seen clearly by social science. The second moment or antithesis is the estrangement of the human condition, the pervasive elusiveness, frequent unreality, and destructive, demonic character of human community.

We are not what we really are, and we cannot seem to will or to achieve what is our deepest nature. The fall does not remove but, rather, warps creation, submits it to conflict and incipient chaos, prevents its fulfillment or realization, and even threatens its destruction. In this antithetical moment the transcendent dimension, the divine, apparent in the first moment as the foundation or ground of the natural, appears only as absent, as hidden, or as judgment and destruction. As a result, a quite new moment, a moment of grace, is necessary if the "nature" promised in the first is to be realized and if the sufferings evident in the second are to be redeemed—and if the divine ground implied in the first moment is to be experienced as present and victorious.

In each of the major themes of this discussion, this dialectic has appeared. What I am here describing is, as is evident, the stuff of our ordinary experience, baffling, paradoxical, and confused until clarified by the right symbolic interpretation. Thus can this set of symbols and this dialectical use of them be validated as most illuminative or adequate to our common experience of life. The true structure of our temporality as destiny and freedom and the true structure of its ground, God the Parent, are obscured in our estranged experience of our temporality and can only be known in full when, in grace, that estranged temporality is accepted and redeemed. Likewise, as now can be seen, the true character, as well as the possibilities of community with nature and with each other, are obscured and elusive until the transcendent principle of community, the Holy Spirit, manifests itself to us. Neither God the Parent nor God the Holy Spirit are "unnatural," irrelevant to what we are and do, unrelated to our ordinary experience, or alien to our own deepest fulfillment. But such is the alienation of that experience from its own intrinsic needs that participation in their power and knowledge of their reality appear as gifts of grace. And it is in their reflection, looking back in their light on the stuff of ordinary experience, or on our experienced creatureliness, our own estrangement and our communion, that at last we understand who and what we are, and what it is that we are to be and to do. A knowledge of God, Parent, Son, and Holy Spirit, is the basis for our understanding of the human and for our enactment of our full humanity—for our courage to be temporal, our openness to possibility, our faith and trust in acceptance, our hope in the future, and for the love which alone can recreate community among all creatures.

SUGGESTED READINGS

Farley, E. *Ecclesial Man.* Fortress, 1975.

Gilkey, L. *Reaping the Whirlwind.* Part 1. Seabury, 1977.

———. *Shantung Compound.* Harper & Row, 1966.

Haroutunian, J. *God with Us.* Westminster, 1965.

Mead, G. H. *The Philosophy of the Present.* Open Court Press, 1932. Cf. *The Social Psychology of George Herbert Mead.* Edited by A. Strauss. Univ. of Chicago Press, 1956.

Niebuhr, Reinhold. *Moral Man and Immoral Society.* Scribners, 1932.

———. *Reflections on the End of an Era.* Scribners, 1934.

Nisbet, R. *The Sociological Tradition.* Basic Books, 1966.

Tillich, P. *Morality and Beyond.* Harper & Row, 1963.

———. *Love, Power and Justice.* Oxford Univ. Press, 1954.

Winter, G. *Being Free.* Macmillan, 1970.

———. *Elements of a Social Ethic.* Macmillan, 1966.

9

THE HOLY SPIRIT AND THE KINGDOM

IN the last chapter I uncovered a strange dialectic connected with community: of all essential aspects of human being it is, like personal identity, the most "natural"; yet of all it is—again like identity—the most elusive. As community is the nature of our finite being, of our self-transcending finitude, so loving community represents both its fulfillment and its endless frustration. Thus the promise of the Gospel is a promise of *reunion*, of the restoration or reestablishment of a "lost community." For what is deeply our nature appears in imaginations fed by estrangement and thus in myths expressive of that situation as something once possessed and now lost, a paradise from which we have all been banned. Yet in these myths (for example, of Eden) the direction backward into a lost beginning, though understandable, is mistaken. As what we genuinely are, loving community represents what we might be, and so what in time we may become. As a consequence, the other significant symbol of loving community, essential for human being and yet now alien to it, is the future messianic reign, the Kingdom of God's rule that is to come.

That the establishment of genuine community among human beings is an act of God, dependent on the divine presence and thus illustrative of the divine rule, is assumed throughout the Scriptures from the story of Genesis, through the establishment of God's rule through his/her law at Sinai, through the mottled history of Israel's betrayal religiously and morally of that commission, to the image in the later prophets of a new convenant, a new people, and so a new messianic reign—all culminating, of course, in the proclamation of the coming Kingdom of God's rule in the New Testament. This identity, or interdependence, of God's rule and of loving human relations is further clarified in Jesus' summary of the whole law as, first, an unconditional love of God and, second, an unrestricted love of neighbor.

As Jesus' proclamation and parables of the Kingdom and the pattern of his own life alike manifested, what was to come was the rule of God, and what *that* meant were new sorts of relations among men and women, relations that negated every oppressive hierarchy, relations of service rather than of exploitation, of being "for others" rather than of using others, and so on. Salvation meant, therefore, reunion in several different dimensions: with God in trust, love, and obedience; with other persons in acceptance, forgiveness, service, and peace; and among wider communities and groups as the fulfillment on earth of God's righteous will for justice and peace. The New Testament symbol of the Kingdom thus brings into a new synthesis the older symbols of the convenant people, of the Law for that people's personal and social existence, of the messianic reign, and of the coming apocalyptic or eschatological deed or advent. And it combines in the proclamation and life of Jesus this complex of relations and dimensions: the reunion in love of persons with God, with one another, with historical communities—and even (in Isaiah and in Paulinism) with nature and the cosmos itself. Thus it is appropriately in terms of the symbol of the Kingdom, central to the teachings of Jesus and to the expectations of the early Christian community, that redemption or salvation is envisioned in Christian theology.

Since, however, this final chapter—and its encompassing part—is also about the Holy Spirit, the question arises: How is the Holy Spirit a fundamental principle of the appearance of the Kingdom? Surely the Spirit is an explicitly substantial aspect neither of the messianic promises in the Old Testament, of apocalyptic expectations in Daniel and Ezekiel, nor even of the proclamation by Jesus of the Kingdom. The Kingdom is clearly eschatological, future, an unaided act of God; the Holy Spirit a principle of the present presence of God in ourselves and in our communities. The Kingdom points to "objective" history and to its culmination for all in something qualitatively new; the Holy Spirit has as the locus of its "work" the inward, the personal; it refers to the workings of grace in ordinary persons in ordinary life; and it seems at its widest to be confined (as in Acts and in John) to the separated or at least differentiated Christian community.

My juxtaposition of these two symbols, Kingdom and Holy Spirit, in order to clarify the Christian belief in salvation, needs, therefore, some defense. First of all, as I have sought to show, the crucifixion and the resurrection, as the culminating aspects of the total event of Jesus as the Christ, effected a significant if not radical transformation of all previous expectations and of the symbols expressive of those expectations: of Messiah, Son of Man, convenant people, law, and divine sovereignty. They also—it should be noted—effected a transformation, as well as a continuation, of the meanings inherent in the teachings of Jesus—a point not often made.

The cross, as I have argued, revealed the depth of the human predicament and the involvement of *all*, all persons and all institutions alike, in the estrangement of history from true community. It manifested the presence of the divine in history, therefore, as at once powerless, vulnerable, and suffering as the essential prelude, in the resurrection, to its victory and triumph. In this way the rule of God, the divine sovereignty over events, promised in the Kingdom and sealed in the resurrection, takes now a dialectical form. God appears in and through what seems most ungodlike—being in and through non-being, life through death; it is, therefore, in judgment and repentence that renewal takes place, in dying to self that new life appears, in and through the powerless and the oppressed that the divine power and sovereignty manifest themselves. Thus are the two *direct* and *undialectical* forms of the Kingdom negated: on the one hand, the direct "building of the Kingdom" by the saints (religious or secular), that is, by unambiguous human activity either through churchly or through cultural power; on the other hand, the establishment of the Kingdom directly by *divine* sovereign action. Cross and resurrection transmuted both an immanent understanding of the Kingdom and also an apocalyptic understanding. The Kingdom, as Jesus had said, comes by *God's* action and also *in* human hearts, and its coming is represented or begun by the event of his life and death. Consequently, in the case of both the divine action and the human response, the new dialectic of death and of new life, of judgment and of grace, of repentence and of renewal through the Holy Spirit, appears. Only if the self dies to itself and is reborn in the Spirit; only if it gives itself in order to be itself; only, therefore, if it is itself by being possessed by God's presence; and only if communities are similarly united by a new spiritual presence can the Kingdom come or does the divine sovereignty appear.

Thus did the total event of Jesus as the Christ redefine not only the traditional understanding of the divine sovereignty and of the expectations that preceded him, but also the expectations of his rule that he himself was understood to have taught. In that redefinition, Holy Spirit and Kingdom come closer together, the former (the Holy Spirit) representing the active, healing, and reuniting presence of God in persons and in community in the historical continuum, the latter (the Kingdom) representing now the goal or the telos of that presence for persons, for communities, and thus for history itself. The spiritual presence, dialectically understood, becomes the *way* the future of God in the Kingdom is introduced into history, the way the eschatological end becomes ingredient in events.

In order to explicate further this unity I am suggesting between the Holy Spirit as the spiritual presence of God in history and the Kingdom as the promised goal or telos of that presence, as the future of God, we must return briefly to two previous discussions: namely, to the emphasis on the communal nature of persons and on the estrangement, both personally and communally, of our human situation. Throughout previous chapters, from start to finish, I have emphasized that there is in the end no separation possible between individual and community, between the personal and the social, between the inner spiritual being of a human and his or her outer, historical being. We arise in and through community, through relations with others, into unique, diverse, and autonomous individuals; correspondingly, the meaning of our individual organic, emotional, intellectual, and vocational life—all we are and do—overflows into community with others and is fulfilled there. Thus, while we can—and should—speak usefully of "inner" and "outer," of a personal, autonomous, spiritual center of human existence *inside* and a communal and historical context of human existence *outside*, we cannot speak of individual and social, private and public, or personal and historical as if they were either antithetical or mutually exclusive categories—as much reflection, both secular and theological, has done. What transpires in the inward person is shaped by the outward social order that that person lives in; in turn, what that outward order is and becomes is in part a result of the inward aims, standards, and loves, the inward health or disorder, of the persons living in and thus, in part, creating and re-creating that order. As Augustine pointed out, a community is bound together by the common, shared love or loves of its members. If these inner loves are sound, so will the outer institutions and the life of the community be sound; if these loves are awry, so will the institutions and social relations of that community be awry. Through the intimate interaction of inner and outer, of personal and social, are both the destructive and healing, the demonic and the redemptive forces of history to be understood and, consequently, the relation of Spirit to Kingdom clarified.

This interaction of inner and outer, of personal spirit and communal structure, of inner existence and outer historical sequences, is vividly illustrated in the character and scope of estrangement. The fundamental root of estrangement in the Christian view is, as has been seen, deeply inward: in an inordinate self-concern, a centering of one's world around the self and its own, a consequent loss of God as that center and so a warping of the relations of the self to itself and to others. We become centered on ourselves, not on God, and "for ourselves" rather than for others. However, this inward disruption has outward social and historical consequences. These consequences are not only evident in broken personal and communal relations and in hostile acts against neighbors and enemies alike, but also in the *forms* that social institutions and social relations take. It is, after all, human creativity, not divine fiat or biological determination, that slowly shapes institutions into the forms they take. Consequently, the warping of that creativity, also an aspect of history, serves to give the disfigured form that all our social institutions manifest. Slavery, tyrranical rule, domination by caste, sex, race; the familiar institutional forms of exploitation, oppression and of coercion, the frozen hierarchies of all social existence—these characteristics of social institutions and social relations are the objective results of inner estrangement. In turn, they lead, as every social analyst since Marx can document, to material and spiritual suffering, to alienation, further broken relations, dehumanization—and finally to the deep and unavoidable temptation to further competition, hostility, and aggression and so to the continuation of sin and of the social forms of sin.

There is, then, a truly vicious correlation of inner and outer, of the inward estrangement of the spirit and of the outward dislocation of social institutions and relations that gives to history its "fallen" character—and causes secular reflection on the human predicament to flip back and forth endlessly from the psychological and the "spiritual" to the social and the institutional; and Christian reflection to emphasize first the Spirit's conquest of inward sin and then the Kingdom's eradication of unjust and coercive institutions. This is understandable because both are involved; and as a consequence, redemption must take place on both levels or, so to speak, at both ends.

In order to understand the roles of Spirit and of Kingdom, of the inward healing through the spiritual presence and the outward effects of eschatological expectations, a useful distinction can be made between the inward sin or estrangement I have discussed and an outward, historical "fate" or fatedness—though, as shall be seen, from a Christian perspective the two are deeply interrelated. The experience of being fated has been universal: an experience of being imprisoned in one's historical existence by forces or structures quite beyond one's control, forces that prevent any free action, any self-direction of life or destiny, any new and creative possibilities from entering, any hopeful future. To be born a slave, in abject poverty, in a lower class or caste, among a people ruled by an outside oppressor or in a situation economically exploited by powers beyond our control—these have been common historical situations where an experience of "fate" has been known. The mythological, philosophical, and theological interpretations and explanations of this experience (for example, that of Karma, of astrology, or of a divine providence) have been as various as the religions and philosophies of humankind. And as modern secular social theories, for example, those of Marxism or of Freudianism, show, these attempts at explanation have not ceased because the experience of being fated continues unabated in extent and unlimited in its destructive intensity. There can be little question that the present rise of religious cults, like a similar rise in the late Hellenistic world, is due in part to an extended experience of being caught by determining forces, of being fated, and so of having neither freedom nor open possibilities for the future.

As the discussion of providence in Chapter 4 showed, the contemporary Christian has as much difficulty assigning the experience of fate as that of sin exhaustively to the divine providence. It is not God's will that our life is suffused with suffering and want, our freedom is seemingly helpless, our self-direction ineffective, our future closed and hopeless. Such an explanation in terms of providence challenges our confidence in the goodness of God too directly and denies as well our certainty that contingent historical causes have also been involved in creating the situation—of poverty, of oppression, or of distructive social conflict—in which we and others find ourselves.[1]

An interpretation, theologically sound and yet in accord with our own historical consciousness, is, I believe, that to experience fatedness is, in fact, to experience the outward, social inheritance that sin or estrangement has left behind itself in history. Fate represents no suprahuman mythological power but the destructive effect on successive generations of warped institutions and distorted social relations. Human creativity—intelligence, ingenuity and will—in all its terrifying ambiguity, has helped to create social institutions; insofar as that creativity is estranged, self-concerned, greedy, hostile, and aggressive, the forms of those institutions will be warped, cruel, oppressive, and exploitative. And long after the creative—and sinful— "fathers" are gone, the institutional results of their labors remain and bequeath oppression, conflict, and suffering to their children and to the children of others.

My generation has experienced this deeply. It inherited the "fate" of the Second World War from its fathers and detested them (at first) for the pride and the blindness that had caused that legacy. But then we bequeathed to our sons and daughters, through a reenactment of the same pride and blindness, the incredible and guilt-ridden morass of Viet Nam and were, in turn, ourselves roundly detested for that fate.[2]

In institutional situations of slavery, political dominance, economic exploitation, racial or sexual injustice, people come to be as fated—unfree, oppressed, in material want, dehumanized, void of significant choices or opportunities—and tempted as are their rulers and exploiters, to further sin. Just as in history freedom "falls" into the inner and subjective bondage of sin and estrangement, so destiny, the given to us in each moment, "falls" into an outer and objective fate, the fatedness of a warped and oppressive social world in which we find ourselves. For there to be redemption in history, for the Kingdom to come at all, there must be a healing both of sin and of fate, a dealing both with the inward estrangement of the spirit and the outward warping of history's institutions. As human existence is both inner and outer, individual and communal, personal and historical, so of necessity is the Gospel both spiritual and social, both religious and political.

The Christian gospel, then, and the redemption it promises, is both spiritual and political, involving both an inward healing of sin and an outward transformation of history's institutions. To deal only with the first, as so much of the sacramental tradition, the kerygmatic or gospel preaching and the pastoral life of the Church have sought to do, is to leave countless humans subject to fate and thus subject not only to endless suffering but also to continual temptation to further sins. It is also highly suspect—both religiously and socially—for a church to preach *inner* redemption alone when it lives in, prospers from, and thereby inescapably blesses *outward* oppressive social institutions. Spiritual liberation is ineffectual and ideological without an accompanying political liberation. On the other hand, for the Gospel to interpret itself only politically, as a commission to deal simply with unjust institutions and the destructive social relations they foster—as many political theologies tend to do—is to leave the deeper issues of sin unbroached and the resources of Christian grace untapped. Political liberation, even if partly achieved, will be ineffectual, and possibly demonic, if the continuing sin of the liberators and their successors is unheeded and unhealed, and the new forms of fate they produce unattended and thus unconquered.

The individual drive toward inward, spiritual acceptance, integrity, and love and the political struggle for institutional justice, communal well-being, and social peace, long considered antithetical interpretations of the Gospel, are *both* essential. Not only are the Spirit that sheds love abroad in our hearts and the Kingdom of God's rule in objective history both central promises in the Scriptural witness and, therefore, if anything is, essential to the divine intention for history. Also inner and outer, personal and social, are inextricable aspects of human existence in history. The Christian witness to God and the promised fulfillment of men and women require that the Gospel be both religious and political, both personal and historical.

I shall conclude this introduction—this brief tour through the strange, possibly alluring, possibly incredible world of Christian belief—with a quick look at four of the contexts, four of the forms of community, in which this dialectical interplay of fate and of sin, of Spirit and of Kingdom, of the worship of God in the present and the promise of God for the future come together to express the Christian vision of the life of faith. My remarks at this point are at best no more than suggestive; a great deal more reflective thought, as well as relevant study, is necessary for the full development of these perspectives.

Recall that in each context the point of redemption or salvation is (1) the fulfillment of what is natural, of what is the essential nature of the human, (2) therefore, the reestablishment or restoration of community, and especially of loving community out of estrangement, separation, and conflict, and (3) that the principle of this reestablishment, because it is the principle of what *is* natural, is the rule or sovereignty of God, the centering of life around the divine center. The centrality of God as the principle of the restoration or fulfillment of the essential nature of the human—as it is, of course, of the creation and preservation of the human—and so as the principle of the establishment or reestablishment of genuine community, forms, perhaps, the basic foundation of Christian understanding and of Christian praxis. This "theonomous" principle[3] is expressed not only in the summary of the law, where the natural love of neighbor is dependent on the love of God, but also in the fundamental doctrines of creation and of providence, which are, for this reason, basic for the present discussion of redemption and of eschatology. Thus the Christian understanding of human being, of culture, and of history are alike theonomous: the autonomous or natural fulfillment of individual human being, of culture, and of history become visible only if the divine is the central principle of each. Thus do the symbols of the Spirit—God's active *presence* in personal and communal existence—and of the Kingdom, God's *rule* in personal and communal existence, come together and interact whatever the communal context we may be discussing.

The *first* communal context I shall discuss may be called the personal, possibly the intimate. It should not be called the individual context, for as I have stressed, to be individuals is to be in relation to others; to have identity and uniqueness, that is individuality, is to participate through these relations in the identity and uniqueness of others— and the norm and goal of these relations of participation is love. In recalling the analysis of estrangement—as a combination of an inward love of self (sin) with warped inherited forms of human relations and institutions (fate)—it can be seen how *both* sin and fate in this sense affect, endanger, and destroy such personal relations, and in so doing weaken and threaten personal identity. Thus a "redemption" of personal relations, the re-creation of love between persons, and thus the restoration of intimate community, have both inward and personal—purely "spiritual"—aspects and structural or "political" aspects; and to each both the presence of the Spirit and the promise of the Kingdom are relevant. I shall discuss each of these aspects in turn.

Traditional theological discussion has, as is well known, concentrated itself on the context of personal relations—on the requirement of love to those with whom we are in close contact—and on the spiritual rather than the political aspects of those personal relations. Thus has that tradition continually defined and redefined the issues of justification and of sanctification, of the relation of the law, the Gospel, and the Spirit to each of them. Granted that we are each of us "sinners," even if we are also believers, how is it that we can love one another? If free will cannot will this sort of love—and, sadly, experience shows it cannot—how is it that grace can enter our inwardly turned, hardened, and defensive-aggressive egos and transform us into loving men and women, persons "for others," as Jesus was? Is renewal possible, as the Gospel seems to promise, and if so, how?

The profoundest answers to these questions have arisen, I believe, through an acute sense of the dialectic that was traced in the chapter on Christology. The renewal of the self in loving community—a goal or ideal set before us by the historical Jesus' life and teachings—becomes possible only through the death of the self to sin and its rising in grace, through, that is, the model set by the themes of the crucifixion and the resurrection. Only if through genuine repentence the self confronts its self-centeredness and bases its life on the gift of grace alone is its life reestablished around its true center, God in the Spirit. Thus, in becoming theonomous through the presence of the Spirit (and they are the same thing), does the self become its true self, its nature; and in becoming its true self (in loving God unconditionally) that other aspect of its nature, loving community with others, becomes possible. The self centered in unconditional concern around itself cannot love others; it is "for itself" and, so, not for them. Only a self freed from itself in God can love others as itself. It is a "justified" self (one now in relation to God), not *through* its love, but in order *that* it may love. Through itself it is only the sinful, self-centered, and, at best, repentant self. As a consequence, it is accepted only by God's mercy and not through its own merit. But in finding itself accepted, and in accepting that gift, it is now truly centered in God, and, so, in potentiality, a sanctified self (the self obedient to the law of love), the self living out of faith in love.

The first work of the Spirit, then, is the awareness or acknowledgment of the judgment of God on the sin of the self, calling forth inner repentence, and the acknowledgment of the mercy of God accepting that self, calling forth faith in God's love and care as necessary conditions of a community of love. These relations of God to the self, of judgment and of mercy, are revealed or manifested in the cross of Christ: here is the basis of "justification" and thus the essential condition for the self's renewal. Correspondingly, the coming in power of the Spirit, of the healing presence of God recreating the creature and "shedding love abroad in our hearts," is manifested in the resurrection and its promise of new life. Thus the Spirit, as the creative presence of God in personal existence, reestablishing loving community in a fallen world, is understood as the spirit of Christ, that is, as present in the dialectic of crucifixion and resurrection, of dying to self and rising in God in order that the love for others incarnate in Jesus be present in history.

The work of the Spirit is thus the work of God's theonomous presence renewing the self which could not renew itself, reuniting it with God, with itself, and with its neighbor: in the coming of repentance, of new trust, of new acceptance of the self, and a new power to love. Its fruits are faith, hope, and love. Its final expression, rare but unforgettable, appears when a person is, as Tillich said, "transparent" to the spiritual presence, when he or she becomes a "symbol" of the divine power and love, expressing both in their own being and so communicating both to others. As repentance and faith represent the final conquest of the demonic side of estrangement, so the presence of the Spirit as filling, directing, and transforming the self into a loving self, represents the conquest of the self-destructive consequences of sin.

Although these themes concerning justification, sanctification, and the presence of grace in and through each, are not new, they remain, I believe, the profoundest symbolic interpretation of the problematic of the self, of the possibility of its renewal and of the new life of the self as both theonomous and in loving community—and, so, finally really itself. It is in this context that what we have called "the new redemptive forces of history" (the new being) manifest in Jesus as the Christ, are given symbolic expression in this dialectic of sin and grace, of judgment, justification, and sanctification through the Spirit; here estrangement and sin are, so to speak, tackled "head on" where they gestate, grow, and increase, in the inner personal center of every man and woman. Here clearly lies the religious center of the Gospel. But if this is so, we may well ask—as countless individual and personal interpretations of the Gospel have asked—how, then, is the Kingdom and its proclamation also central?

As modern theology—in the social gospel and now in the liberationist theologies—has rightly discovered, even the inward healing of the self, now in a new relation to God through grace and the Spirit, is not sufficient. For the inward self that may so relate itself to God—that hears the gospel, that believes, that even repents and seeks to trust—is *historical*, in time, and so in community. It is thus subject, not only to sin, but also to what we have termed fate, to the warping and destructive influence of inherited institutions and social relations that have themselves been shaped by estranged, as well as creative, human beings. This inheritance, in turn, forces the continuation of sin and the destruction of loving community. Examples of this interaction of fate and sin, and so the need for political theology, abound *even in the context of personal relations* (where Lutheran and evangelical piety have thought it could not). Can the master love the slave, and vice versa, in a sharply hierarchical society? Can the maid love her lady, and vice versa? Can workers in a bitterly competitive economic situation—or executives—create loving community (see, for example, Marx, Rauschenbusch, and Horney)? Can personal love cross racial lines in a creative way in a racist society? Can women's love for men, even in the closest of all personal relations, be anything but precarious in a sexist society? The answer in each case is clearly and experientially no. As sin slowly creates in objective historical institutions a fate for generations to come, so, in turn, the inheritance of this fate tempts and even forces those caught within it to anxiety, to competition, to hardness of heart, to defensiveness, to aggressiveness, to conflict, and to cruelty—and so the kingdom of evil, outwardly and inwardly alike, goes on. Love *can* surmount all barriers, to be sure; but time and again loving community is made virtually impossible, snuffed out at inception, soured, finally extinguished by the unjust, oppressive, competitive forms of our social relations and our institutional structures. Freedom is bound by objective, external fate as well as by inward sin. As our common usage of the word "freedom" shows, it has reference to outward, political liberation as well as to inward release and healing. Thus even in the most personal of contexts—for there *is* no "personal" world without social relations, and there are no social relations except those structured by inherited institutional forms—must the Gospel always also be a political as well as a personal gospel.

If this be so, then the Kingdom is relevant to the context of personal relations as is the presence and work of the Spirit. For the possibility of loving community—the clear product of grace—is dependent not only on the inward appearance of repentance, faith, and love, but also on new and cleansed forms of social relations between persons. These cleansed forms of personal relations are those structured by freedom, as the capacity for self-direction and thus dignity; by equality between loving persons so that absorption of the one by the domineering other is less possible; and by order or peace so that a situation of conflict does not prevent the appearance and the continuing existence of love. Love thus, as Tillich reminded us, not only transcends justice; it also depends on it and presupposes it. Love sees what justice requires; justice, in turn, makes possible the appearance and existence of love. Thus the Kingdom, as the symbol of the community and its relations, of the cultural whole that is theonomous in its centering and loving in its relations, is the necessary horizon for the most personal of relations in history. The Kingdom provides the norm for the social context in which love occurs. In providing that norm it both challenges the warped relations of the present and "lures" our social, that is, our political, action into a new and more creative future.

The *second* communal context within which the interdependence of inner and outer, of the redemptive and the political, of Spirit and of Kingdom, appears, is the wider community of the Church. We have seen why in the very beginning the Jesus who was the proclaimer of the Kingdom became himself the proclaimed, the Christ of faith, crucified and raised from the dead—and at least the initial relation of this shift to the dual problems of sin and of fate. How is it, however, that the other great apparent "letdown" of the earliest history occurred, namely that, as Loisy remarked, "While Jesus proclaimed the Kingdom, what happened was the church"? Granted that humans are incurably communal, why should *this* sort of religious community always be there besides family, town, city, nation, and so on? That is, what is the role of ecclesia in personal and historical life; and in that role, how is the presence of the Spirit related to the promise of the Kingdom? This subject is, like all these in the final chapter, endless, and much that is necessary will be omitted from my brief treatment.[4]

The primary role of the Christian community, the ecclesia, in the continuing history of men and women is to provide a locus for those redemptive forces that God's action in Christ had introduced into history. Or, put in terms of the categories uncovered in Chapter 3, that role is to be the bearer of "dependent revelation," witnessing to, re-presenting, and thereby renewing in the successive moments of time the event of Jesus as the Christ and its recreative effects. In this task three elements are central: the Word witnessing to the original event, the sacramental re-presenting of the event, and—rarer but more effective—the "real symbols" represented by persons in community transparent to the divine and thus embodying a new reality of love. It is through these "means of grace" that the Spirit, as the principle of the divine or theonomous presence, is introduced "Christianly" into the lives of successive generations. This does not mean, as I have continually reiterated, that the Spirit does not "blow where it listeth," and so is not also present through other means and in other traditions and in other institutions. But the promise that constitutes the Church is that the Spirit is *here* when the Word is heard, when the divine presence is apprehended in worship and sacrament, and when, through loving community, the reality of grace is known and received. It is, then, because the spiritual presence is the principle of Word, sacrament, and loving community—and *that* is because faith, hope, and love are theonomous—that to proclaim the Word, to hear and acknowledge the Word, to commune through the sacramental elements, and to show forth love in one's existence are all regarded as fruits of the presence of the Spirit. In this sense, the Church as fully the Church, as performing its role, is an "event"; it becomes itself as the locus or symbol of grace, not through itself, its own powers or acts, but through the work and activity of the Spirit. As the Scriptures do not point to themselves but witness to the event of Jesus as the Christ, so the Church does not point to itself—its preaching, its liturgy, its moral excellence, or its loving relations—but to the event it proclaims and the promise of the Spirit for which it hopes and waits.

The wider Christian community, the Church, is therefore subject to the same dialectic of cross as well as resurrection, of dying to self as well as living, encountered in the context of personal relations. Unless the Church is first conscious of its own estrangement and repents, the Spirit is not present in the Church, and the latter's proclamation, its liturgy, its sacramental life, and its corporate relations will be void of the grace it claims. The Church, too, is justified only by the divine mercy—by the cross; and only if it inwardly apprehends this and outwardly shows it, is the creative role of the Church in the world a genuine possibility. The dialectic of death and resurrection—begun in the life and destiny of Jesus and continued in the life and destiny of each believer—appears in the life of the Church as a dialectic of "Protestant principle" and "Catholic substance," to use Tillich's helpful categories. The Church is, on the one hand, the locus of the spiritual presence in time: through Word, sacrament, and its common life—this emphasis and this reality have characterized, empowered, tempted, and endangered the Catholic community. But, on the other hand, only if the Church is also conscious of its fallibility, critical of its faults, repentant for its sins, and thus dependent itself on the divine mercy and grace, will it exhibit with power that spiritual presence. The disunity of the Church in history, caused by the fragmentary witness and insufferable sins of the Church, has in the providence of God become the new possibility of an increased self-understanding, of a growing repentance, and of new levels of community as Catholic forms and Protestant forms realize, for the first time, their essential need for one another. Thus, dialectically through its weakness rather than through its obvious strengths, if appropriated repentantly and truthfully, has the community now the possibility of becoming its intended self, a sacrament or medium of grace for history.

The image of the sacrament or medium of grace for the Church, while apt and instructive about the essential role of the Church, can, however, foster an optical illusion. This is that the Church represents in history a kind of embassy of another realm. So long as it keeps a good rapport (through repentence, faith, and hope) with its "home office," the Church (so this view goes) can mediate to the world around it a message, a norm and a grace the world cannot and will not produce. Thus, like all foreign embassies, the Church sees itself as an institution more shaped by the heavenly realm it represents than by the alien worldly culture in which it happens to reside. This ecclesiastical self-understanding, explicit in Catholicism, implicit in Protestantism, is an illusion because, like the personal and intimate communities just discussed, the Church is itself, from top to bottom, *also* shaped and structured by its world and dependent on that world in many essential respects. Thus, especially when it is least aware of it, it is obedient to the pressures, the norms, and the aims of that world. As the intimate family in a patriarchal culture is patriarchal—whatever the level of its "love"—so the Church in a feudal society reflects that structure, in a bourgeois society is bourgeois, in a racist or patriarchal society is racist or patriarchal, and in a nationalistic society is nationalistic—*unless* it is awake to this danger and is as a consequence *political* in its consciousness.

Moreover, whether it will or no, and whether it intends to or not, its presence as an institution in that given society blesses, secures, protects, and thus furthers the structure and claims of that society; and the individuals that make up the visible community of the Church live in and off that same structure. Thus does the Church represent by its presence a continual, silent, but effective, justification of its society—unless, again, it is political in its consciousness and its responsibility and deliberately treasures what accords with its own norms and criticizes and rejects what does not. As a consequence, if the Church seeks to be nonpolitical, it will represent and support both the injustices that estrangement brings to all societies, our own included, and the religious claims to ultimacy (for example, the nationalistic claims) characteristic of every culture, however secular. Without a political or a prophetic consciousness, the Church can hardly fail to be both oppressive and idolatrous.

If, therefore, the Church feels itself to be holy because and only because it is a medium of the holy gospel and a holy grace—as both Catholic and Prostestant forms are tempted to do—it may be sure it will be found unholy, at best a willing if unacknowledged participant in the evils of its cultural setting and an unconsciously ideological support for those evils, and at worst the explicit ambassador and defender in the name of God of its own cultural world—not to mention the evils it perpetuates on its own if it, as it has surely done, identifies its own truth, its own norms, and its own security with those of God. The social fate that determines, oppresses, and binds men and women towards evil, that continues the kingdom of sin in history, engulfs the Church as well as the individuals and the social communities of secular history. As political consciousness and action are the only human antidotes to this inherited structure of fate in communal life, so are they necessary for the life of the Church. Thus the Church must not only be repentant in general terms about its sins; it must be specifically conscious of its own special social, economic, and political biases, its special temptations, and its peculiar injustices deriving from its particular shape as a very human institution in its own ambiguous cultural setting. And it must be willing to redress them by common action when they are uncovered. A political self-consciousness is as necessary as is a sacramental and a kerygmatic one if the Church is to be the Church.

The culture, then, interpenetrates the life of the Church; and the Church, consciously or unconsciously, involves itself in the life of its culture. These are undeniable social facts. The penetration of the Church by the culture is evident in any glance at the history of the churches in the nations of the West, or at any American church, its interests, aims, standards, and customs. The Church's penetration of a culture is evident to any observer of the pretentions of our own middle class or of the spiritual pride of "religious America" in its interactions with other nations and cultures. The solution is not for the Church to try to abstract itself from politics; so long as it is there at all, it is, as I have argued, political and ideological in its own life and in its influence in the culture. The only antidote is a political component to its consciousness and its common action. This component has three elements: (1) an awareness of the relation of its own norms and aims to its *own* ecclesiastical, social, and political structures, habits, and forms of behavior—of race, sex, property, and so on—that is, for example, who can and cannot be clergy, where authority in Church affairs lies, etc.; (2) an awareness of those aspects of the wider cultural life in which it shares and which support and are supported by its own

Christian norms and aims—for example, the struggle for justice and equality in political, economic, and social affairs, the defense of community, of individuality, of the integrity of nature, and so forth; (3) an awareness of those aspects of its cultural life that are antithetical to its own norms and aims. In relation to the first it must be prophetic, critical, and transformative; in relation to the second, priestly and conserving; in relation to the third, prophetic and radical—and in all three, if necessary, willing to sacrifice itself, and surely its numbers, its direct influence, its wealth, if it would live.

This requirement that the Church possess, proclaim, and act upon a political consciousness, both in relation to itself and to its own life in relation to its world, makes immediately relevant at the heart of its life the symbol of the Kingdom as complementary to that of the Spirit discussed previously. For the symbol of the Kingdom—as evident in its origin in the symbol of the covenant people and in Jesus' preaching—represents the normative *community* implied in the lifestyle and the words of Jesus himself. The Kingdom represents, so Christians believe, God's intentions for (and so the essential nature of) human community as Jesus himself represents authentic humanity (the essential nature of human beings). It is, therefore, from the symbol of the Kingdom—as an authentic and therefore normative society—that the standards relevant to Christian political and social judgments are derived, that the criticism of present social and ecclesiastical realities stem, and that the hopes basic for constructive political action in community and in Church alike flow. The Church is a means of a transcendent grace and the locus of the divine spirit, but it is also a community in the world and of the world. It can be a means of grace and a locus of the Spirit only if it is critically aware of its own involvement in the world's sin and actively dedicated to the transformation of itself and its world. Ironically, now that the danger of persecution for one's faith has receded, it is perhaps only in this "political" involvement in the name of the Kingdom that the spiritual requirement that we must die if we would live can be enacted in reality as well as rehearsed in the Spirit. In contemporary martyrs for racial liberation, for social equality, for the persecuted Jews, for peace, for liberation of conscience and religion, for economic justice appear almost alone in our century a surprising union of the claims of the Kingdom, on the one hand, and the hard dialectic of cross and resurrection on the other.

The *third* context for the interrelation of Spirit and Kingdom in the process of renewal and redemption is, of course, the wider communal context constituted by our social life in cities, states, and nations, by our participation through these communities in the stream of history as a whole, and, finally, by our participation as members of the human community in the community of natural beings. Our treatment here will be skimpy at best, partly because of the obvious extent of the subject and partly because I have recently published a detailed treatment of precisely these issues.[5]

The widest social context of our life is constituted by the human communities of the stream of history and the entire natural world in which these communities appear, live, and then pass on. That this widest context (social history and history in nature) represents the penultimate (next to ultimate) referent of the symbol of the Kingdom, this whole volume has sought to show. The Kingdom is not merely "in our private hearts"—though it is also there; throughout the Scriptures it refers also to historical communities in their widest extent. As has been shown, the originary forms of the symbol of the Kingdom: the covenant people (Israel) called out and established by Yahveh among whom he/she was to rule through his/her law, had clear reference to human, historical community; and the symbol of the messianic reign referred to that historical community, now perfected by new acts of God and now reconciled with a harmonious nature. The New Testament symbol of the Kingdom, moreover, had, in part at least, a future referent, a reference to the culmination of the entire creation in God's time and through his final and decisive intervention. Thus it included what is denoted by my terms "history" and "nature," and it pointed to the perfected union of both in and through the work of God.

The reference of this basic biblical symbol to both social history and nature was, moreover, itself underscored and given empirical meaning by the analysis of human being as at once communal and historical in its essential nature. Whether I spoke of the autonomy of personal belief, the basic temporal structure of our finitude, the social character of our estrangement, or the communal nature of our fulfillment, this theme recurred: individual and social, private and public, personal and historical cannot be separated. Our being and its powers originate in community; we are, decide, and act in community; we are fulfilled, if at all, there. Thus, while the inward, personal referent of the teachings of Jesus and the self-understanding of Christian faith are undoubted, their outward, social and historical references are also so. As Jesus himself represents for Christian understanding the norm and goal for individual life, so the Kingdom represents the norm and goal of objective social and historical existence.

Finally, my analysis of social life uncovered—or sought to—a religious dimension in each historical community in the ethos or vision of reality, truth, and goodness around which each culture is constituted and from which it lives. It is, I noted, this "religious substance" that represents both the ultimate source of creativity and the focus of estrangement in historical community—as it does in individuals. History exhibits the demonic and the self-destructive in its life *because* of this religious element, because of the self-oriented character of the cultural vision, the norms and commitments of any given culture. Implied in this analysis, therefore, is a further point relevant to the role of the symbol of the Kingdom. If normative, authentic community is not and cannot be completely "secular," devoid of this religious dimension, as the eighteenth and nineteenth centuries dreamed, but will—whether it will or no—be constituted by its religious substance, then authentic community must also be "religious" and so in its fulfillment exhibit a normative and authentic religious substance. Such, I argued, was a "theonomous" culture, the essential nature, and thus the goal of human community. The concrete symbol of such theonomous community, and thus the goal of history, is represented by the symbol of the Kingdom, that historical and social community where the divine "rules" and thus where justice, equality, and order represent the objective structures of life as love represents its motivating and binding force. In neither case do psychological and social analyses *prove* a theological interpretation of individual and community, nor establish the direct relevance of the symbol of the Kingdom. However, clearly the unavoidable implications of such analyses are left quite unexpressed and the deepest questions arising from such analyses unanswered without the symbol of the Kingdom as the norm and goal of history's life.

There is an important implication of this argument for our understanding of the Church and its role in social life. As we saw, the Kingdom functioned as a norm and goal of the Church's own life, that reunited community of love which each congregation and the Church as a whole has sought—usually without outstanding success—to be. However the Church may have interpreted this relation of the Kingdom to its own life, seldom has the Church seen the Kingdom as equally, if not so visibly, relevant to the life of the world around it. Now, however, it is evident that if the Church sees itself as unconcerned with the moral and institutional character of the life of its world, the Church denies the full scope of the Kingdom as thoroughly as does the world when the world refuses to recognize the divine rule over its own secular life. A "sacral" Church and a "profane" world, as Tillich powerfully said, have both fallen away from their own essential nature and task since they have separated from each other, the one into a community which is *only* religious, the other into a secular or autonomous society which is *only* cultural. The Kingdom, therefore, stands for a theonomous Church in a theonomous culture. Thus it symbolizes the rule of God in social history as well as in individual hearts and in small religious fellowships. This symbol represents, in turn, the call to objective social structures representing justice, equality, freedom, and order as well as to the piety and personal holiness of a religious fellowship. The Kingdom is the one symbol that unites individual, Church, and social history as expressing the sovereignty of God in each communal realm and thus the norm and goal of each in reunion with the other. As the dual role of the symbol of the Kingdom in relation to both Church and world indicates, the Church cannot be itself without the world any more than the world can be itself without the Church— and individual life and history depend on each for their origin, their continuing reality, and their fulfillment.

It is, of course, in this wider communal context of society as a whole that the question of the meaning of the historical process as a whole arises and thus that the theological issue of a Christian interpretation of history is broached. The obvious answer to this question for our

culture has been expressed in confidence in the development of civilization and of culture, specifically either of the
liberal or of the socialist-Marxist forms of Western culture,
both being based on the scientific, technological, and industrial civilization produced in the modern West and now
exported in one or another of these forms to the entire
globe. Because the continuing progress of this civilization
was so much taken for granted by most intellectuals—it
formed the "religious substance" of modern culture—the
question of the meaning of history was seen as irrelevant or
even "meaningless" and the relevance of a Christian interpretation of that meaning ignored. As our discussion has
indicated, however, this confidence in progress has now
largely dissipated. The awareness of the continuing reality
of our common estrangement has challenged deeply this
answer to the question of the meaning of history as a
whole, and so this ground for confidence and hope in the
future. As a consequence, to both the liberal and the Marxist forms of Western spirituality, the Christian interpretation of history—and so of action or praxis within
history—has a new relevance. In concluding this account
of Christian belief, I shall seek briefly to show the relation
of both Spirit and Kingdom to this fourth context, the
wider question of the meaning and goal of the historical
process.

My description of our creatureliness as temporal uncovered two phases of that temporal process that constituted
both our individual histories and the wider history in
which we live. This is the inheritance from the past which
we name destiny, and the freedom in the present to reshape that destiny in the light of future and thus new
possibilities. It was, I said, through the continuing and
universal providential action of God—and this *was* God's
providence—that these three modes of time—past inheritance, present freedom, and future possibilities—were

united into actuality. Correspondingly, in the discussion of estrangement, I located the problem of historical life in these essential aspects of temporal passage: in freedom we find ourselves to have fallen away from our relation to and dependence on the deeper, creative, and providential ground of history—from God; we have fallen into a self-sufficient and thus inordinate self-love that warps our relation to the past, our freedom in the present, and our relation to possibilities presented to us by the future. Out of this new situation of freedom arises the demonic—self-elevation of the finite creature to an ultimate and unique authority and status in our common existence and thus its aggression against all other forms of life.

Thus also are the actualities, in the widest sense of that term, that our common freedom helps to form in each present warped by the demonic aspect of estrangement; ourselves, our personal relations with others, our work in the world, the events we share in enacting, and, finally, the social institutions we help to build, all reflect this inordinate self-love and this drive toward an infinite security and status in the world. As a consequence, the social and historical inheritance for the next generation is warped, its events warring and chaotic, its motives aggressive and hostile, its institutions unjust and oppressive. The destiny another generation receives from us and, ultimately, from providence has become fate, an exploitative and an unjust social order, a chaotic social situation, a present closed to real experiences or possibilities of freedom, and a future void of significant new opportunities. In this fated inheritance from our own past, the self-destructive aspects of sin appear on both the individual and the social levels: in weakened and empty selves, in barren and unreal relations to others, and in the universal conflict, the radical inequality, and the oppressive institutions that constitute finally the nemesis of each civilization. Thus is the creative side of

history, grounded in providence and actualized by freedom, countered in our actual experience (in the actual experience of the twentieth century) by the demonic and the
self-destructive aspects of historical life. Actual history as
experienced reflects both the creative providence and the
devastating judgment of its divine ground. And so, inevitably, in each culture, when its time comes, the questions
of the meaning of its life and the permanence of its values
arise—no longer at all as meaningless—with urgency and
with poignancy. Is "salvation" possible from sin and fate,
and if so, how?

As my total argument has sought to demonstrate, the
Christian message understands itself as providing answers
to this urgent question, and—although this has not been
universally agreed to—to propose an answer to both aspects of the question of salvation, to the issues alike of sin
and of fate. As our essential nature is constituted by our
inner and outer aspects, a personal, deciding center characterized by trust, by love, and by knowledge, and an outward social being characterized by personal and social relations of all sorts, so the problem of history has this inner
and this outer aspect and must be dealt with on both
levels. Clearly the event of Jesus Christ—his own lifestyle,
his teachings, his death and resurrection—relate most immediately to this primary inner level of the problem, to the
inner aspect of estrangement in our unbelief, our alienation from God, from ourselves, and from others in an
inordinate self-love and a demonic self-concern that ele-
vates us and our own to the center of our world. It is to this
inner, personal center above all that the redemptive work
of the Spirit and thus the redemptive forces of grace, experienced in the life of the Christian community, direct
themselves, and to which its means of grace—namely the
Word, sacrament and loving community—primarily relate
themselves. At its deepest level, the Christian Gospel—

uniting the historical figure of Jesus with the event of his death and resurrection—addresses itself to the inward estrangement from God, from ourselves, and from others characteristic of ourselves; and it is in the healing of that essential estrangement, in the creation of faith, hope, and love, that the redemptive work of the Spirit is most clearly seen and the coming of the Kingdom, as the New Testament says, has already begun.

It is my conviction, shared by most contemporary theologians, that this redemptive work of the Spirit, of the presence of God in the inward life of men and women, is also found in the creative elements of secular communal life and, of course, in the other religions of the Spirit as well—though it is also our conviction that the issue the Spirit there is addressing, and how God has and intends to deal with that issue, are most clearly manifest in the event of Jesus in whom the Spirit dwelt definitively and thus visibly.

As I have tried to show, however, inner estrangement results in outer estrangement as well, and thus no redemption of the inner is possible unless that outer dislocation is resolved. The self-destructive consequences of inner estrangement extend to all, warping, suffocating, preventing any genuine opportunity of loving community, of trust and of hope, and tempting constantly oppressor and oppressed alike into further estrangement. The self-destructive fate of estrangement, visibly and solidly embodied in unjust institutions and chaotic events, can only be dealt with politically, by common action in the objective sphere of history. Inner repentance, new personal trust, and new creative motives—and prayer—may prepare the way to deal with social fatedness; but it takes historical action in all its ambiguity to complete what the inner can only see, plan, and intend. Thus the political reformation of economic, social, and political institutions; the political achievement of order and peace among conflicting powers and groups; the political redistribution of resources, goods, major property, and economic opportunities—and possibly in certain circumstances, political revolution and reconstruction—these are the conditions of new hope for the historical future—as repentance, faith, and new love are for the personal future. Here, clearly political and economic policy, the intricacies and ambiguities of international relations, and questions of social and financial planning enter the scene. But, as is obvious, moral decisions are also crucially involved at every step, and so the questions of the ultimate character of authentic community, of the norm for social community, and thus of the norm and goal of history itself dominate even the most concrete and technical policy decisions.

This political task, necessary for every context of social relations, from the narrow personal to the widest historical relations, calls for hope in the future Kingdom and for reflection on our political present in the light of that hope. In this role the symbol of the Kingdom acts as what we might call a "real utopia." That is to say, this is not a rootless utopia unrelated to the fundamental dynamic forces of the historical past and present, as are any such in a naturalistically-viewed universe. There, although what is ontologically most real is quite void of moral purpose, history itself is supposed in the end to incarnate precisely moral purposes. With the Kingdom, however, the ontological structure and the social goal of history are not in that way at odds; here this utopia finds its grounds in the ultimate reality, power, and purpose of providence and in the supplementary religious work of the Spirit. Since it represents, as has been seen, both the goal of God—as that was manifest in and through the event of Jesus as the Christ—and the fulfillment of essential human nature, it manifests as a symbol the "natural law" or essential telos of society and thus, granted the redemptive promises and activity of God in history, a valid and credible hope for the ultimate future.

In our present, however, despite its reality, it functions as a utopia. As a symbol expressive of justice, equality, freedom, and order, expressive of the bond of love, it is in the starkest contrast to what now is, as that which is not but ought to be. In this transcendent perfection it is the source of continuing and continual criticism of what is now established, of the status quo in its now-evident injustice. If one gift of the Spirit is repentance, then one function of the Kingdom is to provide the symbolic structure in which the disorder of a seemingly orderly present is clearly seen and social repentance becomes possible. The Kingdom is, further, the authentic measure of the worth of each political and economic projection for the future and thereby the criterion for the Christian character of our judgments concerning public policy and program. One of the gifts of the Spirit is love; in public and historical policy love is enacted by an increase of justice. It is the role of the symbol of the Kingdom to help us to decide for what new forms of justice our particular present situation calls. Finally, confidence in the real possibility of the Kingdom under the providential and the redemptive work of God is the necessary basis for the courage and persistence essential for political action. One of the gifts of the Spirit, hope, is the gift of such confidence on which all political action is grounded; one of the gifts of the Kingdom is to help to define or to structure how that hope may concretely be enacted.

As is evident, the Christian understanding of history is complex indeed, as is the web of history itself—replete with apparent necessity and creative freedom, with rational sequences and utter contingency, with fate and with new opportunities, with tragedy and with new beginnings, hardly a story whose character and meaning are obvious or clear. Through belief in God and the manifestation of the divine will in Jesus of Nazareth, the deep mystery that is history is, I believe, clarified, the dynamic forces of history uncovered, and the grounds for confidence and hope established—to, that is, those who are willing to repent for their own involvement in the darkness of our common historical life. These grounds for confidence are, first, the pervasive reality of providence uniting past, present, and future in universal experience so that a creative destiny and new possibilities are continually and unexpectedly present throughout the course of history; second, the appearance, universally in religion and in culture, but definitively and visibly in the event of Jesus as the Christ, of new redemptive forces directed at estrangement and thus crucially supplemental to the continuing and ever-present work of providence; and third, as the two main aspects of these new forces establishing the purposes of God, the work of the Spirit within us and of the Kingdom ahead of us to conquer the two enemies in temporal passage of human fulfillment, namely, sin and fate. In every case, then, human response is an essential aspect of the divine work: in acceptance of our destiny, in affirmation of our freedom; in the courage to dare new possibilities; in repentance for our sins; in new trust in God's mercy and love; in the risk of loving relations with others; and finally in the courage, wisdom, and self-giving required for creative politics. Human creativity is a part of history and thus is that response necessary. But human estrangement is also a part—and thus are the graces of repentance and hope in the Kingdom necessary if that response is to incarnate the forgetfulness of self and the love of justice necessary for creative politics.

Is this, then, all that we can hope? Are sin and fate to be fragmentarily conquered in history by the divine work only so that history—and all its individuals with it—is in the end swallowed up in death? That there will be in the future a terminus to history as to nature as we know it, as there evidently is to our own individual lives, is extremely probable. What then, we may ask, happens to the Kingdom, the goal of God's creative, providential, and redemptive will? Is *it*, then, also swallowed up by death along with the nature and the history God established, nurtured, judged, and cared for? And in that case, one might well also ask, what happens to God, his/her creative intention and his/her redemptive love—are they too swallowed up? The answers to these deeply personal, and yet also clearly reflective, questions, as is obvious, plunge very deeply toward the heart of the Christian Gospel and the meaning of the faith that responds to that Gospel.

Despite the long tradition of philosophical proofs of the "immortality of the soul," it is clear to most contemporary theologians that such proofs turn out, in the modern context, to be closer to what would be termed irrational than rational, against the grain, so to speak, of what seems to be reasonable to the modern person. This is because the consciousness of the unity of body and spirit in a human being is much greater at present than has been in the past; thus, the conception of a "separable soul," both able to continue by itself and representing the identity of the departed, seems almost bizarre to the average thoughtful person—though now less so, I might add, to many under the influence of Indian religions. Since, moreover, to most of modern theology the biblical message on this issue also speaks always of a *unity* of body and spirit in human beings, and thus of a *resurrected* body, and not of a separable soul, these philosophical proofs of the immortality of that separable soul seem as unbiblical as they do unempirical and irrational—though there is certainly no universal agreement on any of this.

For these reasons, most contemporary theologians, insofar as they affirm, as most of them do, a belief in eternal life, regard this belief as the result of their total Christian faith rather than as the consequence of independent rational reflection on life, on death, and on the latter's probable consequences. That is to say, one has confident hope that death—considered as either that of the individual or as that of the race and its history as a whole—does *not* have the final word because of Christian knowledge of and trust in God rather than because of any certainty that our own souls are immortal. One consequence of this ground for a belief in eternal life is that since its certainty is based on our confidence in God rather than on our reflective knowledge of our own postmortal state, modern theology rarely pretends to know anything about the structure or character of eternal life. It believes *that* such is promised and so possible through God's power and love, not *what* it is precisely that all this will "look like."

When one asks further, why does Christian knowledge of and trust in God lead to the confidence that we finite creatures may "inherit"—to use the old term—eternal life in some fashion, we find ourselves in our answer rehearsing most of the religious affirmations and thus most of the theological symbols discussed in this volume. First, if God be the transtemporal ground and source of all finite reality and thus all life, the unconditioned power from which all power to be arises and through which all power to be continues in being, then the divine life clearly transcends the passing away of every creaturely existence. In that sense, God as eternal and as the unconditioned power of being knows and can know no death; the *possibility* of eternal life lies in the eternity and power of the divine life. If, second, the divine love is in truth directed at the fulfillment of each creature that the divine power has brought into being, then it follows that God's will or intention purposes that sharing of the eternal divine life. Third, if the purpose of creation—as the fulfillment of the creature—is the union or reunion of God with his/her creation, the establishment of communion of God with each of us, then that sharing of the eternity of God's own divine life, that reunion with God, is in accord with the fundamental purpose of God's creative will. God's will is precisely for our salvation, as Calvin reminded us. In sum, since salvation is a reunion with God that results in a sharing of the divine life, a knowledge of that will as love for the creature assures us of the actuality of eternal life.

Fourth, and most important of all, the peculiar or unique character of this divine love as agape, as love for even the unworthy, as forgiveness and mercy even towards the sinner, assures Christian belief that the last and most serious barrier to eternal life, namely, sin or estrangement from God himself/herself, is overcome by God's forgiving acceptance of us. This process of reunion with God through grace begins in repentence and new trust; it represents in a fragmentary but real way a new mode of participation in God through the Spirit; and it is a foretaste—incomplete, often fleeting, often elusive—of what seems to be promised in the Gospel. Knowing that in ourselves we are and remain estranged from God, buffeted by doubt and lack of trust, and hopelessly unable to love as we ought, our *basic* assurance of the actuality of eternal life rests as a consequence on our confidence in the divine forgiveness—rests, that is, on what is revealed to us of God's will towards us in the cross and what has been reflectively affirmed through the theories of the atonement.

Fifth, while the basis for Christian confidence rests in the power and the love of God, it has been the Christian experience of the resurrection, and the scriptural witness to it, that has made actual that confidence. What seems *entailed* in the God known in Christian experience has been actually *manifest* in that event, or, better, in that culmination of the total event of Jesus who is the Christ. Thus, while the hope for the future—both of the earthly or historical and of the heavenly or eternal Kingdom—gives shape, as has been shown, to present Christian experience of God in and through the Spirit, it is the experience of God through the Spirit and the faith, love, and hope it generates, that gives grounds for that hope. And in each case, with regard to both the Spirit that is experienced and the Kingdom that is hoped for, it is the central event of Jesus Christ that establishes and molds the faith of the Christian community.

I must add that, in the light of all these grounds for Christian confidence in eternal life, and especially in the light of the divine love as overleaping every barrier, even that of sin and estrangement, I cannot understand our common destiny as a *double destiny*, as including an eternal divine condemnation, as involving the sending of some—because of a lack either of faith or of works—finally and irrevocably to "hell." As I understand the divine love both in Scripture and in experience, it comes to all, even those who refuse it; and when it is refused, it returns, ever and again, seventy times seven, seeking precisely the lost as well as the found. It is this love for the lost that each of us counts on who know ourselves truly and must count on throughout our life here. It is the character of the divine love revealed in Jesus Christ; and it is on the basis of *this* love that we believe, if we believe at all, in heaven, that is in a final sharing in the depth, eternity, and communion of the divine being. If that is so, then this basis of our confidence in heaven must, if our confidence be justified, be the basis of God's dealing with all his/her creatures—even those who may seem to us to be outside the reach of the divine grace. Such unconditioned love, leaping over every barrier—basic to our *own* trust—cannot also imply the exclusion of some, the appearance of a barrier which that love cannot overleap, the reality of an eternal damnation.

It is, then with that interpretation of the promise of the gospel, that I conclude this brief introduction with Paul's amazing and confident cry: "For I am sure that neither death, nor life, nor angels, nor principalities, nor things present, nor things to come nor power, nor height, nor depth, nor anything else in all creation, will be able to separate us from the love of God in Christ Jesus our Lord" (Romans 8:38–39).

NOTES

1. It is interesting that the conviction that unjust institutions (slavery, poverty, imperial occupation) have contingent *historical* causes militates not only against an ascription of those institutions to Divine Providence but also against the assumption that they are "caused" by the Karma in the past lives of the oppressed living under those institutions. A Buddhist philosopher friend in Japan said to the author that it was his *historical* consciousness (not his modern "cosmology") that had forced him to rethink the meaning of Karma. The reason, he said, was his belief that the sufferings of, say, the Eta (an oppressed class in Japan) resulted *not* from what each of them had done in some former life but from quite specifiable *historical* developments in the past, most notably the oppressive actions of the classes and groups that pressed the Eta ruthlessly down and kept them there.

2. As a specific example of this strange dialectic of the generations, my college graduating class (Harvard 1940) at its June commencement (a month after the fall of France) expressed through all four of its class orators a determination "not to go" to the "European" war should we become involved in it. When the then twenty-fifth reuning class of 1915 heard of this, they—the proud veterans of 1918—were horrified. As their senior class passed before us, seated in honor in the stadium as "the reviewing reuning class," they stopped, shook their fists at us, and yelled, "You lily-livered bastards, you'll go!!" We all rose at that and shouted back, "Hell, no, we'll not go!"—and called them some prime names back.

Twenty-five years later at our *own* 25th reunion in 1965, the author, in an address in honor of the dead in our class (a host of World War II veterans *and* JFK!), reminded the assembled classmates, who had fought World War II and were now many of them at the organizing center of the Vietnam War, of this event twenty-five years before. They *too* were astounded and horrified to recall it; they could scarcely believe that in that dim past they had so believed and so acted. As several said to me afterwards—or in words to this effect—"Recalling my own oath in 1940 not to go has helped me to understand my own son who has just burned his draft card!" A strange and disturbing history of three generations is embodied here.

3. Theonomy—a concept used centrally by Paul Tillich—represents precisely the viewpoint expressed in the text, namely, that the fulfillment of the powers, capacities, eros, and goals of the human (or of any creature) are realized only in, with, and through an essential relation to the divine. The divine, then, does not import into the creature any goal, norm, or aim *alien* to the human or to its aims; its dominant and central presence, therefore, fulfills rather than crushes the creature. Thus while it is *transcendent*, the divine is at the same time the *immanent* principle of human existence, essential for its being (creation and providence) and so for its fulfillment (redemption). Theonomy, therefore, contrasts itself with two other concepts: *heteronomy*, where the divine is transcendent and yet "over against," alien to, and so oppressive of the human (a "heteronomous" culture is one in which the religious principle represses and oppresses the creative life of a culture); and *autonomy*, where the creative principles of cultural life are grounded in and appeal to no principle transcendent to the human. To most secular viewpoints theonomy is essentially "heteronomous" and autonomy naturally the answer. To most theists theism is essentially theonomous, and so both heteronomy *and* autonomy in the end are self-destructive. This volume regards itself as one sustained argument for a *theonomous* interpretation of human existence, culture, and history and so against either a heteronomous or an autonomous interpretation of them.

4. For an earlier discussion by the author of the Church, especially the American churches, see *How the Church Can Minister to the World Without Losing Itself* (New York: Harper & Row, 1964); and for a more recent interpretation of the travail *and* the promise of the contemporary Roman Catholic Church, see his *Catholicism Confronts Modernity* (New York: Seabury Press, 1975).

5. See *Reaping the Whirlwind*, (New York: Seabury Press, 1977).

SUGGESTED READINGS

Recent Classics

Barth, K. *Community, State and Church.* Doubleday/Anchor, 1960.
Bennett, J. *Christian Ethics and Social Policy.* Scribners, 1946.
———. *The Christian as Citizen.* Association Press, 1955.
Bonhoeffer, D. *Life Together.* Harper & Bros., 1954.
———. *Ethics.* Macmillan, 1955.
———. *The Cost of Discipleship.* Macmillan, 1966.
Kierkegaard, S. *Training in Christianity.* Princeton Univ. Press, 1944.
———. *Works of Love.* Princeton Univ. Press, 1949.
———. *Attack upon Christendom.* Beacon Press, 1956.
Niebuhr, H. R. *The Responsible Self.* Harper & Row, 1963.
———. *Christ and Culture.* Harper & Row, 1951.
Rauschenbusch, W. *A Theology for the Social Gospel.* Macmillan, 1918.
———. *Christianizing the Social Order.* Macmillan, 1915.
Tillich, P. *Love, Power and Justice.* Oxford Univ. Press, 1954.
———. *Political Expectation.* Harper & Row, 1971.
———. *The Socialist Decision.* Harper & Row, 1977.

Current Discussion

Alves, R. *A Theology of Human Hope.* Abbey Press, 1972.
Bonino, J. M. *Doing Theology in a Revolutionary Situation.* Fortress, 1975.
Braaten, C. *Eschatology and Ethics.* Augsburg, 1974.
Gilkey, L. *Reaping the Whirlwind.* Seabury, 1977.
Gustafson, J. *Theology and Christain Ethics.* Pilgrim, 1974.
Gutierrez, G. *A Theology of Liberation.* Orbis, 1973.
Heilbroner, R. L. *An Inquiry into the Human Prospect.* W. W. Norton, 1974.
Husinger, G., ed. *Karl Barth and Radical Politics.* Westminster, 1976.
Metz, J. B. *Theology of the World.* Herder & Herder, 1969.
Moltmann, J. *The Theology of Hope.* Harper & Row, 1967.
———. *The Crucified God.* Harper & Row, 1974.
Ogden, S. *Faith and Freedom.* Abingdon, 1979.